AF784028

JUSTICE, HUMANITY AND THE NEW WORLD ORDER

For Ross

Justice, Humanity and the New World Order

IAN WARD
University of Newcastle upon Tyne, UK

ASHGATE

© Ian Ward 2003

All rights reserved. No part of this publication may be reproduced, stored in a retrieval system or transmitted in any form or by any means, electronic, mechanical, photocopying, recording or otherwise without the prior permission of the publisher.

The author has asserted his moral right under the Copyright, Designs and Patents Act, 1988, to be identified as the author of this work.

Published by
Ashgate Publishing Limited
Gower House
Croft Road
Aldershot
Hampshire GU11 3HR
England

Ashgate Publishing Company
Suite 420
101 Cherry Street
Burlington, VT 05401-4405 USA

Ashgate website: http://www.ashgate.com

British Library Cataloguing in Publication Data
Ward, Ian, 1963-
Justice, humanity and the New World Order. - (Law, justice and power)
1. Law - Philosophy 2. Jurisprudence 3. Humanism 4. Human rights - Europe - Philosophy
I. Title
340.1

Library of Congress Cataloging-in-Publication Data
Ward, Ian, 1963-
Justice, humanity, and the new world order / Ian Ward.
p. cm. — (Law, justice, and power)
Includes bibliographical references.
ISBN 0-7546-2308-4 (alk. paper)
1. Law—Philosophy. 2. Globalization. 3. Humanism. 4. Humanitarian law. 5. World politics—1989- I. Title. II. Series.

K230.W357 A35 2002
340'.11—dc21

2002074457

ISBN 0 7546 2308 4

Typeset by Manton Typesetters, Louth, Lincolnshire, UK.
Printed and bound in Great Britain by MPG Books Ltd, Bodmin, Cornwall.

Contents

Preface

There is a general mood abroad in modern legal studies, one that demands a fundamental jurisprudential revitalization. The rapidly changing international landscape asks insistent questions. The emergence of a 'new' world order coincides with a broader intellectual desire to emerge from the dominant, but at the same time debilitating, jurisprudences of positivism, scepticism and realism. Not only does the changing international landscape require a new approach to legal theory, but so too does it provide us with the opportunity, even the inspiration. This book is written within this broad context. Legal theory must be able to offer more than analytical rigour or sceptical distrust. It must be able to contribute to the wider debates that surround this 'new' world order. It must be able to present, not just an accurate description of how things are, but also an inspiring prescription of how things might become.

At the same time, this book certainly does not claim to provide a comprehensive theoretical blueprint, some kind of grand unification theory of jurisprudence. It is, instead, the articulation of a series of ideas or impressions, both of legal theory at present, and also of the 'new' world order. Yet, if there is no grand unification theory here, there is, a unifying thesis. This book attempts to argue the case for a legal humanism that has its roots in the attempt, during the late eighteenth and early nineteenth centuries, to recast a non-metaphysical species of natural law. This species can be termed 'romantic' insofar as it aligned itself with the pervasive desire to articulate the idea that a public philosophy is as much an expression of sensibility as it is of sense, as much a matter of effecting justice as it is of describing law. We will investigate this particular intellectual engagement in the two chapters that constitute the first part of this book.

The three following chapters, constituting the second part of the book, present a complementary investigation of the present state of the 'new' world order, of the 'new' Europe and of human rights. It is here that the idea of a new legal theory, of a new legal humanism, must bite. It will be argued that many of the present anxieties that attend to the various facets of the new world order are rooted in the sense that there is a legitimacy gap. In short, this new world order seems to enjoy neither the political nor the intellectual legitimacy that we would like. It appears to pay little heed to all the totems of modern liberal public philosophy, to liberty, to equality, to justice, to democracy, to the rule of law. And yet the new world order exists, irrefutably, and it is here to stay. And so, accordingly, we must search for a public philosophy, and a jurisprudence, that can address these questions of legitimacy. Legal humanism can do this.

The original idea which lies behind this book germinated in a lecture entitled 'Universal Jurisprudence and the Case for Legal Humanism' which I gave during my tenure as Bowker Visiting Professor at the University of Alberta in autumn 2000. It sought, in simple terms, to suggest that the future of legal theory lies in our spending rather more time with the likes of Wordsworth, Coleridge and Shelley, than with Hart, Dworkin or Rawls. In short, the time has come for legal theory to venture beyond its self-inflicted intellectual constraints. The idea that the study of law, in its widest possible sense, *might* be interdisciplinary has passed. It *is* interdisciplinary, radically and irreducibly so. The realization that law is so constituted, by a multiplicity of different voices, at different times, in different situations, is intrinsically humanist, tolerant, liberal and compassionate. And it is for this reason that a text such as the *Lyrical Ballads* or *Prometheus Unbound*, one that is about humanity and compassion, can tell us so much more about that nature of justice than texts such as *The Concept of Law* or *Taking Rights Seriously* ever could.

As I have developed these ideas during the last couple of years, I have benefited from the opportunity of giving various papers in various places, most recently at a human rights workshop at the Law and Society Conference in Budapest last summer. Much of the material recast here in Chapter five was significantly refined following its presentation before the latter audience. To all who have patiently listened, and most particularly to all who have contributed their comments and ideas, I must take the opportunity of expressing my gratitude.

This book does not, I repeat, intend to present a grand, comprehensive theory of law, but it hopes to capture a mood, and to provide a few ideas perhaps. It is an exciting mood. The breaking apart of established intellectual moulds is always exciting. We are asked to rethink the nature of law in a changing world. In order to do this we must first rethink the nature of legal theory as an intellectual discipline. This book is an attempt, albeit a modest one, to contribute to this vital engagement.

I.W.

Introduction: before the Law

An Age of Gold

In the first scene of Shakespeare's *The Merchant of Venice*, the three merchants reflect upon the hazards of the commercial world. Solanio confesses to a state of perpetual anxiety, 'Piring in maps for ports, and piers and road:/ And every object that might make me fear/ Misfortune to my ventures' (Shakespeare, 1964a, 1.1.19–21). Only Antonio seems prepared to hazard a more prosperous resolution. But his hopes are about to be rudely contradicted. It is Antonio who is subject to Shylock's bond, and it is Antonio that the Jew takes 'before' the law in order to effect the terms of the bond.

The central jurisprudential contest is a familiar and ancient one: between the claims of natural and positive law. In its original form, it provided the dramatic heartbeat of Sophocles' *Antigone*, with the protagonist's invocation of the 'unwritten unalterable laws' of the gods against the tyrannical edicts of Creon (Sophocles, 1974, pp.138–9). The pervasive intellectual context was also familiar. The influence of Aristotelian ideas of justice and society had dominated Europe for most of the intervening two millennia, and it was these principles that Shakespeare was so keen to defend. Shakespeare could not have anticipated the challenge of Enlightenment, the critical attempt to balance sense and sensibility, reason and romance. But he did, quite clearly, anticipate the challenge of positive law against the received wisdom of natural justice.

As such, Shakespeare's defence of natural justice is an important signpost for modern jurisprudence. And it is an important signpost for this book, too, for at its heart is the suggestion that modern legal and political thought has lost sight of the idea of justice. It has, instead, become entranced by the idea of law, of rules and regulations and rights. It is, furthermore, this particular forgetfulness, this willful neglect of justice, and with it the cause of humanity, which has played a defining role in the fashioning of our present crisis of intellectual and moral confidence. As Richard Rorty has recently affirmed, the overwhelming characteristic of our present politics is a fundamental and debilitating 'distrust of humanity' (Rorty, 1999, pp.37–8).

The 'new' world order which is currently emerging bears considerable resemblance to that which so troubled Shakespeare. The same economic anxieties that afflicted Solanio afflict us today. The same jurisprudential tyranny that threated Antonio still governs the modern political community. In sum, these constituent anxieties define the modern human condition: the cold calculation of the market and the brutal unsentimentality of the law.

Shakespeare's solution, as we shall shortly see, was to invoke Aristotelian principles of public philosophy. It was a common recourse. Aristotle, and more particularly his *Ethics*, dominated the various strands of Renaissance humanism. In the *Ethics*, Aristotle had presented justice as a 'complete virtue', a supreme example of a virtue that is achieved in relational terms. It is, as such, a constituent of the *telos*, of the 'end' of philosophy. And it is performative, too, something that abets the 'pursuit' of the 'good community' and its realization. 'It is,' accordingly, 'complete virtue in the fullest sense, because it is the active exercise of complete virtue; and it is complete because its possessor can exercise it in relation to another person, and not only by himself' (Aristotle, 1976, pp.63–4, 171–4)

Justice is, then, both 'universal' and 'particular', a metaphysical idea and a political concept. This political concept expresses itself in the form of law, which must always approximate justice in 'particular' situations (ibid., pp.175, 188–90). It is this basic conceptual relation which, as we will see in due course, underpins perhaps the most influential of all 'modern' philosophies of law, that described by Immanuel Kant.

At the same time, whilst they are necessary, neither justice nor the law are alone sufficient for the establishment of the 'good' society. There must be more. There must be equity, the prime example of 'particular' justice, and there must be mercy, friendship and compassion too. There must, in short, be a due measure of sense and sensibility. In chapter eight of the *Ethics*, Aristotle cited friendship as a 'kind of virtue' and something 'most necessary for living'. Friendship is the 'bond that holds communities together', and something which, accordingly, 'lawgivers seem to attach more importance to' than even 'justice':

> Between friends there is no need for justice, but people who are just still need the quality of friendship; and indeed friendliness is considered to be justice in the fullest sense. It is not only a necessary thing but a splendid one. We praise those who love their friends, and the possession of many friends is held to be one of the fine things of life. What is more, people think that good men and friends are the same. (Aristotle, 1976, pp.258–9)

Renaissance humanism was quite entranced by the Aristotelian idea that justice and friendship were complementary constituents of the 'good society'.

It was, accordingly, inconceivable that such a society could be devoid of either, and equally inconceivable that a coherent theory of law could be written without taking account of both. Montaigne explicitly followed Aristotle in maintaining that 'There is nothing for which nature seems to have given us such a bent as for society.' Moreover, 'Of a perfect society,' he affirmed, 'friendship is the peak', and the peak of friendship, in turn, is 'love' (Montaigne, 1993, pp.91–3, 97–8). In his essay *Of Friendship*, Francis Bacon similarly saturated his readers with names of classical scholars who followed Aristotle's lead, who recognized that 'there is no man that imparteth his joys to his friend, but he joyeth more; and no man that imparteth his griefs to his friend, but he grieveth the less'. Ending with a suitably theatrical metaphor, Bacon concluded that, if a man 'have not a friend, he may quit the stage' (Bacon, 1985, pp.141, 144).

Aristotelian ideas of justice and friendship found their definitive expression, at least in Renaissance jurisprudence, in Richard Hooker's *Of the Laws of Ecclesiastical Polity*, written during the last decade of the sixteenth century. Hooker, like Shakespeare, anticipated the challenge of positive law, and he was equally aware of the need to maintain the critical balance of sense and sensibility in a humanist political philosophy. He certainly appreciated the value of reason, for 'Goodness,' he readily acknowledged, 'is seen with the eye of understanding', and 'the light of that eye, is reason'. As Aquinas had pointed out, humanity is bounded by its capacity to reason, and it is human reason which describes positive laws for the common benefit (Hooker, 1989, pp.70, 117–18).

But this does not mean that humanity is solely defined by its capacity to reason. As Hooker's first Book of the *Laws* emphasized time and again, the good society is a natural phenomenon, something which, by definition, is governed by the laws of nature. The desire for law is, after all, merely a function of the desire for natural justice, as well as our insatiable need for 'communion and fellowship'. Hooker even uses Sophocles' *Antigone* as an original authority for this assertion. Only laws that are in accord with nature can be said to be rational at all, for only they can reflect human nature and thereby enhance the sense of human 'fellowship' (Hooker, 1989, pp.82, 87).

Having cited Sophocles, Hooker immediately seeks recourse to St Augustine's imperative, 'Do as thou wouldest be done unto', a 'sentence which all nations under heaven are agreed upon', and then also to the pivotal Pauline injunction, 'love thy neighbour, and all grievous wrongs it banisheth out of the world' (Hooker, 1989, pp.82–3). We will, in Chapter 1, take a close look at the recasting of these injunctions in the legal philosophies of Adam Smith and Immanuel Kant.

And it is to this tradition, of classical Aristotelian humanism tempered by the Augustinian and Pauline injunctions, that Shakespeare has Portia appeal, in Act Four of the *Merchant of Venice*, to a tradition in which compassion and mercy are necessary constituents of justice. Thus, when Shylock at first appears unwilling to modify the terms of the bond, it is to a distinctively Aristotelian idea of mercy and equity that Portia appeals, to a moral 'compulsion':

> The quality of mercy is not strain'd,
> It droppeth as the gentle rain from heaven
> Upon the place beneath: it is twice blest,
> It blesseth him that gives, and him that takes.
> (Shakespeare, 1964a, 4.1.180–83)

And it is universal, embedded in the 'heart', above the 'sceptred sway' of kings alone. It is, indeed, 'an attribute of God himself' (ibid., 4.1.189–90). Thus, she continues:

> When mercy seasons justice: therefore Jew,
> Though justice be thy plea, consider this,
> That in the course of justice, none of us
> Should see salvation: we do pray for mercy,
> And that same prayer, doth teach us all to render
> The deeds of mercy. (Ibid., 4.1.193–8)

Shylock, however is stubborn, and so Portia is forced to engage in jurisprudential niceties. Demolishing the idea that justice is served by the formal enforcement of a positive legal obligation, she proceeds to reveal that the ordinary common law of a Christian commonwealth is anyway infused with the 'quality of mercy', as it is described in England by the equitable prerogatives of the sovereign. It is the common law that will uncover the 'justice' of Shylock's 'bond', thereby rendering its formal enforcement irrational in the most simple and obvious terms, by carrying with it the threat of Shylock's own demise (ibid., 4.1.311–12, 343–8, 351–2; Ward, 1999, pp.127–33).

In this way, Shakespeare extricated himself from the potentially destructive implication that positive law could remain immune from the deeper demands of natural justice. In the final and often neglected Act of the play, the anxious merchants and citizens of Venice are advised to return to the 'sweet harmony' of the 'ancient' world of Belmont with its traditional values of 'love' and 'friendship' (Shakespeare, 1964a, 5.1.57, 306–7). It is, here, ultimately that a settled public philosophy is to be found. The future harmony of England, for Shakespeare, depended upon maintaining a proper appreciation of the central tenets of classical humanism.

*

In subsequent chapters, we will investigate the often torturous fashioning of Enlightenment legal and political thought. This agonizing process was, to use Samuel Taylor Coleridge's famous metaphor, an expression of the 'rage of metaphysics' which possessed late eighteenth and early nineteenth-century intellectual life. It will be suggested that this is the defining moment of modernity. Moreover, it will be further suggested that a residual desire to somehow accommodate the inherited, but increasingly fractious, dynamics of sense and sensibility lay at the very epicentre of this rage.

But before we do this, we must first investigate further the nature of this inheritance, and more particularly the perceptions of law and justice which dominated political thought at the dawn of the Enlightenment. Only then can we progress to an investigation of the critique of modernity. This critique was the essential bequest of the Enlightenment. But against what was it cast?

A typical expression of late Renaissance humanism, its political and legal thought, can be found in the writings of the Hanoverian philosopher, Gottfried Wilhelm Leibniz. Leibniz lived in the past. He dreamt of an 'age of gold', an age when Europe was persuaded that the 'quality of mercy' did indeed 'droppeth as the gentle rain from heaven' (Riley, 1976; 1996, p.243). In 1715, he informed a correspondent that he had 'seen something of the project of M.de St.Pierre, for maintaining a perpetual peace in Europe'. 'I am reminded,' he continued, 'of a device in a cemetery, with the words: *Pax perpetua*; for the dead do not fight any longer.' The tone was wistful. As Europe's seemingly intractable religious wars continued around him, even Leibniz had begun to doubt, for whilst the 'dead do not fight any longer', the 'living are of another humour; and the most powerful do not respect tribunals at all.' Still, he concluded ruefully, it is 'permitted to write romances', to dream perchance, to long for that lost 'age of gold' (Riley, 1996, p.243).

Leibniz's various musings provide us with a compelling testament to the kind of residual classicism with which later Enlightenment *philosophes* would grapple, as they tried to make this essential accommodation between sense and sensibility. At the heart of the 'age of gold', Leibniz described a very particular vision of a 'universal jurisprudence', one that was founded on 'charity' and the 'love of peace, which is so recommended by Jesus Christ' (ibid., p.236). Such a jurisprudence, Leibniz added, is definitive of the humanist intellectual tradition cast by the likes of Erasmus, More and Montaigne.

It is cast also by the likes of Johannes Althusius, whose *Politica*, first published in 1603, was particularly influential amongst late seventeenth-century continental humanists. Althusius' *Politica* prescribed a 'universal' European 'commonwealth', a *respublica*, founded by a series of covenants between constituent 'associations', the authority of which rested in the 'universal association' of humanity, and not, most importantly, in any 'supreme magistrate'. The Pauline injunction was again pivotal, 'Thou shalt love thy neighbour as thyself.' The 'common law' of Althusius' commonwealth is 'nothing other than the general theory and practice of love, both for God and for one's neighbour' (Althusius, 1995, pp.12–13, 19–22, 70–71, 80–81, 139–43).

Leibniz's 'universal jurisprudence' shared precisely these precepts, most particularly the fundamental faith in the idea of a restored *respublica Christiana* as an association of constituent Christian commonwealths. Anticipating the intellectual challenges that were about to descend on the traditions of classical and Renaissance humanism, Leibniz insisted that only a 'universal' jurisprudence could bind such an association together, for only a jurisprudence founded on a coherent philosophy of humanity could maintain the necessary balance between sense and sensibility.

The figure that most starkly personified the intellectual challenge was Thomas Hobbes, the philosopher who sought to replace God with a new 'religion' of the 'state' (Leibniz, 1988, pp.46–50, 61). Like many of his contemporaries, Leibniz reserved an especial venom for Hobbes and his *Leviathan*. Most particularly, he vehemently rejected the idea that sovereignty could be purely political, and that the legitimacy of a legal order might be defined by positive law alone. The legitimacy of any community, he repeatedly affirmed, must be described by certain principles of natural or 'universal jurisprudence'. Otherwise there is nothing to protect humanity against the venal ambitions of any number of absolute tyrants who 'recognize no longer any judge but the sword'. If 'we listen to Hobbes,' he confirmed, 'there will be nothing in our land but out-and-out anarchy' (ibid., pp.118–19, 136–45; Riley, 1996, pp.36–8, 93–6, 205–15; Jolley, 1975).

Predictably, against Hobbes, Leibniz cited the revered figure of Aristotle, the master of 'universal' jurisprudence, the man who placed legal theory within a wider public philosophy which was itself founded upon a fundamentally humanist theory of ethics. A proper, 'universal', concept of 'justice', must be one that tends to the 'good' of the whole community, for 'one always finds his own good in the general good' (Leibniz, 1988, pp.50, 57, 60). In his *Opinion on the Principles of Pufendorf*, Leibniz paid fulsome homage to Aristotelian natural justice. 'Aristotelian philosophy,' he opined, 'bases all of the virtues splendidly on universal justice; and we owe it not only to ourselves, but also to society, above all to that in which we find ourselves with God, by the natural law written in our hearts, that we have a soul imbued with free thoughts, and a will which tends constantly toward the just' (ibid., p.69).

But Leibniz's 'universal jurisprudence' did not simply reproduce Aristotle uncritically. The particular context, of the translation of European humanism from late Renaissance to the early Enlightenment, necessitated a particular revision of Aristotelian jurisprudence. So Leibniz added two essential components. The first was the Platonic notion of totality which underpinned St Augustine's *City of God*. In his *Monadology*, Leibniz advocated a metaphysical atomism, and held that 'The totality of all spirits must compose the City of God, that is to say, the most perfect state that is possible.' For 'This City of God, this truly universal monarchy, is a moral world in the natural world, and is the most exalted among the works of God.' Civil law was, thus, placed within a wider public philosophy of the earthly City of God, which was itself nothing other than a 'sufficient' emanation of the City of Heaven (ibid., p.3).

The second component was the Pauline idea of justice as 'charity', or more particularly the 'charity of the wise', a 'habit of loving' which defines the virtuous Christian, and which, moreover, is most likely to be found in the educated godly magistrate (ibid., pp.98–9). The essential imperative was that expressed in chapters twelve and thirteen of the *Epistle to the Romans*: 'Owe to no man any thing, but to love one another: for he that loveth another hath fulfilled the law' (Romans 13:10). Charity, for Leibniz, is an innately jurisprudential concept, one which should determine all human interactions, a 'universal benevolence, which the wise man carries into execution in conformity with the measures of reason, to the end of obtaining the greatest good' (Riley, 1996, pp.58–60). In a short treatise on *True Piety*, Leibniz affirmed that 'one cannot love God, who is invisible, if one does not love his neighbour, who is visible'. Moreover, those who 'reduce justice to rigour' and nothing more, by which Leibniz clearly intended to implicate the Hobbesians, 'fail altogether to understand that one cannot be just without being benevolent' (Leibniz, 1988, p.19).

In his most substantial commentary on 'universal justice as charity', the *Codex Iuris Gentium*, Leibniz placed a particular stress on the impressionistic nature of such a jurisprudence, and on the necessary and 'sufficient' function of the imagination in perfecting a Christian humanism. He observed:

> And since the contemplation of the beautiful is pleasant in itself, and a painting of Raphael affects a sensitive person who understands it, although it brings him no material gain, so that he keeps it in his eye, as the image of a thing which is loved; when the beautiful thing is itself capable of happiness, this affection passes over into pure love. (Ibid., p.171)

Leibniz was certainly not inclined to abandon everything to experience. In a long critique of Locke's *Essay on the Human Understanding*, he argued strongly that, whilst a political philosopher must take note of 'sensible experience', it should not be thought that such experiences are 'sufficient'. Experience cannot 'give us' either 'particular or individual truths' (Leibniz, 1973, pp.150–51). What politics must do is emulate art. It is only in this way, as Leibniz asserts, that the 'men of our times' can be encouraged 'to humanize themselves' (Leibniz, 1988, p.171). This recourse, amongst humanists, to art and to the faculty of aesthetic judgment, is striking. We shall return to it repeatedly in this book, with Smith and Kant, and then with any number of Enlightenment romantics such as Godwin, Shelley and Whitman. We shall also encounter it amongst latter-day romantics, such as Albert Camus and Herbert Read and, more recently still, Richard Rorty and Martha Nussbaum.

'Charity,' Leibniz affirmed in the *Codex*, 'is a universal benevolence, and benevolence the habit of loving or of willing the good', so that 'Love then signifies rejoicing in the happiness of another, or, what is the same thing, converting the happiness of another into one's own' (ibid., p.171). This, for Leibniz, is what a 'universal' public philosophy should do. It should set itself to resist the Hobbesian attempt to translate legal science into a study of particular governments, and instead embrace once again the Aristotelian notion that justice is a matter, at its root, of cultivating the 'friendships' which define humanity (ibid., pp.195–6). At the heart of the *Codex*, Leibniz advanced a *ius gentium* which could bind together once more the 'republic of Christian nations', providing an overarching political morality which could accommodate the relativity of human laws, without compromising the sanctity of divine law and Christian ethics. The 'highest degree of right' in a European public philosophy, he concluded, could only be 'piety' or 'charity', a 'city of God' indeed (ibid., pp.172–5).

Leibniz was a romantic by his own admission. And his legal and political thought has often been dismissed as utopian, even naïve. The triumph of legal positivism was barely a century away. Natural law would pass into abeyance, sensibility would be cast outside the realm of jurisprudence. And the *respublica* would stay divided and dissolute. Yet, as we squint uncertainly into a new millennium within which it is clear that emaciated theories of positive law will have no place, and as we contemplate instead the case for a revitalized and distinctive legal humanism, there is a certain resonance in Leibniz's 'universal jurisprudence'. The thought that 'justice' is something that is 'useful to the community', a community moreover 'let it be recalled, not of a few, not of a particular nation, but of all those who are part of the City of God and, so to speak, of the state of the universe' suddenly seems rather apposite, perhaps even compelling (Riley, 1996, p.260).

The End of Philosophy

The idea of a 'universal' jurisprudence has been out of fashion for two centuries. As we shall see in the next chapters, variants would be championed by the likes of Smith and Kant, and even Rousseau and Godwin. But few jurists put much stock in principles of natural justice, fewer still spend much time worrying about the demands of compassion and sentiment, of friendship and love. There is nothing romantic about modern legal and political thought. This is its essential weakness.

In very large part this weakness, this absence of sentimental substance, is the result of a wider intellectual scepticism, perhaps even cynicism. Against the charms of an 'age of gold', against the claims of reason and the 'good society', and justice indeed, it has been suggested that we are programmed for indeterminacy and disillusion. Armies of existentialists, post-structuralists and post-modernists, have accounted for our particular melancholic seduction. We are always going to be seduced by promises, by imagined utopias, they tell us, and we are always going to be disappointed.

One of the most influential of these modern sceptics is Jacques Derrida. The very essence of Derrida's notorious theory of deconstruction is the consistent refusal to accept any assumed truths, least of all those pretended by reason or science or law. As Derrida has emphasized in his recent *Specters of Marx*, the deconstructionist and post-modern enterprise is very much the product of a particular intellectual engagement with Enlightenment attempts to refashion classical humanism. Thus, whereas this book opened by suggesting that the predicament of Solanio and Antonio is symbolic of the impending 'rage of metaphysics', Derrida argues that precisely the same is true of the agonies experienced by Shakespeare's eponymous Prince in *Hamlet*.

The claim that *Hamlet* defines the modern condition has often been made. According to Jan Kott, for example, no text in modern literature better describes the fate of humanity, 'tormented by thoughts of the fundamental absurdity of existence' (Kott, 1967, p.56; Eagleton, 1986, pp.71–3; Bassnett, 1993, pp.148–9). In his various reflections on the 'rotten state' of Denmark, on 'the question' of providence and human determinism, Hamlet articulates concerns about the human condition that are as pressing today as they were four centuries ago.

It is this claim that is taken on by Derrida. At the very end of the scene that follows his famous muse on the 'question' of being, Hamlet announces that 'The time is out of joint' (Shakespeare, 1994, 1.5.196). It is this utterance which, according to Derrida, continues to haunt us. We cannot make sense of our presence. Hamlet's reflection on our existential condition undercuts the pretensions of Enlightenment, of sure and steady progress towards an ideal human and political condition. Human existence is not about certainty, still less certain progress. Its very marrow lies in its unpredictability, in an essential existential uncertainty. As Hamlet muses elsewhere, 'The readiness is all. Since no man, of aught he leaves, knows aught, what is't to leave betimes? Let be' (ibid., 5.2.219–20). Maybe we are indeed programmed for disillusion? Maybe it really is meant to be this way?

Hamlet's statement has been echoed by another of the great sceptics of the twentieth century, Martin Heidegger. As the Second World War turned inexorably against Germany, Heidegger could only despair of a 'planet' that was 'in flames', and in which 'human nature is out of joint' (Dallmayr, 1993, p.23). Aside from the political context, of acute personal disillusionment at his abandonment by a political movement to which he had happily sold his soul a decade earlier, there is an immediate intellectual context to this statement. By the 1940s, Heidegger was thoroughly immersed in a pivotal engagement with Friedrich Nietzsche; an engagement that, as Derrida has himself acknowledged, would chart the course of subsequent post-modern critical theory (Derrida, 1989, pp.9–15).

Nietzsche, of course, had concentrated his assault against the 'decadence' of modernity on the Aristotelian idea of goodness and the good society. His was a 'campaign against morality', against the 'falsity of instinct' that has been propagated by the later Judaeo-Christian disciples of classical philosophy (Nietzsche, 1979, pp.95, 129–34). Socrates, he affirmed in *The Birth of Tragedy*, represented nothing more than a 'subtle form of self-defence against the truth', an attempt to deny the deeper truth that there is no truth beyond art (Nietzsche, 1993, pp.4–8, 60–72). The political conclusion inherent in Nietzsche's critique was uncompromising. The pretensions of the state, and the tyranny of its laws, rest with the presumption that Socratic man, 'theoretical man', has gained access to the 'truth'. 'The state,' Nietzsche affirmed, 'has no unwritten laws more powerful than the mythical foundation that guarantees its connection with religion and its growth out of mythical representation' (ibid., p.109).

In *Thus Spoke Zarathustra*, Nietzsche presented his anti-hero as the harbinger of an anti-humanism which would soon sweep across Europe and raze the idols of rationalism to the ground. Our 'howling and cries of distress,' he observed, would only get louder before they could be quieted. So long as humanity kept its faith in the assurances of Enlightenment, it could never truly assert itself. As he observed in a wonderfully resonant metaphor, if we are ever to experience freedom, we must first learn to 'dance on the feet of chance'. Only by rejecting the humanism prescribed by the 'spittle-licking and fawning' cast of philosophers, priests and lawyers can we reinvest the idea of humanity itself (Nietzsche, 1969, pp.41–52, 186, 196, 290).

When he emerged from his study of Nietzsche, and as he sought to make some sense of the destruction that had been wrought on Germany and the ideology of National Socialism, Heidegger sought to explain the extraordinary, and grotesque, turn of events, in terms of a fundamental flaw at the heart of the Enlightenment's promise. In his *Letter on Humanism*, published in response to Jean-Paul Sartre's attempt to present existentialism as an extension of Kantian humanism, Heidegger suggested that classical and Enlightenment humanism had mutated into a dehumanizing totalitarian *techne*, by which he meant an acute concern with objectivity and the pretences of science.

In his essay *The Question Concerning Technology*, Heidegger would later suggest that technology would ultimately devour the humanity that had borne it. Humanity had abrogated its particular responsibility for thinking about 'Being'. It had resigned its commission to science. The most immediate expressions of this, he famously suggested, were tractor-farming and gas chambers. But another, no less significant expression, as he had already affirmed in his *Basic Problems of Phenomenology*, was the law. By pretending that the law is innately rational, by immersing ourselves in the myths of jurisprudence, of the 'science of law', we are abrogating our deeper responsibilities to individual justice (Heidegger, 1972, pp.193–7, 315–17; 1992, p.135).

It was this sense of responsibility which, Heidegger argued, had to be 'retrieved'. In his later writings, he sought recourse to a metaphor of pathways to a clearing, or *Lichtung*, a place of true enlightenment in which humanity would think 'more primordially' of the essential '*humanitas* of men', of the 'truth of Being'. What humanity needed to do, in simple terms, was to reach back beyond the perverted humanism of the Enlightenment, and its Socratic roots, beyond the delusions of metaphysics, to a revitalized humanism or *humanitas* (Heidegger, 1972, pp.204–14, 231–42).

In 1962, Heidegger penned one of his final essays, entitled *The End of Philosophy and the Task of Thinking*. Philosophy, he suggested, had 'entered its final stage'. In place of the 'incessant frenzy of rationalization', there would, he prophesied, be a renewed interest in the 'possibility of truth', in the revitalized, non-metaphysical humanism of *humanitas* which he had extricated from Nietzsche. The 'possibility of truth', he concluded, is our only possibility for hope, our only recourse from the disillusion which is otherwise the pervasive experience of our lives (Heidegger, 1972, pp.374–8, 387–91). Even Heidegger, it seems, in his very darkest hours, was prepared to place some hope in the possibility of hope. We shall return to this particular thought at the very close of this book.

*

The events of the twentieth century appear to compound the pervasive intellectual mood of scepticism and cynicism. The Nietzschean dismissal of Aristotelian idealism seems unanswerable. As Walter Benjamin famously observed, the 'Angel of History' looks back on the intervening two centuries and perceives merely 'one single catastrophe which keeps piling wreckage upon wreckage' (Benjamin, 1973, p.259). The two world wars, and most particularly the seemingly endless series of holocausts wreaked by all various ideologies of terror and totalitarianism that blotted the century, have become symbolic of our grotesque capacity for inhumanity.

Jean-François Lyotard, one of the harbingers of present-day post-modernism, famously suggested that Auschwitz had 'silenced' modernity, stripped it of its haughty presumption of progress and perfectibility. In this sense, it represents the starkest of symbols, the epitome of Enlightenment perverted (Lyotard, 1988, pp.3–5; 1990, pp.4–5, 28). It is a thought that finds an echo in Ionesco's observation that the 'world of the concentration camps' was 'not an exceptionally monstrous society'. Rather, 'what we saw there was an image, and in a sense the quintessence, of the infernal society into which we are plunged every day' (Marcuse, 1991, p.80).

George Steiner asks the question, 'How is one to address oneself, without a persistent feeling of fatuity, even of indecency, to the theme of ultimate inhumanity?' More precisely, why were our 'humanistic traditions' so inadequate when it came to opposing 'political bestiality'? Steiner's conclusion is uncompromising. Genocide is not 'some monstrous accident in modern history'. Rather, it is 'deliberate enactment of a long, precise imagining'. The capacity for such 'bestiality' lies at the heart of an intellectual tradition which has been perverted, that is no longer fired by the 'passionate adventure of spirit and emotion' that 1789 momentarily described. Instead, our culture currently lies in a state of 'toxic' decay. We have abandoned 'ideas' and sublimated ourselves before the idols of scientific 'truth', and so now live our lives in a condition of debilitating 'ironic pessimism'. We have developed the 'technical competence to build Hell on earth', but we have lost the capacity to 'bring sweetness and light to men' (Steiner, 1971, pp.17–18, 31–2, 47–8, 64–5, 105).

This is what is so tragic, and so disturbing too: the sheer predictability of it all. Three years before the horrors of the Somme, the Russian composer Igor Stravinsky presented a ballet, the *Rites of Spring*. The music was disruptive, and the dancers fell over themselves. The audience was as shocked as it was bewildered. The idea for the ballet, Stravinsky recorded, was that of 'ritual' slaughter, in which a 'sacrificial virgin dances herself to death'. Less than a year later, Europe was engulfed in mass slaughter (Eksteins, 1989).

The conclusion is eminently sobering. If there is a 'rotten heart', as Hamlet feared, then surely it must lie within each of us? The experiences of the twentieth century merely appear to have reinforced the residual scepticism that lay at the heart of the Enlightenment, the scepticism against which Leibniz wrote, but which could still be found even amongst the most canonical of progressive eighteenth-century texts. It is, thus, the kind of scepticism that underpinned Alexander Hamilton's observation in the *Federalist Papers*, that the 'latent causes of faction' are 'sown in the nature of man'. Laws exist in order to quell the 'passions of men' which 'will not conform to the dictates of reason and justice without constraint'. For James Madison, writing in the same context, the irreducible conclusion was just the same; the whole purpose of the American Constitution was to protect Americans from each other, to offset the 'danger of disturbing public tranquillity by interesting too strongly the public passions' (Madison *et al.*, 1978, pp.124–5, 149–50, 314, 319–20).

Perhaps Hobbes was right, perhaps our lives are meant to be 'nasty, brutish and short'? Not only are we programmed for disappointment, so too do we appear to be programmed for self-destruction. How else can we explain the serial horrors of the countless holocausts of the last century? More pertinently, perhaps, is there anything we can do to prevent their gruesome recurrence?

In his *One-Dimensional Man*, written during the early 1960s, Herbert Marcuse suggested that we could indeed aspire to a rather more elevated human experience. A generation of radicals was enthused by the thought that the horrors of the twentieth century were not rooted in human nature, but rather were the incidental product of systems of government that could be reformed. Post-war governments in particular, he argued, had failed to appreciate that the 'totalitarian tendency' of technology represents the greatest challenge to humanity. Marcuse's 'one-dimensional man', like Francis Fukuyama's more recent 'last man', is one who has resigned his power of self-determination to the oppressive tyrannies of science and its pretended truths. Marcuse, too, recognized that the balance of sense and sensibility had been lost. The 'romantic space of imagination' has been 'concealed' by the 'arrogance' of reason. If 'hope' is to be retrieved, it is this space, this power of the 'imagination', which must be reawakened (Marcuse, 1991, pp.1, 56–67, 123, 248–57).

The recourse, once again, is to the faculty of the aesthetic judgment, to art and to poetry, to the romantic sensibility. It was to this that Albert Camus appealed in the wake of the Second World War, to an 'aesthetic moralism'. It is the artist who 'truly argues for love of one's neighbor' (Camus, 1974, pp.237–40, 266). And it was to art that Nietzsche had also turned half a century earlier. It is 'only as an aesthetic phenomenon,' as he repeatedly asserted in *The Birth of Tragedy*, that 'existence can be justified'. The divorce of reason from sentiment was the ultimate 'tragedy' of modernity

(Nietzsche, 1993, pp.7, 60–72). We must hold this thought. It is compelling, and we shall return to it time and again throughout this book.

Though only half of it had passed, Camus described 'our twentieth century' as 'the century of fear'. The root of this fear lies in humanity's disconnection, in a fundamental failure to relate. 'We live,' he suggested, 'in terror because dialogue is no longer possible, because man has surrendered himself entirely to history, because he can no longer find that part of himself, every bit as real as history, that sees beauty in the world and in human faces.' Following Heidegger and Nietzsche, and anticipating Marcuse too, he laid the responsibility for our disconnection in an over-reliance on 'abstractions, bureaucracies and machines, absolute ideas, and crude messianism.' For those of us 'who can live only' with 'the friendship of men, this silence means the end of the world' (Camus, 1991, pp.117–18). The same metaphor once again: that of silence. The events of the last century have silenced the pretensions of the age of reason.

And so, as Camus concluded, we exist now in a kind of suspended animation, trapped between 'hell and reason' (ibid., p.111). The advance of reason has created this hell on earth, the capacity for oppression, exploitation and destruction. But it is not a necessary fate. It is merely our particular expression of reason. The horrors that have afflicted the last century were horrors designed by humanity. This capacity will always be present, but the expression need not be. We can imagine something else, something better. We can, in short, re-imagine humanity. But if we are to do so, we must return first to the crucible within which modern society was forged, to Coleridge's 'rage of metaphysics'. We must, in short, return to modernity's critical decision, to sacrifice the claims of sentiment, of the politics of compassion indeed, to the voracious, all-consuming, appetites of reason, of political and legal science.

Before the Law

In Chapter 9 of *The Trial*, Franz Kakfa placed Joseph K. in the Cathedral. Here he encountered a priest, who proceeded to tell him the Parable of the Doorkeeper. The parable tells of a man who comes 'before the Law', described in terms of a doorway guarded by a doorkeeper. At the man's inquiry, the doorkeeper refuses entry, simply suggesting that it might be 'possible' in the future. The door to the law 'stands open', and the man is clearly tempted to enter, but the doorkeeper warns him that there are many more doors, and each is similarly guarded. The presence of the law, it seems, is infinite. The man, who had arrived expecting that he would be able to enter the law, is taken aback and takes a seat that is offered him outside the door. There he waits, in occasional conversation with the doorkeeper. Towards the end, he perceives more clearly 'a radiance that streams immortally from the door of the Law'. But still he declines to force his entry. Finally, he inquires, 'Everyone strives to attain the law', so 'how does it come about, that in all these years no one has come seeking admittance but me?' This is his final question, and the doorkeeper 'bellows in his ear' the following reply: 'No one but you could gain admittance through this door, since this door was intended only for you. I am now going to shut it' (Kafka, 1953, pp.234–7).

The parable is a parable for the whole novel. Joseph drifts from one chapter to another, encountering all kinds of characters and situations in an attempt to find somebody who can tell him what he is accused of. He is never told. When he challenges the priest who told him the parable, the priest duly suggests that the 'doorkeeper deluded the man'. The priest is evasive; such an interpretation might be Joseph's, but it enjoys no greater authority. Indeed, there is no greater authority to be had, and this perhaps is the most disturbing conclusion to be drawn, the conclusion that Joseph is unable to grasp. Joseph's fate, like that of the man before the Law is self-inflicted. When he took his seat upon the stool, the man did so 'of his own free will'. The delusion, it seems, lies elsewhere. The doorkeeper, the priest reminds Joseph, is a man of 'duty', not 'pity' (ibid., pp.237–8, 241). The Law is an institution, whether it be the Law of the scriptures or the law of the community in which Joseph lives. The same, of course, is true for all the various communities in which modern humanity today resides. It deals in duties and delusions rather than in pity or compassion. And if we sense a lack of proper balance between duty and pity, it is for us, for humanity, to take the responsibility of demanding their realignment.

Kafka's Parable is often deployed by critics of modern jurisprudence. It is perceived to be a symbol of the failings, and more particularly the delusions, of law. More than that, it is seen to be a symbol for the wider tyrannies of modern society. The law is used as a semiotic of the failings of modernity, of the promise of Enlightenment lost. Of course, there is no sure interpretation of the Parable. As the priest reminds Joseph, there are merely 'opinions' about the meaning of the parable; just as, perhaps, there are merely opinions about the meaning of law, or indeed the Law (ibid., p.239). But what is undoubtedly significant is the fact that, in conveying a sense of bleak hopelessness, of a life without ultimate purpose, of a life of parables and delusions, Kafka chose to deploy a jurisprudential metaphor. Law is presented as the ultimate expression of delusive hopelessness. We are, again, supposed to be shocked by this revelation, horrified, like Joseph, that the law should be used as a metaphor for deception, for turning 'lying into a universal principle' (ibid., p.243).

In a brief essay on Kafka, Albert Camus suggested that his novel 'expresses tragedy by the everyday', revealing the absurdity of human existence in the very ordinariness of life. This, Camus suggests, is exquisitely humanist, not least in the fact that it denies the possibility of authoritative interpretation. If the anxieties which afflict Joseph K., and indeed Mersault, are those which necessarily afflict humanity, then each of us is empowered to make our interpretation of his fate, for we are all part of this 'tragedy'. This, Camus concludes, ensures for us the 'hope of escape' (Camus, 1975, pp.112–24).

A slightly different interpretation is provided by Derrida, who prefers to emphasize the bleaker, innately jurisprudential aspects of Kafka's novel. According to Derrida, *The Trial* is about the role of the law in suppressing our own existential potential for self-determination. Of all the intellectual disciplines, law is the one which is least inclined to permit interpretive creativity. Such an interpretation chimes with Derrida's own writings which emphasize a critical distinction between the humanistic aspirations of justice and the brutalizing, homogenizing 'force' of law (Derrida, 1992, pp.181–20). This distinction between justice and law is, of course, absolutely central to our present ambition, to reinvest a 'new' humanism. The fate of such a humanism depends upon retrieving and reasserting the primacy of justice over law.

Regardless of its various interpretations, Kafka's Parable impresses the illusory quality of law. Such a conclusion should disturb us. Modern society clings to the law as a source of truth. It does not need to be a source of metaphysical truth, but the law is supposed to provide a rock of stability in a sea of social and political turmoil. Law is not supposed to be a matter of 'opinion'. Still less is it supposed to be an illusion. And yet the idea that the law is essentially illusory has found an expression in various revered jurisprudential texts. The famous distinction between the 'dignified' and the 'efficient' parts of the constitution lies at the heart of Walter Bagehot's *The English Constitution*. Rules and regulations might make government work, but it is the 'Gothic rituals' of the constitution that delude citizens into assuming its legitimacy. The English constitution, Bagehot rightly concluded, is nothing more than a 'charmed spectacle' (Bagehot, 1963, pp.60–68, 98–100, 248).

And once again the insight was certainly not lost on Shakespeare, whose very last play, *The Tempest*, revisited the same themes as *The Merchant of Venice*, the situation of law and justice in an emergent 'new world' the dynamics of which appear to be essentially anarchic. In such a world, as Prospero came to realize, much would depend upon the ability of magistrates to maintain the charms of their 'rough magic', upon nurturing the faculty of sensibility as much as the science of reason (Shakespeare, 1964b,

1.2.73–7; 4.1.156–7; Epil.4–13). As Aristotle had long ago advised, if political communities are to hold together, the politics of friendship and compassion remains just as vital as the science of laws.

*

Enlightenment promised many things, as we shall see throughout this book. In terms of political aspiration, it promised liberty, equality and fraternity. It articulated the rhetoric of rights, of sovereignty and democracy. Such political concepts both described and abetted the moral progress or, to use Kant's phrase, the 'disposition' of the human race. Their demise, therefore, or at least the perception of their demise, is a central concern. The invention of a liberal jurisprudence was one of the defining events of the Enlightenment; the science of law, the idea that law might be described by means of some kind of internal coherence or discipline, quite outwith any received metaphysics of nature or theology, still less sentimentality. Once again, therefore, its apparent failure is of the utmost importance. But before we embark upon a closer examination of this jurisprudence in the following chapters, and the possible effect of its failure in modern society, and particularly our much-vaunted 'new world order', we should first investigate further the extent of this presumed failure.

The idea of right, as we shall see, was one of the clarion calls of Enlightenment jurisprudence. The critique of rights has, accordingly, invested much of its energies in trying to detonate our residual faith in liberal rights. The essential weakness in 'liberal rights consciousness', we are often informed, lies in its inability to conceive of 'human freedom as self-expression and growth in and through community' (Klare, 1981, p.479). Rights are nothing more than 'illusions' and 'myths' (Tushnet, 1984, p.1363). 'Exactly what people do not need,' we are told, 'is their rights.' What they need, instead, is the reinvestment of 'actual forms of social life', the facility to reassert the 'communal nature of human understanding' (Gabel and Kennedy, 1984, pp.2–4, 10–15, 34–5). Clearly, therefore, the critique of rights builds inexorably into the critique of liberal conceptions of democracy, and indeed justice and humanity. We shall flesh out this assertion shortly.

The recent tenor of critical legal scholarship builds on earlier realist jurisprudence, of the kind which gained its summative statement in Oliver Wendell Holmes's observation that law is not a 'brooding omnipresence in the sky'. At the core of present-day legal scepticism, however, is the suspicion that rather too many of us still think that it is. Liberalism's ability to perpetuate certain myths of legal transcendence appears little diminished. There is still a residual faith in the idea that the law somehow reflects certain absolute, and by definition unarguable, values. The existence of certain rights is merely the most startling of these myths.

The critique of sovereignty complements that of rights. They are, we are often told, twin delusions. Moreover, the advance of the 'new world order', of a politics that is somehow 'beyond' the nation-state, adds further weight to this particular accusation. As we shall see in due course, when we take a closer look at the evolution of the 'new' Europe, the idea of sovereignty as a coherent, integral concept is no longer credible, if indeed it ever was. If sovereignty is intended to denote the concentration of supreme authority in one determinate institution or person, as suggested by the likes of Locke or John Austin, then there is clearly little room for the concept in either the 'new' Europe, or indeed the 'new' world order. For in this order, and this Europe, the talk is of 'pooled' sovereignty and 'variable geometry', of subsidiarity and balanced competences.

The demise of sovereignty is as often welcomed as it is regretted. The overweening nation-state all too readily begat the horrors of nationalism. The jurisprudence of sovereignty, in turn, all too easily lent a spurious legitimacy to these horrors. Sixty thousand troops died on the first morning of the Somme, all pretending that they were defending the sovereignty of Belgium. The demise of rights is perhaps more likely to bring a tear to the liberal eye. As we shall also see, much credence is still attached to the idea of civil and indeed human rights. Indeed, for many, particularly those who rejoice over the 'end' of history, the assumed advance of human rights is a prized trophy. The idea of human rights still has a number of champions, even if it has just as many critics.

Amongst the jurisprudential and political icons of Enlightenment, perhaps none is supposed to shine more brightly than that of democracy. It is the great unalloyed treasure of Enlightenment political thought. Pretty much everybody claims an affinity with democracy, even if the vast majority of 'democracies' today fall far short of what an idealistic Enlightenment democrat, such as Tom Paine or William Godwin, would have hoped. And yet, as Vaclav Havel has graphically suggested, our modern politics is characterized by a basic 'distrust' of democracy, one that lies in

> the limited ability of today's democratic world to step beyond its own shadow, or, rather, the limits of its own present spiritual and intellectual condition and direction, and thus its limited ability to address humanity in a genuinely universal way. As a consequence, democracy is seen less and less as an open system that is best able to respond to people's basic needs; as a set of possibilities that must be continually rediscovered, redefined, and brought into being. Instead, democracy is seen as something given, finished, and complete as is, something that can be exported like cars or televisions, something that

the more enlightened purchase and the less enlightened do not. (Havel, 1998, p.179)

Whilst Havel's observations are made within the particular context of the 'new' world order, they are just as apposite with regard to the 'old'. The affliction is a shared one. Indeed, it is mutually constitutive. Michael Sandel speaks of a pervasive 'democratic discontent' within and without the *anciens régimes* of the classical nation-state (Sandel, 1996, p.3). Likewise, the phrase 'democratic deficit' has become a byword for jurisprudential criticism, not just of the European Union, but of its constituent member states too. Cold statistics reinforce the sense of democratic disillusionment. Barely half of America could be bothered to vote for either of the candidates in the November 2000 presidential elections. A meagre 60 per cent turned out in the UK general election in spring 2001. The turnout for successive European Union elections is derisory.

Even if we make little effort to defend sovereignty, even if we still choose to decry ideas of fundamental rights, we should all agree at least on the need to address the apparent failures of modern democracy. As Carl Schmitt advised us nearly a century ago, and with some poignancy, democracy is not a given, any more than it is an entitlement. By its very nature, democracy permits the anti-democrat to shout as loud as the democrat (Schmitt, 1988, pp.32–9).

At the heart of this book lies the familiar argument that the Enlightenment, rather than offering a clear and coherent philosophy of untrammelled progress, actually described a whole series of such contradictory impulses. The internal contradictions within democracy, like the various ambiguities and indeterminacies which pervade the theories of right and sovereignty, are merely particular expressions of this wider critique. They are, in essence, products of the central tension of the 'rage of metaphysics', the relation of sense and sensibility, reason and romance. Jurisprudence, as we shall see, attempted to overcome this intellectual strife by the simple, and crude, expedient of banishing sensibility. The serial injustices of modernity, made ever more apparent by the advance of the 'new' world order, are the inexorable product of this crudity.

Sense and sensibility, reason and romance, scepticism and liberalism: all essential tensions which lie at the heart of the Enlightenment, and which describe our present intellectual anxieties. It was always intended that the law would somehow ride above these ambiguities. Whereas justice, the great conceptual treasure of Leibniz's 'age of gold', sought to somehow accommodate the interests of the universal and the particular, the rival claims of reason and compassion, the leviathan of modern law would simply articulate, and enforce, established jurisprudential truths. Law would be the rock of stability, the rock upon which the passions of humanity, of sentiment, justice and compassion, would be broken.

In the end, liberalism sold its soul, sacrificing the claims of justice and humanity to the pretended surety of the law. And so today we live in a world of laws and lawyers, of rules and regulations. We are possessed of what John Austin termed a 'habit of obedience'. We have become obsessed with the law. We vest our hopes in the law. The law, as Nietzsche foretold, has become our new god, the lawyer our new priest (Nietzsche, 1969, pp.76–7). The accusation is echoed today by Alasdair MacIntyre, who rightly asserts that the caste of 'lawyers' rather than 'philosophers' has become the 'clergy of liberalism' (MacIntyre, 1988, p.344). The bare statistics reveal the extent of this Faustian pact. In 1970, there were approximately 250 000 lawyers in the United States. By 2000, there were four times as many. There are 18 000 lawsuits in America every year; hardly surprising, perhaps, in a nation in which prenuptial agreements can include rights to sexual activity and in which visitors to Disneyland have a legal right to expect Mickey Mouse to keep his mask on during opening times (Esler, 1998, pp.84–99).

This is an absurd situation; a world gone mad indeed, or least one that has lost any sense of reason and balance. Writing once again at the dawn of the Enlightenment, Jonathan Swift ridiculed a world in which so great a faith was placed in the authority of the lawyer. There is, as Swift's Gulliver advised, a 'society of men' trained 'in the art of proving by words multiplied for the purpose, that white is black, and black is white, according as they are paid'. Such men are lawyers, and no other 'society' is so determined 'to pervert the general reason of mankind in every other subject of discourse' (Swift, 1985, pp.297–8). All humanity's hopes, for justice and reason and equity, are placed in the one institution that is trained to pervert truth and to argue against the cause of justice.

The eschatological in Swift realized that law is merely a means, something shaped by human hands; enriched perhaps, but just as likely soiled. We began this introductory chapter with Shakespeare, and there is no better place to end. As we have already seen, time and again, when he sought to describe the condition of humanity, Shakespeare returned to the defining theme, the essential tension between law and justice. And on each occasion, the threat is clear. The failure of justice is the root of anarchy. It is the threat which lies behind the Butcher's notorious cry in *Henry VI part 2*, 'Let's kill all the lawyers' (Shakespeare, 1969, 4.2.73). It is also the threat that hovers above Solanio and Antonio and their fellow merchants, the utter destruction of their markets and their society. When Hamlet muses that time is 'out of joint', he also reflects that it is more immediately described by 'law's delay' (Shakespeare, 1994, 3.1.72). At the root of a 'rotten state' lies a failure of law and justice.

The insight is as valid today as it was four centuries ago. As we shall see in due course, there is much that is rotten about our present society, and all the states in which we live, our nation-states, our regional states, our international and indeed transnational states. The reason is simple. We failed to heed the implicit warnings carried in Solanio's musings, and Hamlet's. We have forgotten the vision of humanity articulated by Portia, just as we have cast out the jurisprudence which she, like Leibniz indeed, defended. We have reached a stage where the 'end' of philosophy appears to carry with it the 'end' of justice, perhaps even humanity. It is, as Joseph K. reflects, a 'melancholy' conclusion.

Yet there is hope, as even Nietzsche recognized. For at the 'end' of philosophy lies the prospect of a renaissance, of 'a moment of supreme coming-to-oneself on the part of mankind'. The humanism after which Nietzsche, like Heidegger, strove may seem rather elusive. It is supposed to be. Our present yearnings, for the principles of universal justice, for equality, respect and dignity, for a principle of democracy, might seem to be rather more prosaic. But they express the same essential craving. Nietzsche cited an ancient Indian inscription which, he suggested, hung over the doorway to the future, 'There are so many daybreaks that have not yet dawned' (Nietzsche, 1979, pp.95–6). Our only hope is that he is right.

PART I

1 Sense and Sensibility

The Religion of Humanity

In 1838, John Stuart Mill published an essay on Jeremy Bentham in the *London and Westminster Review*. Two years later he published a complementary essay on Samuel Taylor Coleridge. According to Mill, they were 'the two great seminal minds of England in their age'. There was, he further hazarded, 'hardly to be found in England an individual of any importance in the world of mind', who 'did not first learn to think from one of these two' (Mill and Bentham, 1987, p.132.). The shape of the nineteenth-century English culture was framed by these two thinkers and what they sought to represent, sense and sensibility. But the holistic implication of Mill's tribute masked a deeper anxiety. For whilst there was 'hardly' a mind that had not learnt from one or the other, there were very few minds that had been nurtured by both. Mid-nineteenth-century England was schizophrenic, some of its citizens devoted to the pursuit of science and utility, others to sentiment and sensibility.

Mill admired the iconoclast in Bentham, the 'great subversive', the first to 'speak disrespectfully of the constitution'. It was Bentham who 'expelled mysticism from the philosophy of law'. With a certain admiration, Mill even likened Bentham's vitriolic critique of lawyers and the practice of law to Jonathan Swift's more famous observations in *Gulliver's Travels*. But, despite all this, Bentham's utilitarianism was problematic: the obsession with 'interminable classification', the determination to reduce everything to a 'science', the apparent absence of a moral dimension, the inability to account for 'moral approbation or disapprobation' (Mill and Bentham, 1987, pp.139, 152–3, 160–62). Above all there was the 'incompleteness of his own mind as a representative of universal human nature'. Mill's castigation of this sorry deficiency was uncompromising:

> In many of the most natural and strongest feelings of human nature he had no sympathy; from many of its graver experiences he was altogether cut off; and the faculty by which one mind understands a mind different from itself, and

> throws itself into feelings of that other mind, was denied him by his deficiency of Imagination. (Mill, Ibid., p.148)

Bentham, in other words, was emotionally retarded. He lacked the essential and defining capacity of the emotionally literate, the 'power by which one human being enters into the mind and circumstances of another' (ibid., pp.149, 173).

The extent of Mill's venom can perhaps be understood when placed in the context of his own particular self-doubts. In his *Autobiography*, Mill recalled the torments caused by his early introduction to Bentham, and the growing sense that analytical jurisprudence alone should not be permitted to chart the 'destiny of mankind in general'. One of the things which most served to condemn Bentham was his dislike of poetry. Mill, in contrast, read vast quantities of poetry, particularly Wordsworth and Coleridge, as if in doing so he might be able to imbibe the spirit of humanism, and thereby somehow recreate an intellectual bridge between the dynamics of utility and the sentiments of the *Lyrical Ballads*. It was Wordsworth, Mill acknowledged in his *Autobiography*, who 'saved' him (Mill, 1989, pp.111–13, 119–23).

As the *Autobiography* further revealed, Mill never really escaped his father's shadow. James Mill had been a prominent member of the intellectual circle that surrounded Bentham in London. Another member of that circle was Bentham's jurisprudential protégé, John Austin. If the younger Mill needed any further evidence of the depths to which an emotionally illiterate jurisprudence might descend, he needed only to finger through a copy of Austin's recently published *Province of Jurisprudence Determined*. For Austin, the study of jurisprudence was little more than a study of 'sovereign' bodies, 'commands' and 'relative duties'. It was certainly not something that should allow itself to become entrapped in the 'muddy speculation' and 'senseless fictions' of such things as rights, liberties or sensibilities. Law might be of assistance in the pursuit of justice, even in the improvement of human society, but there again it might not (Austin, 1995, pp.19–20, 38–57, 64–6, 80–99).

In many ways, Austin's *Province* represented something of a caricature of legal positivism. Bentham's *Introduction to the Principles of Morals and Legislation* evidenced a far greater awareness of the countervailing tensions of sense and sensibility. At the same time, however, it did prescribe the distinction between positive law, law as it 'is', and legal morality, law as it 'ought' to be (Bentham, 1982, pp.11–16). Mill readily appreciated the distinction, but was enormously troubled by the implication that only the former is part of the 'province' of jurisprudence. Enlightenment had promised more. The cause of future progress depended upon the instrumental role of law in promoting justice and morality. There had to be more to jurisprudence than Austin's simplistic, and ultimately emaciated, account of legal rules.

At the same time, Mill's support for the poetic mind was not unalloyed. In his complementary essay on Coleridge, he readily admitted that the great poet was an 'arrant driveller' when it came to dealing with metaphysics and science. But in comparison with Bentham, Coleridge 'saw so much farther into the complexities of the human intellect and feelings', and it was for this reason that he recognized that political communities were cultural and emotional artefacts, expressions of a 'strong and active principle of cohesion' (Mill and Bentham, 1987, pp.178, 193–5). In his earlier essay, an *Attack on Literature*, Mill had already affirmed that, in the final analysis, the 'progress' of civilization is at least as dependent on the 'genius' of men such as Coleridge as it is upon anything that science could divine (Alexander, 1967, pp.24–5).

Mill was particularly interested in Coleridge's journey to Germany during the first years of the nineteenth century, and his subsequent conversion to the writings of Immanuel Kant and the 'German school'. Though he had doubts regarding Kant's attempt to present a 'science' of the mind, Mill readily approved their shared determination to reinvest a sense of 'moral obligation' against the rather more ethically emaciated scepticism of Hobbes or Locke. The idea that the political imagination might, as Coleridge alleged, be an intrinsic expression or 'positive command of the moral law' fascinated Mill (Mill and Bentham, 1987, pp.184–9; Coleridge, 1997, pp.279, 284).

*

Indeed, it fascinated a generation, not least one of Mill's closest intellectual associates, the novelist George Eliot. In a series of essays and translations of the major works of German 'Higher Criticism', including Friedrich Strauss's *The Life of Jesus* and Ludwig Feuerbach's *The Essence of Christianity*, published in the *Westminster Review*, Eliot advocated a 'religion of humanity', one that recognized in the 'idea of God' an 'extension and multiplication of the effects produced by human sympathy' and which championed the 'love of the good and the beautiful'. Drawing on the earlier traditions of Kantian humanism that had inspired Coleridge a generation earlier, the Higher Critics argued that man alone, as Feuerbach put it, 'is the God of man' (Eliot, 1990, p.462; Jay, 1979, pp.207–43). If the inspiration looked back to Kant, the prognosis looked forward to Nietzsche.

But, for Feuerbach, the 'religion of humanity' was certainly not intended to be the precursor to a melancholic existentialism. Quite the reverse. The reassertion of humanity was the unfulfilled promise of Enlightenment. It reeked of a pragmatic hope; of the kind, perhaps, that is today recommended by the likes of Richard Rorty or, to a certain degree, Francis Fukuyama. As Feuerbach asserted in his *Essence of Christianity*:

> My fellow-man is the bond between me and the world. I am, and I feel myself dependent on the world, because I feel myself dependent upon other men. If I did not need man, I should not need the world. I reconcile myself with the world, only through my fellow-man. Without other men, the world would be for me not only dead and empty, but meaningless. (Eliot, 1990, p.461)

This attitude, almost post-modern in tone, was continued in Feuerbach's description of the human faculties:

> Wit, acumen, imagination, feeling as distinguished from sensation, reason as a subjective faculty, – all these so-called powers of the soul, are powers of humanity, not as an individual; they are products of culture, products of human society… Love, which requires mutuality, is the spring of poetry; and only where man communicates with man, only in speech, a social act, awakes reason. (Ibid., p.462)

For Feuerbach, a humanist politics was, by definition, a relation of sense and sensibility, and Eliot was wholly taken by this idea too. There had, she observed, 'perhaps been no perversion more obstructive of true moral development than this substitution of a reference to the glory of God for the direct promptings of the sympathetic feelings' (ibid., pp.65–7).

Positive religion had conspired with positive law to annihilate the natural sentiments of humanity, and it had done so, primarily, by erasing the roots of human association and compassion, what Eliot termed, in a commentary on the poet Cowper, 'that genuine love which cherishes things in proportion to their nearness, and feels its reverence grow in proportion to the intimacy of its knowledge' (ibid., p.213). It is this emotional delinquency in matters of social justice which needed to be redressed. In a review of Carlyle's *Life of Sterling*, she praised the author for his ability to paint a picture of compassion, the 'love of good and beautiful in character' which is, she added, 'after all, the essence of piety'. In another essay in the *Review*, Eliot affirmed her view that it was 'not as a theorist, but as a great and beautiful human nature, that Carlyle influences us' (ibid., pp.301, 344).

A revived humanist 'religion' could only be conveyed through an 'extension of our sympathies', through the 'picture of human life such as a great artist can give', and it is this which Eliot endeavoured to do (ibid., p.110). Amongst the best examples of this aspiration are some of the earlier works, written in the immediate wake of translating Strauss and Feuerbach, such as the *Scenes of Clerical Life* and *Adam Bede*. It is in the latter novel that Eliot's heroine Dinah is able to reinvest a sense of humanity and compassion by preaching a 'religion of the heart' to a community that is otherwise riven by the discords of evangelical dissent and radical democratic politics (Jay, 1979, pp.220–34; Pyle, 1995, pp.155–7).

Mill's affinity with Eliot's 'religion of humanity', which according to Maurice Cowling describes the essence of his entire moral philosophy, finds an explicit statement in his *Essays on Religion*. It is here that Mill famously aligns the 'golden rule of Jesus of Nazareth', the rule which St Paul described in his famous injunction to 'love thy neighbour', to the 'spirit of an ethics of utility'. Both, according to Mill, were philosophies of disinterest, philosophies which could, therefore, devote themselves exclusively to the interests of humanity, untrammelled by any deeper metaphysics or ideology (Cowling, 1990, pp.77–93).

The younger Mill had already written a series of essays, during the early 1830s, about the relation of politics, philosophy and poetry. It was in these essays that he made his influential distinction between the kind of 'emotional' poetry of the 'poet', such as Shelley and the more 'thoughtful' poetry of the 'cultivated' mind, such as that of Wordsworth and Coleridge. It was the latter which really attracted Mill; 'thoughts, coloured by, and impressing themselves by means of, emotions'. Certainly, it was the 'cultivated mind' which, he thought, must be deployed anew in the cause of social and political progress (Alexander, 1967, pp.49–78).

As his *Autobiography* later confirmed, Mill had constantly sought to somehow effect a balance between Benthamism and the kind of philosophy found in the verses of Wordsworth and Coleridge. The 'progress of civilization', as he had affirmed in his *Attack on Literature*, depended upon it. Progressive politics is founded upon the ability to educate humanity 'to love truth and virtue for themselves', and this is what a poet can do so much better than anyone else. Poets, as he again affirmed in another essay written during the early 1830s, *On Genius*, deal in the 'whole'. In other words they think in terms of the 'whole' individual, the sensitive and the 'sympathetic' as well as the sensible (ibid., pp.22–3, 27, 36–7).

Despite his own ultimate adherence to the basic principles of utilitarianism shared by his father and by Bentham, Mill retained a fundamental commitment to the balance of sense and sensibility. Indeed, as he argued insistently in his essay *Utilitarianism*, published in 1861, the philosophy of utility is a humanist philosophy, one that is therefore founded on this balance. His later campaigns, for the poor or for female suffrage, were expressions of this basic commitment. In an eloquent passage in *Utilitarianism*, he described the process by which the human condition might be alleviated by the reinvestment of principles of humanity:

> The social state is at once so natural, so necessary, and so habitual to man, that, except in some unusual circumstances or by an effort of voluntary abstraction, he never conceives himself otherwise than as a member of a body; and this association is riveted more and more, as mankind are further removed from the state of savage independence.

The interests of the individual and the society within which they live become 'inseparable'. The 'collective interest' becomes paramount:

> Not only does all strengthening of social ties, and all healthy growth of society, give to each individual a stronger personal interest in practically consulting the welfare of others; it also leads him to identify his feelings more and more with their good, or at least with an ever greater degree of practical consideration for it. He comes, as though instictively, to be conscious of himself as a being who of course pays regard to others. The good of others becomes to him a thing naturally and necessarily to be attended to, like any of the physical conditions of our existence. (Mill and Bentham, 1987, p.304)

Moreover, as a consequence, 'the smallest germs of the feeling are laid hold of and nourished by the contagion of sympathy', around which can then be 'woven' a 'complete web of corroborative associations'. As we shall see shortly, these particular passages are striking in their resonance with both Kant's categorical imperative and Adam Smith's idea of the 'impartial spectator'. The 'motives' of 'interest' and 'sympathy', sense and sensibility, find a common expression in the congruent concern of the individual and the community, and the duties which flow from it. Justice, indeed, becomes a function of this balancing of interests and duties, something dedicated ultimately, to the promotion of individual and social 'good' (Mill and Bentham, 1987, pp.305, 334–8; Cowling, 1990, pp.40–41, 82–3).

Although it is often suggested that Mill's *Principles of Political Economy* should be read as a kind of footnote to Adam Smith's *Wealth of Nations*, there is a commitment to social distribution which gives the lie to the idea that his economic theory somehow consolidated a neoliberal abandonment of humanist principles. Indeed, as we shall see shortly, the misconception is equally relevant to readings of Smith. The extent of Mill's commitment to forms of 'social cooperation' is reinforced by the *Chapters on Socialism* which he published after *Political Economy*. 'Suffice it to say,' Mill affirmed, 'that the condition of numbers in civilized Europe, and even in England and France, is more wretched than that of most tribes of savages who are known to us.' Such a state of affairs is neither just nor even necessary. It confounds the 'irresistible claim upon every human being for protection against suffering'. It confounds, indeed, the very 'idea' of humanity (Mill, 1994, pp.382–3, 425–6). There can, Mill concluded, be no genuine liberty without a basic equality of resources. And neither can there be any credible claim to progress. The responsibility of the enlightened liberal is to remember that progress is something that must be enjoyed by all. Otherwise, it is not progress at all, and neither is it liberty.

A Jurisprudence of Sentiment

A century before Mill voiced his concerns, it was apparent to many that the countervailing demands of sense and sensibility represented the greatest intellectual challenge of the Enlightenment. And no one worked harder to address this challenge than Adam Smith, whose treatise *The Theory of Moral Sentiments* was intended to provide the foundations for precisely such a balanced and comprehensive public philosophy. In the end, such a comprehensive statement would prove elusive, and instead Smith bequeathed his renowned treatise on economics, *The Wealth of Nations*, together with an altogether less coherent, scattered set of *Lectures on Jurisprudence*. It is one of the great tragedies, not only that *The Wealth of Nations* should be so often misunderstood as some kind of authority for an extreme, even anarchic, neoliberalism, but that generations of jurists should largely neglect Smith's attempt to lay the foundations for a 'general' jurisprudence in the *Theory* and the *Lectures* (Ross, 1995, pp.418–20: Griswold, 1999, pp.9–24).

As more recent scholars have suggested, a closer look at the earlier texts reveal a jurist who was deeply committed to received ideas of the 'good society', who betrayed a fundamental distrust of radical liberal ideas of untrammelled commerce, and who maintained a fixed adherence to the inherited humanist notion that the study of human relations is irreducibly aesthetic. As we shall see shortly, Smith's 'natural' jurisprudence is, indeed, founded on the belief that political morality is generated by a series of impressionistic reflections, which can then generate a mutually sympathetic engagement. Such a perception of politics and morality emphasizes, above all, that Smith was an intensely humanist philosopher, someone whose ideas were entirely founded on a particular view of humanity and its progressive well-being (Griswold, 1999, pp.119–24; Haakonssen, 1981, pp.147–51; Werhane, 1991, pp.7–17, 177–80).

But what was Smith's particular vision of humanity, and how did it underpin his idea of a 'general' jurisprudence? The answer to the first part of this question could be found in *The Theory of Moral Sentiments*. Indeed, there is much in the *Theory* which lays clear foundations for the answer to the second part as well. The opening passages of the *Theory* are instructive:

> How selfish soever man may be supposed, there are evidently some principles in his nature, which interest him in the fortune of others, and render their happiness necessary to him, though he derives nothing from it except the pleasure of seeing it. Of this kind is pity or compassion, the emotion which we feel for the misery of others, when we either see it, or are made to conceive it in a lively manner. (Smith, 1976, p.6)

The rest of the *Theory* is devoted to explaining, and also applauding, the extent to which a concern for others is not merely a voluntaristic complement, but an integral part of a philosophy of self-interest. It is from this driving, intensely human, desire to promote self-interest that a concern for others is derived.

The dependence upon the Christian ethic of love was acquired most obviously from Hutcheson, who had resolved all virtue to the idea of benevolence. This was then tempered with a measure of classical Stoicism, some Aristotle and a lot of Cicero. For Smith, the ideal humanist remained the 'prudent' man, the man of 'virtue' and 'duty' and 'self-command' and, above all, of 'balance' (ibid., pp.212–17, 237–9, 267–72, 287–97; Griswold, 1999, pp.179–84; Fitzgibbons, 1995, pp.16–19, 46–52). Whilst the hero of *The Wealth of Nations* might be the rational economic actor, the hero of *The Theory of Moral Sentiments* is the man who appreciates the proper balance of sense and sensibility.

Later in the first book, Smith can thus conclude:

> And hence it is, that to feel much for others and little for ourselves, that to restrain our selfish, and to indulge our benevolent affections, constitutes the perfection of human nature; and can alone produce among mankind that harmony of sentiments and passions in which consists their whole grace and propriety. As to love our neighbour as we love ourselves is the great law of Christianity, so it is the great precept of nature to love ourselves only as we love our neighbour, or what comes to the same thing, as our neighbour is capable of loving us. (Smith, 1976, p.25)

An interest in others is, thus, both a 'precept of nature' and a virtue. It is what defines the character of the 'prudent' man. As he says later, in the second book of the *Theory*, the 'man of the most perfect virtue' is 'he who joins, to the most perfect command of his own original and selfish feelings, the most exquisite sensitivity both to the original and sympathetic feelings of others' (ibid., p.152).

This idea of 'sympathetic feeling' represents Smith's most original contribution to the inherited philosophy of classical humanism. Yet it is not, of course, entirely original. In his *Treatise of Human Nature*, David Hume has already noted that 'No quality of human nature is more remarkable, both in itself and in its consequences, than that propensity we have to sympathize with others, and to receive by communication their inclinations and sentiments, however different from, or even contrary to, our own' (Hume, 1978, p.316). The influence of the 'exceedingly ingenious' Hume is pervasive. It was from Hume that Smith inherited his central belief that jurisprudence was 'natural' or general. In his *Enquiry Concerning the Principles of Morals*, Hume had affirmed that the very 'notion of morals implies some sentiment' so 'universal and comprehensive as to extend to all mankind' (Hume, 1966, pp.110–11).

It was also Hume who suggested that moral judgment is founded on reflective human perception, ultimately upon feelings and 'sensations'. Indeed it was this that reinforced his assertion that ethics and jurisprudence were 'natural' and general. 'Men,' Hume suggested in his *Treatise*, 'always consider the sentiments of others in their judgment of themselves' (Hume, 1978, pp.295–6, 375). All 'perceptions of the human mind,' he famously asserted, are 'impressions', forms of 'resembling'. Sympathy, indeed, is 'nothing but a lively idea converted into an impression'. In this way human beings acquire a 'strong and lively sense' of the condition of others, and, by reflection, of themselves. And the same, of course, is true of justice. More precisely, 'tis only from the selfish and confin'd generosity of men' that 'justice derives its origins'. Justice, in short, is founded on selfish passion. Furthermore, and this is another insight that clearly had a profound effect upon Smith, 'in treating of the passions' it is apparent 'that men are mightily govern'd by the imagination'. If justice is located in the 'passions', it is also described by the 'imagination' (ibid., pp.1–11, 211–12, 319, 385–6, 495, 534).

In the *Theory*, Smith duly affirms that the sensible human being can sympathize with others through the exercise of the 'imagination'. In other words, individuals can apply their own experience of the same 'feelings' in similar, or even dissimilar, contexts to the particular context within which the other is situated (Smith, 1976, p.75). The importance of 'sympathy' in simple terms, is that it elevates the individual above mere 'self-interest':

> The man who, not from frivolous fancy, but from proper motives, has performed a generous action, when he looks forward to those whom he has served, feels himself to be the natural object of their love and gratitude, and, by sympathy with them, of the esteem and approbation of mankind. (Ibid., p.85)

And it is the 'thought' of this 'approbation' which thus fills the mind with 'cheerfulness, serenity, and composure'. 'Humanity,' as Smith affirms elsewhere, 'does not desire to be great, but to be beloved' (ibid., pp.85, 166).

In this sense, 'sympathy' determines our regard for others. We crave sympathetic treatment, and so we crave sympathetic relations. We need to be loved, and so we are prepared to love others. In this way we learn to judge sympathetically, and judiciously. This is the very essence of Smith's renowned idea of the 'impartial spectator'. 'Every faculty in one man,' Smith asserts, 'is the measure by which he judges of the like faculty in another.' Accordingly, 'I judge of your sight by my sight, of your ear by my ear, of your reason by my reason, of your resentment by my resentment, of your love by my love.' There is no 'other way of judging' (ibid., p.19).

In this way we are intensely dependent on our reciprocal relation with others, and we can conceive of neither morality nor politics outwith this condition. Indeed, a 'good' society is one in which the public 'tranquillity' is preserved by precisely this kind of sympathetic 'conversation'. 'Nothing', Smith affirms, is 'more dreadful' than 'solitude' and nothing more likely to dissolve the human bonds of duty, respect and compassion than silence. Politics, for Smith, is all about improving our capacity to judge ourselves and others through the faculty of refined 'conversation'. Throughout the *Theory*, Smith repeatedly affirms the extent to which mutual 'love' and 'respect' are nurtured by the 'happy commerce' of human interaction. Indeed, such 'commerce' is the mark of a 'humane and polished' society. There is nothing more 'joyous' than the cultivation of 'friendship', and nothing more conducive to social 'harmony' (ibid., 23, 38–40, 46–7, 84–5, 153, 207). As he confirms in the closing passages of the *Theory*, the 'great pleasure of conversation and society arises' from a 'certain harmony of minds, which like so many musical instruments coincide and keep time with one another' (ibid., p.337).

*

Of course, 'justice' is something quite distinct. It is the 'last and greatest of the virtues', and something that cannot be 'left to the freedom of our own wills' (Smith, 1976, pp.79, 269–70). It is for this reason that Smith makes the distinction, both in the *Theory* and then again in greater depth in his *Lectures on Jurisprudence*, between law, which is merely an expression of politics and conversation, and justice which is constituted by 'nature'. Sets of laws, or constitutions, as Smith affirms in his discussion of 'Utility' in the *Theory*, 'are valued only in proportion as they tend to promote the happiness of those who live under them'. 'This,' furthermore, 'is their sole use and end' (ibid., pp.185–7, 190).

At the same time, while it may be a natural 'virtue' and thus something very different from law, justice remains an essentially 'negative' element in social order, something that exists to define the boundaries of the human condition. In the *Lectures*, Smith would develop this insight into a putative theory of rights. To this extent it too is judged in terms of its utility. Accordingly, while justice is the 'main pillar that upholds the edifice of society', it cannot itself promote a benevolent or enlightened society (ibid., pp.81–2, 86; Griswold, 1999, pp.228–9: Haakonssen, 1981, pp.85–7, 99–104). It merely protects it, and thus provides the necessary conditions within which love and compassion can flourish. This, for Smith, describes the essential balance in an Enlightened public philosophy, between sense and sensibility, between justice and compassion. As he confirms in the final chapter of the *Theory*, 'moral sense' must be understood as the marriage of the one virtue that can 'properly be given', namely justice, and the 'sentiments of the heart' which by their 'nature' deny sure definition (Smith, 1976, pp.328–9).

The Theory of Moral Sentiments was always intended to provide the groundwork for a comprehensive public philosophy, a critical constituent of which would be a 'general' jurisprudence of the 'moral sense'. The final passages of the *Theory* were clearly written as a link to this anticipated treatise. Although Smith never realized his ambition to publish a definitive text on the subject of natural jurisprudence, a series of lectures given at Glasgow University in 1762–4 and 1766 were recorded by students and are sufficiently substantive as to provide us with a reasonably clear picture of what Smith intended.

Smith's jurisprudence was geared by his overarching belief in progress. Adopting the approach which he inherited from Hutcheson and Hume, and through them from Montesquieu, Smith expressed his commitment to the idea that a 'natural' jurisprudence was an evolutionary jurisprudence, and that the role of law was meant to be progressive and instrumental. In his discussion of 'public jurisprudence' in the 1766 report, Smith aligned this belief in progress with a residual faith in the Aristotelian idea of the good society. The art of government, he suggested, lay in arousing the popular 'sentiment' so that citizens 'sympathize' with those that seek to lead them, 'admire their happy situation, enter into it with pleasure, and endeavour to promote it'. Most obviously, 'most all laws and regulations tend to the encouragement' of those 'arts' which promote the cultivation of land and the prosecution of trade. All 'law and government have these as their final end and ultimate object'. Making reference to the *Theory of Moral Sentiments*, Smith repeated that such laws must always seek to nurture the natural inclination to promote self-interest, and thereby effect the 'general' improvement of society (Smith, 1978, pp.337–8, 401).

This did not, of course, mean that law should be intrusive. As he impressed in both the *Lectures* and *The Wealth of Nations*, the presumption remained that law should be minimal in its impact upon society. His famously ambiguous statements on smuggling reinforce this particular attitude, as do his various comments on oppressive taxation and tariffs. Too many laws create too many criminals. While smuggling might violate the law, this is not the same as 'violating' the laws of 'natural justice'. Once again, positive law and natural justice are two very different things; one an instrument, the other an end. It was this core belief that defined Smith's commitment to the ideas of a natural and 'general' jurisprudence (ibid., pp.343–4, 383; Ross, 1995, pp.23, 120–22).

The distinction between 'positive law' and 'natural jurisprudence', originally described in the closing passages of the *Theory*, remained at the very heart of the *Lectures*. Given that modern society is naturally progressive, the nature of positive laws will vary in relation to the nature of the society in which they are employed. The more advanced a society is, the more its laws reflect this developed appreciation of human 'sentiments'. Positive law thus follows the dictates of natural, progressive, jurisprudence (Smith, 1976, pp.340–41; Werhane, 1991, pp.78–82; Haakonssen, 1981, pp.148–50). A prime example here is the law of contract, which has developed as a response to humanity's natural inclination towards self-interest and improvement. Contract, for Smith, is also a good example of a legal instrument which has evolved in response to a mature appreciation that the individual good is congruent with the wider public good (Smith, 1978, pp.9–10, 86–102).

Just as the final passages of the *Theory* looked forward to the anticipated treatise on natural jurisprudence, so too Smith's final lectures in 1766 explored some of the material that would later emerge in a more developed form in the *Wealth of Nations*. The government of markets, Smith suggests, like the government of societies, depends upon a proper appreciation of self-interest and sympathy in the condition of others. A 'prosperous' society is one that somehow converts the natural sentiments of 'self-interest' into a wider Aristotelian appreciation that the individual interest cannot be cleanly distinguished from that of society itself. It is for this reason that Smith concludes with a cautionary discussion of the 'disadvantages of the commercial spirit', namely that the 'minds of men are constructed and rendered incapable of elevation, education is despised or at least neglected and heroic spirit is almost utterly extinguished'. Such a 'spirit', in short, is one in which the relation between self-interest and the interest of others has been broken. Ultimately, societies that devote all their energies to such an endeavor destroy themselves (ibid., pp.540–41; Fitzgibbons, 1995, pp.153–6, 172–6).

As ever, a 'prosperous' society, like a 'good' society, is one in which there is 'harmony' between sense and sensibility, between law and justice and compassion. It is this 'harmony' which confirms that a jurisprudence is indeed 'natural'. As Smith argued in his concluding lectures on international law, the essential characteristic of any society at war with itself, or indeed societies at war with themselves, is the absence of 'sentimental' engagement. The effect of such 'spite', moreover, can only be to impoverish all parties, and tend, ultimately, to their mutual destruction. International law, like any other form of law, must be founded on the facility of each party to sympathize with the other (Smith, 1978, pp.391–2, 547; Werhane, 1991, pp.96–100).

The idea that sympathy or compassion should be something of immediately jurisprudential import might seem rather odd today, particularly perhaps in the discipline of international law and relations. Jurisprudence, we are told, deals in laws, in rules and regulations, in constitutions and statutes and cases. Even international law is supposed to deal in this currency. But this was not how Smith saw jurisprudence. It has even been suggested that so determined was Smith to explore further this intrinsic relation between positive law and justice and compassion, that he could never bring himself to complete his intended treatise on jurisprudence. The more he looked to define a 'science' of law, the more impossible the aspiration seemed to be (Griswold, 1999, pp.83–94, 149–50, 257–8).

And Smith was not alone in his commitment to a 'natural' jurisprudence that was founded on a fundamental belief in the instrinsic relation between the ideas of justice and compassion. A decade later, George Mason could be found drafting the Virginia Declaration of Rights, a forerunner of the American Declaration, and in Article 16 suggesting that all Virginians, whilst they possessed an array of inalienable rights, had above all a 'mutual duty of all to practice Christian forbearance, love and charity toward each other' (Klug, 2000, p.74). Smith would have approved such a duty. And so too would Immanuel Kant, to whom we shall now turn. For Kant was a firm admirer of Smith, 'the man,' he noted, 'who goes to the root of things' and who looks at every subject 'not just from his own point of view but from that of the community'. Kant was just as determined to maintain a critical balance between sense and sensibility in Enlightenment public philosophy.

The Starry Heavens and the Moral Law

The events of 1789 hit Europe like a thunderbolt, thrilling some, horrifying others, fascinating all. Across the other side of the continent, tucked away in his beloved Koenigsberg, the greatest of all Enlightenment legal philosophers, Immanuel Kant, was ebullient. The French revolution, he declared, like that in America a decade before, proved the 'moral disposition of the human race' (Kant, 1991c, pp.182–3). Eight years later, Kant completed his final, definitive treatise on public philosophy, his *Metaphysics of Morals*. For many jurists, the *Metaphysics* is the founding text of modern legal thought. It is, but it is also far more than this. For the *Metaphysics* is a far more rounded text, a far more humanist text, than is often appreciated.

There is much in the *Metaphysics* about legal rights, but there is much, too, about respect and virtue and compassion.

But, before we take a closer look at the *Metaphysics*, it is essential to place it within the context of Kant's wider philosophical 'architectonic'. In 1781, Kant published the first of his three *Critiques*, the *Critique of Pure Reason*. The introductory passages to the first *Critique* set the mood. The sceptical reaction against metaphysics, he suggested, was 'not produced by lightness of mind, but by judgment of the age, which has matured and no longer tolerates being put off with illusory modes of knowledge'. His was, he declared, the 'genuine Age of Criticism, to which everything must submit'. And he continued:

> This calls upon reason to undertake anew the most difficult of tasks – that of knowing itself – and to institute a tribunal that will assure to reason its legitimate claims while dismissing its groundless pretensions; not by enforced decrees, but in accordance with its eternal and unalterable laws. This tribunal is the critique of reason itself. (Kant, 1988, p.xi)

Because order was defined by the faculty of reason, any metaphysics had to be reoriented to the individual, to the 'moral self'. In simple terms, reason is immanent, and because of this liberating. If pure practical moral reason is located within the self, then we alone can self-govern, self-create and self-determine. Understanding is created by the cognate subject, and not by any metaphysical object.

Kant's famous distinction of the *apriori* and the *aposteriori* flowed from here: the distinction between the idea of something, and our experiential approximation of it. As we shall see shortly, this is a critical mechanism for understanding a Kantian theory of law; for the idea of law or right, and our experiential approximation of it, can, accordingly, be very different. The capacity for human creativity, for the contribution of the 'moral self' lies within this distinction. It distinguishes the tyranny of metaphysical truths and their laws from the jurisprudential expressions of the 'free-will'.

This key distinction was taken up in Kant's following two works, the *Groundwork for a Metaphysics of Morals* and the second *Critique*, the *Critique of Pure Practical Reason*. The idea of the 'free-will' is the keystone of the *Groundwork*. The entire text was devoted to refining maxims of behaviour, duties which obliged everyone to act in accordance with the precepts of the categorical imperative, the 'supreme principle of pure practical reason'. In its generic form, the imperative was described in the following terms: that 'I ought never to act except in such a way that I can also will that my maxim should become a universal law' (Kant, 1964, p.70). The universality of the imperative was critical. It prescribed a public morality to which all cognate individuals should adhere.

This universalism was impressed still further in Kant's affirmation that the moral self, as the ultimate source of reason and morality, must be the 'end' of any metaphysics:

> For rational beings all stand under the law that each of them should treat himself and all others, never merely as a means, but always at the same time as an end in himself. But by doing so there arises a systematic union of rational beings under common objective laws – that is, a kingdom. (Ibid., p.101)

The *Groundwork* was written in anticipation of the second *Critique*, upon which he was already working, and which was to reaffirm the central importance of the moral law as the foundation upon which the entire 'architectonic' was set. As he famously observed at the conclusion of this *Critique*, 'Two things fill the mind with ever new and increasing admiration and awe, the oftener and more steadily they are reflected on: the starry heavens above me and the moral law within me' (Kant, 1956, p.161). The moral law is given as 'an apodictically certain fact', for the 'same subject, who is also conscious of himself as a thing in himself, considers his own existence, so far as it does not stand under conditions of time, as determinable only through laws that he gives himself through reason' (ibid., pp.97–8).

It is for this reason, because morality is immanent to the self, that the moral self also acquires certain responsibilities with regard to others – as was, indeed, suggested by the idea of the categorical imperative. If the moral self is the 'end' of any critical philosophy, then the duties owed towards others, the 'end' of 'community', becomes the 'end' of a public philosophy too (Sullivan, 1989, pp.25–6, 85–7, 152).

*

A Kantian public philosophy could, then, be clearly discerned within the construction of the first two critiques; an idea of free-will determinative of the moral self, and an array of conceptual networks of practical duties. But before we take a closer look at Kant's most obviously political works, including the *Metaphysics of Morals*, it is important to appreciate the full import of his third *Critique*, the *Critique of Judgement*. The fact that generations of Kantian jurists have preferred to concentrate on the *Metaphysics* is perhaps understandable. It seems to be Kant's definitive statement of jurisprudence, and its most immediate intellectual context appears to be provided by the first two *Critiques* and the *Groundwork*. But a failure to fully appreciate the position and the purpose of the third *Critique* is a critical error. The third *Critique* is an intensely political critique, for at its heart is a determination to maintain a balance of sense and sensibility within the entire Kantian 'architectonic'.

The essential tenor of the *Critique of Judgement* is one of reflection, of 'thinking the particular' as Kant put it, of mediating the 'great abyss' that had opened up between reason and sensibility. This abyss, Kant now realized, could no more be bridged by reason alone than it could by any classical or theological metaphysics. There was certainly no abandonment of morality, still less of the moral self. As he affirmed in the first volume of the *Critique*, it is 'only as a moral being that we acknowledge man to be the end of creation' (Kant, 1991b, 1. 407, 444). But, more than before, Kant was prepared to concede a degree of relativism to the creative capacity of the political individual, a concession which was, however, sharply defined within the boundaries of a constructive communicative rationality.

The definitive statement was to be found in section 40 of the *Critique*, in the 'faculty' of the *sensus communis*, a 'critical faculty which in its reflective act takes account of the mode of reflection of every one else, in order, as it were, to weight its judgement with the collective reason of mankind'. This, he continued, 'is accomplished by weighing the judgement, not so much with actual, as rather with the merely possible, judgements of others, and by putting ourselves in the position of everyone else, as the result of a mere abstraction from the limitations which contingently affect our own estimate' (ibid., 1. 151). There are various resonances here, not just with Kant's own categorical imperative, but also very obviously with Smith's idea of the 'impartial spectator'.

Much of the rest of the third *Critique* is dedicated to a discussion of the constituent critiques of aesthetics and teleology. Both sought 'harmony' between reason and sensibility. Inevitably, Kant was drawn into esoteric discussions of the indeterminacy of 'ends', discussions which could only undermine the attempt to maintain a distinction between the faculties he was trying to bridge. If the moral self is indeed the 'end' of any moral or political philosophy, there is nothing to prevent that same self judging political 'ends' differently. Conceptions of the beautiful vary, just as must conceptions of the moral good. They are not irreducibly contingent, because they are bound by the *sensus communis*. But neither can they be confined within any autonomous self. Politics, in other words, already unhinged from the illusions of metaphysical truth in the first two *Critique*s, is now further detached from any pretence that it might be defined by an immanent morality.

So is the third *Critique* really a political treatise? Someone who clearly thought so was Samuel Taylor Coleridge, whose *Biographia Literaria* paid fulsome tribute to 'the illustrious sage of Konigsberg', whose ideas 'took possession of me as with a giant's hand'. More particularly, Coleridge was fascinated by the 'hints and insinuations', within Kant's writings, that the truly critical faculty was the faculty of the imagination. As the *Biographia* made plain, Coleridge was quite convinced that it was only through the exercise of this faculty that human relations could be properly mediated (Coleridge, 1997, pp.89–90). As we have already noted, in due course this thought captured the minds of a generation of mid-nineteenth century intellectuals, including John Stuart Mill and George Eliot.

If this is so, if Coleridge's interpretation of Kantian metaphysics is correct, then the imagination is indeed a necessarily political faculty. Coleridge was committed to the idea that poets had an avowed political and moral responsibility, to promote the 'best interests of humanity' (ibid., pp.23–4, 41–4, 175). It was this that led him, after many tortuous years of intellectual journeying, to Kant and the German school of romanticism, to the uncompromising belief that the 'cultivation of judgement', like indeed the cultivation of sympathy, was 'a positive command of the moral law'. The term 'cultivation' was vital. Coleridge consciously deployed it in order to signify a new form of 'public-spiritedness' that could be set against the more traditional notions of civic humanism which had been perverted by the 'commercial spirit' (ibid., pp.279, 284: Leask, 1998, pp.108–16, 124–5).

We shall take a closer look at the kind of politics espoused by the likes of Coleridge, along with Wordsworth and Shelley and others, in the next chapter. In many ways, Coleridge's interpretation of Kant provides a bridge into this rather different intellectual world: one in which the realm of rights, rather than being part of delicate balance, of sense and sensibility, is radically relegated to a position of almost incidental import. But for now it is worth emphasizing the extent to which the third *Critique* evidenced the extent to which philosophers such as Kant were desperate to somehow maintain this essential balance. It also reveals how very difficult this proved to be.

Coleridge's interpretation of Kant has been taken up more recently by a range of scholars. Paul Crowther has suggested that it is the 'capacity to humanize' which makes the third *Critique* irreducibly political. For Paul Guyer, too, a Kantian politics must be established on the twin foundations, of the categorical imperative and the faculty of judgement (Crowther, 1989, pp.165, 172–4; Guyer, 1993). This particular interpretation of Kant has also been promoted by a number of scholars who pay intellectual obeisance to the Nietzschean elision of politics and aesthetics. Gilles Deleuze, for example, has recently argued that the third *Critique*, like any treatise which was devoted to the 'ends' of human existence, has to be intensely political (Deleuze, 1995, pp.62–3). Jean-François Lyotard likewise suggests that the *sensus communis* unlocks the door to a distinctively post-modern philosophy, one in which the claims of reason are finally dismissed from the pantheon of political morality. Henceforth, politics must be seen to be as much a matter of sensibility as of sense; more so, indeed (Lyotard, 1988, pp.132–3, 155–8, 169).

Two of Heidegger's most famous pupils add further weight to this particular interpretation of Kant. In his *Truth and Method*, Hans-Georg Gadamer suggested that the third *Critique* should be recognized as the 'Critique of Critiques', the keystone in the grand edifice of Kantian moral and political philosophy, one that finally destroys any pretence that there are moral absolutes upon which some kind of atemporal politics can be founded (Gadamer, 1975, pp.29–51). Similarly, according to Hannah Arendt, it is in the 'faculty' of judgment that Kant had uncovered an entirely new, and radical, way of describing politics. It is, moreover, the logical 'end' of the critical project, and as such must be read as a complement to the *Metaphysics of Morals*. It was only once Kant had thought through the implications of the 'particular', of the power of the 'free-will' to create understanding, that he could properly compose a coherent treatise on public philosophy. There is a certain chronological credibility to this assertion, for it was only upon completing the third *Critique* that Kant seemed able to devote his energies undiluted to the question of politics (Arendt, 1982, pp.10–28, 34).

Arendt championed Kant as the 'all-destroyer of metaphysics', the man who finally dismantled the sclerotic principles which had perverted western philosophy for two millennia. What the third *Critique* revealed, Arendt suggested, was the impossibility of asserting objective truths. Instead, Kant is drawn inexorably towards a politics of 'common meaning', of 'common sense' indeed. Politics becomes a matter, not just of reason, but of sentiment and attachment, of accommodating a multitude of relative beliefs, interests and interpretations. In her final lectures on Kant, Arendt went further still, and placed her hero at the vanguard of a movement towards radical liberal politics, towards what we associate today with ideas of 'communicative action' and 'participatory politics'; a politics of what she termed essential 'sociability' (ibid., pp.61–4, 72–7).

*

And so, finally, to the *Metaphysics*. The *Metaphysics*, as is well known, takes the Kantian idea of the moral self and transposes it into the world of real politics. Effecting this transposition, as Kant had declared half a century earlier, was to be his ultimate ambition. Underpinning the entire enterprise is a determination to establish constraints upon the 'free-will' which can maintain practical political liberty without descending into an abstruse anarchy. These constraints are, of course, the duties or maxims generically described by the categorical imperative. But what is striking about the *Metaphysics*, though often rather neglected, is the fact that the mature public philosophy which Kant prescribes comes in two constituent forms: a 'Doctrine' of rights and a 'Doctrine' of virtue. Only a philosophy that recognizes their mutual constitution can be properly termed critical, or indeed humanist.

Kant's holistic public philosophy is, then, constituted in part by law and in part by the Aristotelian idea of sociability or mutual respect, the idea which the likes of Arendt, Deleuze and Lyotard are so keen to impress. And the governing principle of both, of law and respect, indeed the dynamic which binds them together, is the categorical imperative. What this means is quite simple; the idea of 'respect' for human dignity is no less essential for an enlightened political community than the idea of a 'right'. It is duty which bridges the two aspects of a humanist public philosophy (Kant, 1991a, p.51; Ward, 1997, pp.26–35; Teson, 1998, pp.3–6). The 'Doctrine of Right', of course, prescribes external constraints on behaviour; positive laws, or 'acquired rights', which express approximations of the 'one innate' idea of right. The 'Doctrine of Virtue', on the other hand, describes internal constraints, ethical duties, of 'inner freedom', which express an essential humanity or 'sociability' (Kant, 1991a, pp.186, 198).

Kant describes the second Doctrine as 'the science of how one is under obligation even without regard for possible external lawgiving', and develops this further in terms of an idea of virtue that is dedicated, not just to self-improvement, but to realizing the 'happiness of others' (ibid., pp.191–2, 211). These are the duties, far more than those of positive law, which reveal the 'moral disposition' of the human race. And to overlook their position in the *Metaphysics* is to make a serious mistake. Kant was fully aware that the interests of humanity require the promotion of moral sensibility. He had resolved this much in his third *Critique*. The 'happiness of others' is an 'end' which every citizen is under an ethical 'duty' to promote. Moreover, the 'principles' of 'mutual love' and 'respect' are not to be understood as mere 'feelings', but as a matter of both reason and sentiment. They are the definitive 'duties' of 'humanity' (ibid., pp.243–51).

In this sense, as Paul Guyer has emphasized, the 'Doctrine of Virtue', with its more particular duties of 'love' towards others, represents the very apex of a Kantian humanism (Guyer, 1993, pp.31–2, 304–84). And, accordingly, it is wholly mistaken to conceive a Kantian jurisprudence, including any Kantian idea of human rights, outwith these critical, but so often forgotten passages in the second 'Doctrine'. Modern jurisprudence has paid due reverence to the Kantian idea of 'right'. It has too often failed to note that the 'duty to cultivate the compassionate' has just as central a place in a Kantian political philosophy (Kant, 1991a, pp.250–51).

It is important, at this point, to note the bridge between the two 'Doctrines' in the *Metaphysics*. That bridge is provided by Kant's discussion of 'cosmopolitan right', the final brief chapter at the end of the first 'Doctrine'. Whilst the idea of 'cosmopolitan right' describes certain 'rights' pertaining to humanity, it also represents a striking example of the principle of mutual respect for human dignity, of a morality which prescribes 'obligation even without regard for possible external lawgiving'. The presence of 'cosmopolitan' right becomes the mark of a mature international order. But it also makes something more. The acknowledgment of cosmopolitan right, once again, confirms the 'moral disposition' of the human race. It is, indeed, an ultimate expression of the idea of the moral law itself.

Kant has long enjoyed a predominant place in the pantheon of international lawyers and advocates of human rights. Fernando Teson, for example, cites Kant as the first to place the 'normative individual' at the centre of a putative international law (Teson, 1998, pp.1–3). This reputation is fully justified, for Kant was indeed amongst the first to explore the idea of a cosmopolitan order, one which was defined by the relation of citizens across national borders. Prior to the events of 1789, he had already commented on the possibility that the establishment of some kind of international order would represent the epitome of Enlightenment politics. In his essay, an *Idea for a Universal History with a Cosmopolitan Purpose*, he argued that the 'history of the human race as a whole' could 'be regarded as the realisation of a hidden plan of nature' to effect a 'perfect political constitution as the only possible state within which all natural capacities of mankind can be developed completely' (Kant, 1991c, pp.41–53).

Such a conclusion, of course, chimes with that which emerged from Kant's tortuous intellectual voyage through the *Critiques* and the *Groundwork*. There is no doubting the irreducibly universalist aspirations of Kant's wider critical project. The categorical imperative, like the 'kingdom' of ends, demanded the recognition that each moral self was bound to all others by certain duties. The sense of 'fraternity', so strong amongst contemporary radicals such as Rousseau and Godwin, as we shall see in the next chapter, is striking. It was this innately universalist impulse which underpinned Kant's exuberant response to the events of 1789, his resolution that the 'revolution' had 'aroused in the hearts and desires of all spectators,' in other words right across Europe, 'a sympathy which borders on enthusiasm' (ibid., p.182).

Kant's interest in the idea of 'cosmopolitan right' must be understood within the context of this contemporary excitement. As the 1790s progressed, he became more and more committed to the idea that 'cosmopolitan right' might represent an epitome of a balanced right, an expression of sense and sensibility in the political relations of individuals and nations. In *Per-*

petual Peace, he emphasized that the distinguishing factor of 'cosmopolitan right', as opposed to 'international right', is that it is based on the 'universal state of mankind'. Kant was not arguing for some kind of transnational legal authority, but he was arguing for a conception of 'transcendental' public law; intimating that the establishment of a 'perpetual peace' would be founded on a proper appreciation of shared humanity between citizens rather than merely nations. International law was merely an intermediary stage as humanity progressed towards the 'end' of universal cosmopolitan right (ibid., pp.98–100, 106–9, 125–7)

This same broad schema was followed in the *Metaphysics*. Following discussion of the 'Right of Nations', which charted the law relating to international relations, and which, interestingly, was described in terms of a 'league of nations', Kant contrasted the idea of 'Cosmopolitan Right'. The 'rational Idea of a peaceful, even if not friendly, thoroughgoing community of all nations on the earth', he suggested, is not merely a 'philanthropic' aspiration, but something 'having to do with rights'. With a certain prophetic prescience, Kant affirmed that such a 'Right' would be necessary in order to mitigate the rigours of 'commerce'. The ill-treatment of citizens of other states is a 'stain of injustice' that militates against the 'moral disposition' of the weight of enlightened humanity. By definition, the failure to observe even these minimal principles of cosmopolitanism is to reduce humanity to the level of beasts (ibid., pp.156–9).

When he came to describe, and prescribe, the jurisprudence of Enlightenment, Kant presented 'cosmopolitan right' as the centrepiece of a coherent public philosophy. Nothing could better describe the judicious balance of sense and sensibility, and nothing was more essential if humanity was indeed to attain a state of 'perpetual peace'. For Kant, the idea of a 'good society' was always meant to describe a transnational state of humanity. In the final analysis, for Kant as for Smith indeed, the interests of humanity, and its anticipated progression toward Enlightenment, were as dependent upon virtue and compassion as they were upon law or right.

2 Prometheus Unbound

The Passions of Men

In the summer of 1790, thousands of French men and women swore oaths to the principles of the revolution in various ceremonies across the country. Cities tried to outdo one another, spending vast sums on ever more ostentatious ceremonies. Teenage girls dressed in white bobbed up and down in boats on the Rhine at Strasbourg all confirming their virginity for the benefit of France. Mass adoptions were popular. A vast temple of Concord was constructed in Lyon. The seminal event took place in Paris, at the Champs de Mars, and was conducted by Talleyrand and Lafayette. An 'altar to the Fatherland' was constructed beneath an 'Arc de Triomphe'. The ceremony was intended to identify the France of 1790 with the Rome of Brutus, Cato and Cicero. All the institutions were present, the king, the church, the government; all pretending to be the sponsors of a new republicanism, the embodiment of 'liberty, equality and fraternity' (Schama, 1989, pp.504–13).

Four years later, following the Jacobin revolution, a very different ceremony took place at the Champs de Mars, a 'Festival of Supreme Being'. Talleyrand had fled to London, where his arrival caused great excitement amongst the likes of Charles Fox and the radical democrat, William Godwin. The new power in France was that of Maximilien Robespierre. The new religion was the 'cult of sensibility' and the new intellectual deity was Jean-Jacques Rousseau, the man revered by Mary Wollstonecraft as 'the Prometheus of Sentiment'.

As Robespierre later reported to the Convention, the Festival was intended to sanctify a new 'Creation', a new 'divinity' born, as he had confirmed on the day, of 'liberty and virtue'. A month earlier, he had announced that the Festival would celebrate 'the relations between moral and religious ideas with republican principles'. The relation was not easily defined. Robespierre certainly struggled. 'The true priest of the Supreme Being,' he declared, 'is Nature itself; its temple is the universe; its religion virtue; its festivals the joy of a great people assembled under its eyes to tie the sweet knot of universal fraternity and to present before it the homage of pure and feeling hearts' (ibid., pp.831–6).

The accommodation of sense and sensibility clearly troubled Robespierre. On the one hand, he was keen to underline his own popular association with the Rome of Cato and Cicero. Sense mattered. But, to Robespierre, sensibility mattered even more. The tortured rhetoric of spring 1794 was a testament to the difficulty of this accommodation. The 'cult of sensibility' vied with the 'age of reason', the age of love-letters and romance with the age of constitutions and civil rights (Dart, 1999, pp.25–42, 46–8, 59–62, 66–75; Wingrove, 2000, pp.13–14).

When he was asked whether the French revolution was a success, Mao-Tse Tung famously replied that it was too early to tell. There is certainly a sense that the intellectual and political inheritance remains unclear. Like Robespierre, we are still struggling to make sense of sensibility. Perhaps more particularly, we are still trying to make sense of Rousseau. The late eighteenth century was entranced by Rousseau. Robespierre certainly was. So too was Kant, who even went so far as to suggest that the publication of *Emile* in 1762 was an event comparable with the 1789 revolution itself.

Rousseau, too, thought that *Emile* was his best work, the work that encapsulated his entire philosophy of life. At its heart is the determination to infuse politics with the natural passion which drives humanity. The concentrated exploration of sex, compassion and love is aimed at educating *Emile*'s audience not merely in the arts of private life, but in the governance of public life too. If politics is about human relations, then politics is about compassion and love, about ensuring that all citizens are 'submissive' only to the 'voice of friendship' rather than the 'great and useless' science of jurisprudence (Rousseau, 1991, pp.418–19, 457–8).

The radical import of *Emile* was not lost on the authorities in Geneva, who had the book burnt in public. An 'unparalleled fury', as Rousseau termed it, swept across Europe (Rousseau, 1953, p.545; Strong, 1994, pp.6–7). *Emile* was not merely iconoclastic: in its advocacy of a common education in the virtues of sensibility, it was also implicitly democratic. Rousseau was fond of describing himself as a Promethean, someone who brought the light of sensibility and democracy down from the intellectual gods. It was this implication that attracted Kant's attention. By the very act of writing, Rousseau sought to educate humanity, to nurture a 'natural' democracy through the facility of an imaginative political dialogue. 'He who imagines nothing,' Rousseau observed, 'feels only himself; in the midst of mankind he is alone.' The study of all is the 'condition' of all (Rousseau, 1991, pp.42, 214).

It is the very fact that this study is universal, that everybody engages in adjudging the 'condition' of others, that makes politics a matter of 'sensibility', of the 'sentiment of common existence'. Coining a phrase that struck a particular resonance with Kant, Rousseau referred to this as the sixth sense, 'called the common sense'. Whilst 'reason alone teaches us to know good and evil', it is 'conscience which makes us love the former and hate the latter'. It is our moral sensibility which makes us act upon what reason reveals. 'Make the language of the mind pass through the heart, so that it may make itself understood.' Rousseau urged. 'I repeat, cold arguments can determine our opinions, not our actions. They make us believe and not act. They demonstrate what must be thought, not what must be done' (ibid., p.323).

The mark of social progress lies in the translation of 'self-love' into a love of others. And for this to happen we must be able to draw on our imaginative capacities. It is here that education becomes, once again, central. For while sensibility might be natural, it is also capable of perfectibility. Before we can study politics and society, 'we must begin by knowing the human heart' (ibid., pp.97–8, 135–57, 213, 236; Wingrove, 2000, pp.32–3; Still, 1993, pp.83–92). There is a very obvious resonance here with Adam Smith's idea of the sympathetic 'spectator'. But whereas Smith, like Kant indeed, struggled heroically to maintain the balance between reason and sentiment, Rousseau leant inexorably towards the latter. It is 'our passions', he confirmed, that are the ultimate 'instrument of our preservation' and our 'freedom'. It is these passions that are 'enchained' by moral sentiment, and which then find their mature statement in an appreciation of 'friendship', 'pity' and 'compassion'. The exercise of such 'social virtues brings the love of humanity to the depths of one's heart'. Civic virtue finds its ultimate expression in the 'love of mankind', which in turn 'is nothing other than the love of justice' (Rousseau, 1991, pp.212, 219–22, 250–52).

The education of Emile is autobiographical in the sense that it describes the education of humanity. There is an implicit politics here, one that was refined further in Rousseau's *Confessions*, written just three years later. The two texts are commonly described as complementary, their intense subjectivity announcing a radically different, and intrinsically democratic, conception of politics. For Rousseau, genuine democracy lies in the facility to express compassion and respect for others, and the knowledge that such a facility is reciprocal. The thought found subsequent expression in the countless confessions of later 'romantics', from Goethe and Wordsworth to Trollope and Mill. For each of these, following Rousseau, the personal and the political were inseparable (Strong, 1994, pp.9–12; Dart, 1999, pp.9–15).

The intense subjectivity of the *Confessions* was announced on the very first page: 'I am unlike any one I have every met; I will even venture to say that I am like no one in the whole world.' No amount of 'stifled' ideology can change that simple truth (Rousseau, 1953, p.17). And no statement has more thoroughly determined the subjectivity of a humanist politics. The 'impossibility of attaining the real person' through philosophical reflection means that politics can never be anything more than a sequence of 'impressions' defined by the 'creative imagination' (ibid., pp.398–9). The 'cult of sensibility' admits this impressionist politics, and treasures it, for it describes an intrinsically humanist philosophy, one that focuses upon our ability to translate love and compassion into the virtues of freedom, equality and tolerance. Whilst they might, at first glance, be thought to distract political attention, the idyllic portrayals of Savoyard villagers dancing and picnicking together were intended to subvert. Theirs is a simple politics, to 'love and serve humanity', to promote the 'genuine love of truth and justice'. Theirs is a politics that is lived by 'all' (ibid., pp.231–3, 263, 427).

If *Emile* and the *Confessions* described Rousseau's philosophy of sensibility, the political translation found its most compelling, and influential, expression in the *Discourse on Inequality*, published in 1754, and then eight years later in *The Social Contract*. In the *Confessions*, Rousseau recounted how he had been inspired to compose his *Discourse* whilst walking through the woods of Saint-Germain. It was here that he stripped 'bare' the 'naked nature' of humanity, and 'demolished' the 'petty lies' of political ideology. The more he walked, the more he engaged in 'deep reflections' and the more he became convinced that the politics of the future must be based upon the retrieval of original ideas of the human condition (Rousseau, 1953, pp.362, 388).

Humanity, Rousseau concluded, has become distanced from its natural sentiments. In particular, it has become detached from the first 'natural virtue', the 'universal' virtue of 'compassion' (Rousseau, 1984, pp.99–101). It is for this reason that humanity tolerates inequality and suffering. It is for this reason, too, that it tries to shroud this inequality behind the 'moral inequality' of 'positive law', the 'fraudulent' fictions of legal institutions such as contracts and courts of law. The ambition of the *Discourse*, accordingly, is to reinvest the 'cause of humanity', and to do so, as ever, by redressing the imbalance of sense and sensibility. Reason makes plain the inequality of the human 'condition', but only 'passion' can make us care enough to do something about it (ibid., pp.77, 89, 137).

If the *Discourse* was intended to describe the 'origin' of inequality, the solution was to be presented nearly a decade later in *The Social Contract*, published in 1762. The essential sentiment was unchanged: the need to retrieve the freedom and equality that defined the 'natural' condition of humanity. As the opening sentence of the first book of *The Social Contract* famously states, 'Man was born free, and he is everywhere in chains.' Moreover, to 'renounce freedom is to renounce one's humanity, one's rights as men and equally one's duties' (Rousseau, 1968, p.49).

But whereas the *Discourse* lingered over this 'natural' condition and its renunciation, *The Social Contract* suggested that the retrieval of freedom necessitated the embrace of civic society. The central idea here was that of the 'general will', a 'sovereignty' that 'is formed entirely of the individuals who compose it', and which indeed serves to define the political identity of the commonalty or 'common sense'. The 'general will' becomes the expression of the evolved political 'condition', a matured moral sensibility (ibid., pp.63–5, 150–53; Dart, 1999, pp.22–5; Wingrove, 2000, pp.37–44).

This idea of the 'general will' captured the contemporary imagination, perhaps because it seemed to be so mystical, even nebulous. Sieyes defined it in terms of *patrie*, of common compassion and purpose, a shared interest in the liberty and equality of others, not just within France but beyond (Schama, 1989, p.444; Dart, 1999, pp.25–6). In his *Political Economy*, Rousseau made a comparable affinity with *patrie*, the political manifestation of the 'greater whole' which humanity can most readily come to 'love'. In *Emile*, Rousseau had placed the understanding of the 'general will' at the very end of his student's education. An obligation to the 'general will' is the only obligation that a free citizen should have (Rousseau, 1991, p.462; Wingrove, 2000, pp.151–64).

In language that was consciously resonant of Aristotle, Rousseau affirmed that a 'state' is established in order to translate the sentiment of the 'general will' into the politics of the 'common good'. In order to do this, humanity needs certain 'positive' laws and institutions. But such laws must always be understood to be 'acts of the general will', and in accord with a 'universal' or natural 'justice' (Rousseau, 1968, 69–72, 80–83). It is here that Rousseau could thus affirm the intrinsic relation between liberty and equality, and fraternity. The idea of the state is legitimated by an appeal to commonalty that is both rational and sentimental. It found a typical expression in the declaration of excited revolutionaries such as Charles de Ferrière, 'Oh my France, amiable and good people, I have made an eternal alliance with you. Before this day I had no *patrie*; now I have one and it will always be dear to me' (Schama, 1989, p.338). The implicit fraternity of the 'general will' made politics personal. It made people care about liberty and equality, and not just for themselves.

*

Whilst Robespierre traded on the totemic figure of Rousseau, and popular fondness for the man known affectionately as the 'Jack of Hearts', many amongst the more intellectual circles revered a very different icon. Whereas Rousseau had become the arch-priest of the 'cult of sensibility', Voltaire had been the arch-priest of anti-clericalism, the great champion of reason, the hero of men such as Talleyrand and Condorcet. It was Voltaire's spirit that presided at the 'altar to the Fatherland' in the Champs de Mars in 1790, the spirit that famously declared that it was a moral responsibility to declaim the judicial execution of one human being, simply because we too are human.

The progress of Enlightenment, Voltaire held, depended upon the thorough destruction of both mysticism and metaphysics. His *ABC* sought to destroy all the 'devilish perverseness' of mystic theology, and in its place present the simple principle of natural justice. Just laws are the 'daughters of nature'. In political terms, justice demands liberty and equality, and the laws necessary to secure them. 'To be free, to have only equals,' he affirmed, 'is the true, natural life of men.' The 'human race', Voltaire affirmed, has been waiting too long for justice. It has been too long distracted by 'soothsayers and wizards'. Now, courtesy of the 'perfection' of 'reason', its time had come (Voltaire, 1994, pp.84, 110–14, 125–6, 164–7).

As his contemporaries noted, in many ways Voltaire's spirit would have found its more congenial home outside France, in America perhaps, or possibly even Britain. Voltaire was uncompromising in his criticism of the 'cult of sensibility' and the kind of naturalist utopia advocated in Rousseau's *Social Contract* (ibid., pp.202–3). Constitutions, not woodland pathways, were humanity's guide. Voltaire was, accordingly, far more impressed by the English constitution, and the ideas of men such as Montesquieu and Locke (ibid., pp.172–4, 198). It was these men who similarly impressed the founding fathers across the Atlantic, and there is little doubting the extent to which the American revolution provided an inspiration for many in France at the time of the revolution. 'It is in the heart of this new-born republic,' the Abbé Gentil declared, 'that the true treasures that will enrich the world will lie' (Schama, 1989, pp.21–9, 47–8).

Rousseau and Voltaire, then, could be said to represent the alternative dynamics of the Enlightenment, of sense and sensibility. And, in some ways, so too did the Jacobin and American revolutions: one shrouded in a romantic mysticism, the other crowned by a fervent belief in the role of constitutions. If the events of 1789, and more intensely those of 1793–4, were inspired by the *Confessions* or *The Social Contract*, the settlement, and the sentiment, of 1776 were cast in the image of the *Federalist Papers* or Tom Paine's *Common Sense*.

Common Sense, which had appeared anonymously on the streets of Philadelphia in early 1776, made much of constitutions. Of course, so did the revolutionary National Assembly in Paris. But the American revolution was always far more influenced by lingering memories of the 'good old cause' and the 'great and glorious revolution', and all the other mythologies of English liberal democracy. It was within this tradition that Paine cast his later *Rights of Man*, as well as his *Common Sense* (Paine, 1987, pp.90–92). And the kind of constitution he envisaged, therefore, was always intended to be defensive. 'Society,' Paine alleged, 'is produced by our wants, and government by our wickedness', and so accordingly, whilst 'society in every state is a blessing', the presence of 'government even in its best states is but a necessary evil' (ibid., pp.66–7).

Paine's equation set society against government, and left constitutions to hold the ring. In his *Rights of Man*, he suggested that constitutions cast in this role expressed the 'spirit' of 'Reason' in politics (Paine, 1985, pp.208–9). Like the Abbé Gentil, moreover, he was convinced that this 'spirit' had now crossed the Atlantic. 'The cause of America,' he affirmed at the outset of *Common Sense*, 'is in great measure the cause of all mankind' (Paine, 1987, p.65). The prospect of a 'new' world excited Paine and Gentil in pretty much the same way as that of a 'new world order' is supposed to excite us today. Certainly, young America put much stock in its constitution. Richard Rorty describes an almost crusading zeal for the various aspects of its still tender 'civic religion' (Rorty, 1998, pp.9–15, 20–24, 30–31, 35–7).

It was this that led so many in the 'old' world to admire those who had sought to forge the 'new' one. In France, for example, there was a particular reverence for Benjamin Franklin. According to Turgot, it was Franklin who had 'seized the fire from heaven and the sceptre from tyrants' (Schama, 1989, p.44). Franklin was a Promethean, determined, as his 1782 *Address* on the abolition of slavery revealed, to retake the 'luminous and benign spirit of liberty' in order to rid his country of any 'debasement of human nature' which must, of necessity, 'impair the social affections' of a 'man's heart'. Franklin's was the cause of 'humanity'. But it was also, as his *Autobiography* repeatedly affirmed, the cause of constitutions. It was in the cause of constitutional propriety that America had been forced to go to war against its colonial masters (Franklin, 1986, pp.186–91, 244–5).

An examination of the *Federalist Papers* further adds to the sense that those who sought to draft the constitution, while proudly proclaiming the cause of humanity, were altogether less starry in their admiration for human nature. James Madison advised his 'fellow Americans' that they should 'perceive a finger of that Almighty hand' in their constitution (Madison *et al.*, 1978, p.246). But the most prominent digits were those of John Locke and Tom Paine. And someone whose fingerprints were most certainly not to be found was Jean-Jacques Rousseau. Madison's Almighty smiled far more benignly on the cult of rights than he did on the cult of sensibility.

The reason for this was simple. As Alexander Hamilton observed, the 'latent causes of faction' are 'sown in the nature of man'. Whilst there was a due measure of optimism regarding the constitution as an expression of human progress, there was an equal sense that laws exist in order to counter those 'passions of men' which 'will not conform to the dictates of reason and justice without constraint'. For Madison, the whole purpose of representative government was to offset the 'danger of disturbing public tranquillity by interesting too strongly the public passions' (ibid., pp.124, 149–50, 314, 319–20). Involve the people too much in politics, and they will get too excited. Little reverence here for the innate humanity of the noble savage. When 'the pot boils', James Otis warned in 1776, 'the scum will rise'. Ten years later, fellow revolutionary James Price was equally blunt. 'When a man who is only fit to patch a shoe attempts to patch the state, fancies himself a Solon or a Lycurgus,' he warned, 'he cannot fail to meet with contempt' (ibid., p.24). Prometheus needs to be bound. Citizens need constitutions.

A Universal Sense of Mankind

The English were fascinated by the French revolution. Some welcomed it. 'How much the greatest event it is that ever happened in the world and how much the best,' proclaimed Charles Fox. Paine exulted at the possibility that his homeland would finally embrace the 'spirit' of 'reason' already experienced in America and France. Even Edmund Burke was momentarily taken by the 'wonderful Spectacle'. Others were not so sure. Burke turned against the revolution with a vengeance, and composed his *Reflections on the Revolution in France* in an attempt to horrify his countrymen with a picture of anarchy and mayhem. Horror was a popular sensation. Lord Auckland feared that 'the whole world may go Mad, that all Governments may break to Pieces' (Ward, 2000, p.138).

In October 1793, Prime Minister William Pitt decided to move against the establishment of a Jacobin Convention in Edinburgh. He feared that the London Corresponding Society, and similar organizations, would be tempted to follow the example of their Scottish brethren. London was, at that time, decidedly on edge. The Habeas Corpus Act was already suspended, and a special parliamentary committee was investigating all kinds of alleged conspiracies. There was a very genuine sense that revolution was around the corner. Three prominent radicals, Horne Tooke, Thomas Hardy and John Thelwall, were arrested, and presented before the Grand Jury by the Lord Chief Justice on a charge based on a statute of Edward III which defined high treason as any act which did 'compass or imagine the Death of the King' (ibid.).

At the same time, an anonymous pamphlet was published in the *Morning Chronicle*, entitled *Cursory Strictures on the Charge Delivered by Lord Chief Justice Eyre*. Its forensic dismantling of Eyre's charge concluded with the apposite observation that plenty of Englishmen and women 'imagined' the King's death, some with horror, some without. Moreover, if the countenancing of reform was treason, then just about any 'card club, bench of justices, or even a Cabinet Council' could be considered treasonable. The government looked as ridiculous as the charge (Locke, 1980, pp.76–86).

The man who had rendered them so was the darling of the London societies, William Godwin. His *Cursory Strictures* confirmed a reputation which was already well established by the publication of his vast tract, an *Enquiry Concerning Political Justice*, a text dedicated to furthering the central mantra of Enlightenment, that 'the interest of the human species requires a gradual, but uninterrupted change' (Godwin, 1985, p.251). Amongst all the many and varied voices of political radicalism, Godwin's was perhaps the loudest. It was certainly the one that carried the most resonance in 1793. According to William Hazlitt, Godwin's *Enquiry* was recognized to be the 'abode' of 'moral truth', while the man himself 'blazed as a sun in the firmament of reputation', for 'wherever liberty, truth and justice was the theme, his name was not far off' (Hazlitt, 1964, p.202).

Liberty, truth and justice. The inspiration of Rousseau and events across the Channel cannot be doubted. Godwin was hugely taken with Rousseau, and the idea that 'every man would make his confessional' and the 'human species' should be 'the keeper of his conscience' (Dart, 1999, pp.59, 83–5). Yet, for Godwin, liberty, truth and justice were also intrinsically English principles, the principles indeed of the 'good old cause', of the English commonwealth idealized by the likes of Milton and Lilburne. The *Enquiry Concerning Political Justice* was written in order to argue precisely this, resurrecting the spirit of the 'good old cause', and recasting it in the language of late eighteenth-century political utopianism. Liberty, equality and fraternity were disinterred from English history, and re-described in terms of radical democracy, of a rational anarchy indeed. Much later in life, in his *History of the Commonwealth of England*, written during the 1820s, Godwin emphasized once again his belief that the idea of radical democracy found an original expression in seventeenth-century English radicalism (Morrow, 1991).

At the heart of the *Enquiry* lies the same basic tension which so occupied the likes of Hume and Smith, as well as Rousseau: between the virtues of Aristotelianism and the nihilism of Hobbes. For Godwin this tension was rather more ambiguous, because he was attracted both to the Aristotelian idyll of the community of rational, virtuous citizens and to the emergent utilitarianism of the Humean sceptic. In the 'Summary of Principles' which opened the *Enquiry*, Godwin acknowledged the basic utilitarian premise that the 'true object of moral and political disquisition is pleasure or happiness', while also affirming that it must be in 'the improvement of reason that we are to look for the improvement in our social condition'. 'Reason is the only legislator,' he affirmed, 'and her degrees are irrevocable and uniform.' But, at the same time, the principles of 'virtue' are just as much refined by the nurturing of 'kind and sympathetic feelings' (Godwin, 1985, pp.75–9, 509).

The accommodation of sense and sensibility was as essential to Godwin as it was to Hume, Smith or Kant. The 'great stream of voluntary actions', he affirmed, are as dependent upon 'decisions of the understanding' as they are on 'immediate impulses of sense'. In seeking this accommodation, Godwin was committing himself to the essential intellectual and political creed of the Enlightenment. As the very first pages of the *Enquiry* impressed, the happiness of the individual could only be founded upon the rational 'improvement' of humanity as a whole (ibid., p.97; Kramnick, 1972).

The Aristotelian in Godwin craved society, and the accommodation of the free individual in it. The purpose of politics is to pursue the 'general good' (Godwin, 1985, pp.165–6). Like Kant, and for precisely the same reasons, he immersed himself in the idea of the free will. And like Kant too, he also recognized the presence of a 'moral law' which is 'enjoined upon us by dictates of enlightened reason'. But, unlike Kant, Godwin argued that there was a second form of political 'regulation', the 'interest of the community', and that is determined by the construction of 'opinion'. This does not mean that politics is defined by nothing more than sensation and 'impulse'; but it did mean that it could not be discerned by the definition of the moral law alone. The utilitarian in Godwin insisted that the 'subject of moral enquiry' would always be defined by the measure of 'Pleasure and pain, happiness and misery' (ibid., pp.128, 221, 345–55).

It is this acknowledgment of the moral law, and moral 'duties', along with the concentration on reason, which founded Godwin's political idea of radical democracy, and which made it constructive, rather than, as subsequent critics have eagerly implied, nihilistic. The situation of the moral law affirmed that the purpose of radical democracy must always be to ensure the progression of principles, of liberty and toleration, 'the moral equality of mankind', and most importantly justice, the ultimate 'appellation for all moral duty'. Where radical democracy, and Godwin, differed from so many of his contemporaries lay in his belief that this progression could only be achieved by reaching beyond a narrow concern with juristic rules, and instead seeking to redefine the kind of politics to which the 'whole family of mankind' aspires (ibid., pp.169, 183, 308).

This intensely humanistic impulse was well captured in his specific discussion of democracy in the fifth book of the *Enquiry*:

> Democracy restores to man a consciousness of his value, teaches him, by the removal of authority and oppression, to listen only to the suggestions of reason, gives him confidence to treat all other men with frankness and sympathy, and induces him to regard them no longer as enemies against whom to be upon his guard, but as brethren whom it becomes him to assist. (Ibid., p.490)

Godwin never sought to deny the idea of truth. It was indeed, the 'road to the improvement of mankind' (ibid.). But it is a truth that can be located in the idea of a humanity, defined by the facility of conversational exchange, rather than any grand metaphysical 'truth'; a humanity that is nurtured by 'a spirit of universal kindness', and which promotes political exchanges unhindered by 'narrow resentments or angry invective'. It is a truth bred of toleration and the willingness to listen to others with 'sincerity'. Such a conception of truth is not merely pragmatic, in that it allows for the inevitability of political change, but is also principled in that it allows individuals to exercise the creative capacities of self-determination which define humanity – or at least the Enlightenment conception of it. It is for this reason that Godwin describes the free will in terms of empirical response rather than Kantian metaphysics, as the 'offspring of circumstances and events' rather than 'any original determination that they bring into the world' (ibid., pp.97–8, 247–53, 308–21).

The precise focus of Godwin's tract was England and its 'shibboleths', the 'shrine of positive law and political institutions' (ibid., pp.70, 87). Godwin's utilitarian pragmatism was dedicated to casting down these jurisprudential icons. A constitution, he declared, is 'an abstract idea', an 'imaginary existence', and so to express 'affection' to a constitution, as the likes of Edmund Burke had suggested in his *Reflections on the Revolution in France*, is 'altogether unintelligible'. It is significant that one of the 'shibboleths' that Godwin was keenest to cast down was that of 'love of our country', one that is always used to encourage thousands of the deluded to sacrifice their lives to satisfy the self-interest and blood-lust of various ruling elites (ibid., pp.509–13, 569–73, 685–95). In order to counter this irrationality, each institution of government must be 'divested of its present mysterious appearance', not just monarchy, which is self-evidently a 'species of government essentially corrupt', but also the established church, with its 'system of blind submission' to 'fantastic' dogmas, and most importantly, the law, with its catalogue of spurious rights which are nothing other than an expedient for 'regulated force' (ibid., p.69).

The destruction of received institutions is therefore the prerequisite of radical democracy. Although very few read Godwin's *Enquiry*, formidably long and just as formidably expensive, the same message could be found in his novels, perhaps most obviously the hugely successful *Caleb Williams*, a novel which, by Godwin's own admission, was the 'offspring' of that same 'temper of mind' (Locke, 1980, p.62). The misfortunes which attended Caleb, inflicted upon him by a corrupted system of government, provide an obviously literary complement to the more immediately political critique of the *Enquiry*. It is only through a sequence of legal cases and trials, at which the injustice of institutionalized law is made plain, that Caleb comes to realize the absurdity of his naïve belief that it is the 'privilege of an Englishman to be sole judge and master of his own actions'. It is, in fact, the institution of the law that precisely robs Englishmen of their freedom, and with it their humanity (Godwin, 1982, p.159; McCracken, 1969; Butler, 1982).

The argument both in the *Enquiry* and in *Caleb Williams* is, then, the same. Only when society has been levelled will the free individual be able to pursue the virtue which Aristotle and others have repeatedly suggested is the ultimate purpose of life. It is government which prevents the exercise of the free will and also the progress of humanity. It is 'an evil, an usurpation upon the private judgement and individual conscience of mankind'. The very essence of democracy is to give vent to this 'unspeakably beautiful' doctrine of 'private judgement' (Godwin, 1985, p.208). In many ways, the close of the third book of the *Enquiry* encapsulated the essence of Godwin's political and moral philosophy:

> It is earnestly to be desired that each man should be wise enough to govern himself, without the intervention of any compulsory restraint; and, since government, even in its best state, is an evil, the object principally to be aimed at is that we should have as little of it as the general peace of human society will permit. (Ibid., p.251)

It is, then, the concentration on the exercise of private judgment, of the rational free will that underpins Godwin's particular 'species of anarchy', an anarchy that, far from being nihilistic, 'cultivates thought' by means of the democratic exchange of 'opinions'. The 'fallacious uniformity of opinion' always masks the reality of intellectual and political tyranny, whereas 'conversation accustoms us to hear a variety of sentiments, obliges us to exercise patience and attention, and gives freedom and elasticity to our disquisitions' (ibid., pp.289–90, 567–8, 665–6).

Driven by this determination to nurture the processes of 'common deliberation', Godwin recommended the radical decentralization of power to occasional 'assemblies' of parishes. Such a form of government would necessarily encourage civic responsibility, educating citizens in 'positive sincerity' as well as releasing the creative capacity of their free will. All citizens would dedicate their lives to self-government, to making themselves and others 'free, virtuous, and wise'. Godwin never denied the need for society, or for certain forms of democratic government. Government, as he frequently admitted, is a 'necessary evil'. But he did deny the need for governments that seek to dictate what people should believe, think and say (ibid., pp.231, 408, 536–51).

Although his writings may have been revolutionary, Godwin was never so sure about the wisdom of bloody insurrection, the 'tumult and violence' which had occurred in France. 'Headlong zeal' rarely puts an end to 'mutual animosity', while political parties and factions merely negate the exercise of individual thought and free-will. In a letter written at the end of the 1790s, he rather whimsically declared that 'Discussion, reading, enquiry, perpetual communication, these are my favourite methods for the improvement of mankind.' Associations, he added, never focus on the 'progress of truth'. The 'universal sense of mankind', nurtured by a willingness to converse and to experience a 'variety of sentiments' and 'opinions', he assured readers of the *Enquiry*, will render violent political revolution unnecessary. The progression of humanity will be marked by the ultimate appreciation that the 'love of our neighbour is the greatest ornament of a moral nature' (ibid., pp.272–4, 282–90, 547–50, 565, 604, 620, 787–94).

No one better understood what Godwin was saying, perhaps, than Samuel Taylor Coleridge. In 1795, Coleridge penned his *Sonnet to William Godwin*, which included the following tribute:

> And hymn thee Godwin! With an ardent lay;
> For that thy voice, in Passion's stormy day,
> When wild I roam'd the bleak Heath of Distress,
>
> Bade the bright form of Justice meet my way –
> And told me that her name was Happiness. (Coleridge, 1969, ll.11–15)

As a tribute it is entirely fitting: to a man who dared to imagine that the interests of humanity lay in the politics of genuine democracy and the philosophy of universal love.

*

Writing in 1814, the Bishop of London, William Howley, recalled the horror of the French revolution and likened the event to the rampages of the Beast of the Apocalypse. Three years later, the Beast appeared once again, in a field just outside Manchester. Sixty thousand had gathered in order to listen to a number of prominent radicals, including the famous Henry 'Orator' Hunt. Participants had been drilled for weeks before, and marched to the fields carrying banners proclaiming 'Votes for All' and 'Reform or Death'. Haunted by memories of the Luddite riots in 1812, and then again by the Corn Law riots of 1815 and 1816, the Manchester magistrates decided that the 'whole bore the appearance of an insurrection', and sent the yeoman cavalry to capture Hunt. When the prey proved to be rather elusive, the magistrates ordered in the Hussars. Within fifteen minutes, eleven people were dead and four hundred lay injured.

Away in the Alps, discussing metaphysics and free sex with Byron, Percy Bysshe Shelley expressed his outrage in *The Mask of Anarchy*. The slaughtered Mancunians, he suggested, were murdered because they aspired to be democratic citizens. They had been slaughtered by the forces of tyranny, the real anarchists who ruled in blatant disregard of nature and harmony. The poem pivoted around the distinction between a rational anarchy which defined justice, and an irrational anarchy which sought to 'mask' tyranny. The opening stanzas alluded to various leading public figures, including Castlereagh, Sidmouth and Lord Chancellor Eldon, as well as the various institutions of government, the church, the king and the law. All were responsible for the massacre. All were anarchists. It was 'Anarchy' who came up behind 'On a white horse, splashed with blood'. He

> wore a kingly crown;
> And in his grasp a sceptre shone;
> On his brow this mark I saw –
> I am God, and King, and Law'. (Shelley, 1971, ll.30–37)

Government, rather than democracy, was consonant with anarchy. All the deceits of governmental tyranny, all the 'pomp' and 'pageant', were unmasked, the 'Lawyers and priests, a motley crowd', the 'pensioned Parliament', the 'hired murderers' who keep kings on thrones (ibid., ll.51, 58–61, 65, 85).

Shelley has long enjoyed the reputation as the most political of the English romantic poets. For him the poetry and the politics of liberation could not be distinguished. As he famously suggested in his essay *A Philosophical View of Reform*, poetry is the truest form of revolutionary idealism; poets are 'the priests of an unapprehended inspiration, the mirrors of gigantic shadows which futurity casts upon the present', the 'unacknowledged legislators of the world' (Foot, 1990, pp.29–84).

It was, of course, a sentiment which he shared with Godwin, whose daughter Mary he married. Although the influence waned, Shelley always paid fulsome tribute to Godwin as his intellectual mentor. In his famous letter of introduction to Godwin, written in 1811, by which time the 'sun' in the radical firmament had passed into a deeper shadow, Shelley invoked the memory of a 'luminary too dazzling for the darkness that surrounds him'. A second letter went further, suggesting that on reading the *Enquiry* Shelley had become convinced that airy metaphysics must give way to a more solid commitment to the politics of romanticism; 'I beheld in short that I had duties to perform', the duties of an unacknowledged legislator (Holmes, 1995, pp.79–105).

Although his overt enthusiasm would dissipate, disappointed by the apparent lack of a residual revolutionary vigour in his mentor, Shelley continued to carry the Godwinian argument, committed to the belief that the fate of radical democracy depended upon the forging of a politics that was matured by poetic sentiment. In a later letter to Godwin, Shelley attributed his poem *The Revolt of Islam* to a 'series of thoughts which filled my mind with unbounded and sustained enthusiasm', thoughts which had been inspired both by Godwin's *Enquiry* and by the French revolution, an event which he termed 'the master theme of the epoch in which we live' (ibid., p.346).

Composed in the same year as *The Mask of Anarchy*, the *Revolt* announced 'an experiment on the temper of the public mind', written in the hope of 'kindling within the bosoms of my readers a virtuous enthusiasm for those doctrines of liberty and justice, that faith and hope in something good, which neither violence nor misrepresentation nor prejudice can ever totally extinguish among mankind'. In writing the poem, Shelley added, he hoped to paint a 'succession of pictures' which could illustrate the possible 'growth and progress' of an 'individual mind' towards its final expression in the 'love of mankind' (Shelley, 1971, pp.32–5; Holmes, 1995, pp.401–2).

Against the tyrannies of 'helpless misery' which had descended upon Europe, of 'Tyrant and slave, victim and torturer, bent/ Before one Power', of the 'lust' for power which sought to suppress human instincts, the *Revolt* set the idyll of a 'free and equal' society, a world liberated by 'reason's mightly lore' (Shelley, 1971, ll.715, 730–31, 737–8, 995–6, 1043). The Hermit encountered in the fourth Canto, a sage whose wisdom is founded in his power of 'language', advises Laon of 'mighty hopes', of a 'pure law/ Of mild equality and peace', a 'Paradise/And not a dream' of 'Pity and Peace and Love', forged by the conjunction of 'Science, and her sister Poesy' (ibid., ll.1517–18, 1540–42, 2210–11, 2255–6, 4643–4)). The role of language is critical in the achievement of a 'free and equal' society, for it is 'Words' alone which are 'the lore of truth in hues of flame', and it is 'human words' that 'found sympathy/ In human hearts', ensuring that 'those/ Who grow together cannot choose but love' (ibid., ll.2686–8, 3541–2, 3573).

When he drowned in the Gulf of Spezia, Shelley had been trying to conclude the rather poignantly entitled poem, *The Triumph of Life*. The essential theme of the *Triumph*, the endless challenge of unmasking the 'countenance' of humanity, had been set in his previous, and last, great epic,

Prometheus Unbound, a poem which he hoped would represent 'a great work, embodying the discoveries of all ages' (Holmes, 1995, p.475). The central themes of *Prometheus* are consistent: the overcoming of tyranny by the democracy of language, by a 'speech' that can infuse a 'sense of love' and 'bind' the 'human heart' (Shelley, 1971, 1.1.621, 651, 2.4.63, 66, 72, 3.4.102). Reason frees Promethean man, whilst language mediates the indeterminacies of politics and human relations. The idyll which Prometheus established is one where 'thrones were kingless, and men walked/ One with the other even as spirits do,/ None fawned, none trampled', where 'hate, disdain, or fear,/ Self-love or self-contempt, on human brows' is 'No more inscribed' (ibid., 3.4.131–4).

The anarchy of tyrannical government will be overthrown by the anarchy of democratic government, of a politics of duties and responsibilities which describe the political life of enlightened men and women. Ultimately, it will be a democracy of 'Familiar acts' rendered 'beautiful through love', a democracy of equality and liberty, of

> Man, one harmonious soul of many a soul,
> Whose nature is its own divine control,
> Where all things flow to all, as rivers to the sea. (Ibid., 4.4.400–403)

A Warmer Love

In a pivotal passage of *The Prelude*, William Wordsworth recalled a series of discussions with a young French revolutionary, Michel-Arnaud de Beaupuy, 'about the end/ Of civil government, and its wisest forms', of 'self-respect, and virtue in the few' (Wordsworth, 1936, 9.321–3). On one occasion, the two men famously encountered:

> … a hunger-bitten girl,
> Who crept along fitting her languid gait
> Unto a heifer's motion, by a cord
> Tied to her arm. (Ibid., 9.510–13)

Wordsworth recalled the impact of the girl. 'In agitation', Beaupuy exclaimed, 'Tis against that/ That we are fighting', and Wordsworth 'with him believed/ That a benignant spirit was abroad/ Which might not be withstood' (ibid., 9.517–20). Wordsworth, famously, had been hugely taken with the French revolution, racing to France himself in order to better experience the excitement. 'Bliss was it in that dawn to be alive/ But to be young was very heaven', he later recalled in *The Prelude* (ibid., 11, 108–9).

But as the prophecies of Burke and Bentham seemed to come true, as revolutionary France staggered from one bout of savagery to another, Wordsworth turned against the ideology of revolution with a venom. Abjuring his former fondness for the 'Dances of Liberty', Wordsworth cast successive revisions of *The Prelude* in order to detach the interests of humanity from the fetishes of ideology. 'I looked for something which I could not find,' he confessed of his earlier fascination with the revolution, 'Affecting more emotion than I felt.' He had become a 'bigot' to ideology (ibid., 6.348–9, 371, 9.70–73, 11.108–9).

Very obviously, *The Prelude* represented Wordsworth's own particular commitment to the idea of the democratic confessional. In doing this, as John Stuart Mill observed, Wordsworth was making an irreducibly political statement. *The Prelude* presented itself as an intensely political work, precisely because it was so polemical in its rejection of political ideology. Appalled by the perceived loss of ideals, embarrassed by his apostasy, Wordsworth radically realigned his own political beliefs and values. Henceforth, he declared, it would be poetry rather than politics, and political rights, that would preserve the spirit of humanity. In his *Lines Composed a Few Miles Above Tintern Abbey*, Wordsworth made a collective confession for a disillusioned generation. The poet returned, from France, from the lures of ideology, to 'repose', to reflect:

> In hours of weariness, sensations sweet,
> Felt in blood, and felt along the heart;
> And passing even into my purer mind,
> With tranquil restoration: – feelings too
> Of unremembered pleasure: such, perhaps,
> As have no slight or trivial influence
> On that best portion of a good man's life,
> His little nameless, unremembered, acts
> Of kindness and of love. (Ibid., ll.27–35)

It was here, in the appreciation of a 'warmer love', that Wordsworth would be able to hear once again

> The still, sad music of humanity,
> Nor harsh nor grating, though of ample power
> To chasten and subdue. (Ibid., ll.91–3)

In many ways, *Tintern Abbey* was the defining poem in the *Lyrical Ballads*, the collection he published along with Coleridge in 1798. Wordsworth had agonized over the order of the collection, and it is no coincidence that it concludes with *Tintern Abbey* (Johnston, 1998, pp.397–400, 588–91).

Of course, the *Lyrical Ballads* were themselves published to make precisely this statement, that a 'natural' politics must be retrieved from fabricated ideologies. Again, the famous 'Preface', composed solely by Wordsworth, was a statement of deep political intent. The poems, it declared, were intended to 'speak a plainer and more emphatic language', the 'language really used by men' (ibid., p.734). Coleridge had happily deferred to his mentor. He was merely a 'kind of Metaphysician', the kind of man who is seduced by ideology and never able to detach himself fully from its gaze. Wordsworth, by way of contrast, was a 'great, a true Poet', someone who could envision a new politics. Despite his own crisis of self-confidence, Coleridge fully recognized the genuinely revolutionary implication of the *Ballads*. Annihilating the pretended distinctions of public and private by which classical liberalism sought to operate, the *Ballads* invited a new form of democracy, a politics of poetic conversation (Hazlitt, 1982, pp.62–3; Johnston, 1998, pp.571–83).

In the twelfth book of *The Prelude*, Wordsworth made reference to his vocation as a 'youthful traveller' meeting 'the wanderers of the earth' as he 'wandered from day to day'. The allusion is to the composition of the Salisbury Plain poems, originally cast in 1791 and then revised intensively through to 1794, and then again periodically for another decade. It is generally recognized that the origins of Wordsworth's redefinition of politics can be found in these poems. In some ways, they are his most intensely humanist, precisely because their emotion is so raw. In 1794, Wordsworth's anger was undiluted. Before the composition of *The Prelude*, before his reflections overlooking Tintern Abbey, the poet had already acknowledged a particular responsibility: to root out the political and social deprivations of the human condition and to paint its horrors on a public canvas.

At the heart of one of the most evocative passages of *Incidents Upon Salisbury Plain*, is Wordsworth's harrowing account of his encountering a gibbet and a corpse:

> It was a spectacle which none might view,
> In a spot so savage, but with shuddering pain;
> Not only did for him at once renew
> All he had feared from man, but roused a train
> Of the mind's phantoms, horrible as vain,
> The stones, as if to cover him from day,
> Rolled at his back along the living plain. (Ibid., verse 10)

No amount of ideology could explain this.

Law, humanity, politics; all condemned, all responsible for such a spectacle. Though Wordsworth abjured ideology, he was never fully exorcised of a Godwinian iconoclasm. An undue and uncritical reverence for institutions, particularly institutions which could permit such savagery, was just as dangerous as a reverence for ideology. Wordsworth turned away from both, and it was this rejection which, as we have already noted, caused John Stuart Mill so many sleepless nights.

*

Whilst Mill was lying awake in his bed worrying about Wordsworth and Bentham, Henry David Thoreau was tucked away in the backwoods of Massachusetts, musing on the inheritance of 1776, and wondering what had happened to the spirit of democracy. The product of his reflections was *Walden*, an account of his retreat into nature, and a classic study within the tradition of humanist utopias. From the very outset, *Walden* describes the alienation of modern humanity, of lives lived in 'quiet desperation', so 'occupied with factitious cares and superfluously coarse labors of life that its finer fruits cannot be plucked by them' (Thoreau, 1986, pp.48, 50).

It was for this reason that Thoreau retreated to Walden, to 'live simply and wisely', and to 'transact some private business', to commune not just with nature but with himself. The emphasis on the 'private' is critical. It directs humanity away from ideologies and market-places towards an inner sanctuary, to a 'more ethereal life'. Ultimately, such a communication is revelatory, and what it reveals is the moral self, the innate capacity for justice and harmony which resides in all of us. What Thoreau really discovered by the pond is the simple fact that 'Our whole life is startlingly moral', and that the only obedience that is natural is not to civil constitutions, but to the 'laws' of the inner 'being'. There is an obvious resonance here with Kant's idea of the 'moral law'. But whereas Kant described the moral self in terms of a critical faculty of reason, for Thoreau this revelation comes to us solely through the 'senses' (ibid., pp.62, 84, 114, 120–22, 266, 371).

The America that Thoreau idolized in *Walden* represented a universal humanism, an accord with a natural divinity that enjoyed a far more immediate affinity with Rousseau than with anything to be found in the *Federalist Papers*. As we have already seen, the idea that the 'cult of sensibility', having been cast out of Europe, had crossed the Atlantic, enthused many. Alexis de Tocqueville was certainly intrigued by the possibility, and it found a common expression in the writings of French exiles. Lucy de la Tour de Pin, who fled to America during the Great Terror, recounted a 'joy beyond words' on encountering 'the green fields, the flowering trees' and all the 'lakes strewn with small forested islands that looked like floating gardens'. (Schama, 1989, pp.863–4).

There is, moreover, much here that enjoys an obvious resonance with Wordsworth's return to nature: the idea of a natural, as opposed to ideological, politics. *Walden*, like *Tintern Abbey*, is a testament to a politics that abjures ideology. Men and women of Thoreau's generation immersed themselves in metaphysical, as well as political, reflection, trying to work out the implications of their revolution. The interest in transcendentalism that Thoreau shared with his sometime mentor, Ralph Waldo Emerson, was born of this gestation, as was the comparable rejection of ideology which underpinned this new intellectual divinity.

In *Walden*, Thoreau described an equivalent 'reverence' for nature and virtue, one that, once again, sought to balance sense with sensibility:

> Once or twice, however, while I lived at the pond, I found myself ranging the woods, like a half-starved hound, with a strange abandonment, seeking some kind of venison which I might devour, and no morsel could have been too savage for me. The wildest scenes had become unaccountably familiar. I found in myself, and still find, an instinct toward a higher, or, as it is named, spiritual life, as do most men, and another toward a primitive rank and savage one, and I reverence them both. I love the wild not less than the good. (Thoreau, 1986, p.257)

The prose might seem to be rather different from that employed by Adam Smith, or even Rousseau. But it was this kind of 'wildness', as Thoreau described it, that thrilled those who clung to the idea of Prometheus truly unbound.

The cause of humanity, which for Thoreau and Emerson was the only cause with which the American revolution could be legitimated, depended upon the revival of 'private lives'. It is the compassionate relation of individuals which seals a community, not the pretensions of political ideology. Again, the resonance with the likes of Wordsworth and Coleridge is striking. The critical difference, of course, lay in their very different reaction to the idea of democracy. For Wordsworth, democracy took the form of another ideology, another distraction from the natural harmony of 'beauteous forms'. For Thoreau, however, democracy was hardly an ideology, more a theology, a matter of transcendental faith.

The overwhelming power of this faith was evidenced in his famous essay *Civil Disobedience*, published in 1849. The principles of natural justice and democracy, Thoreau suggested, legitimate civil disobedience. Indeed, they make a preparedness to be disobedient a positive responsibility of the good citizen. The 'right to revolution', he asserted, is the only right which 'all men recognise'. Godwin would have purred. The dichotomies between law and justice, government and democracy lie at the heart of *Civil Disobedience*. 'Law,' it proclaimed, 'never made men a whit more just' (ibid., pp.385–7, 389, 395–6). The venom of *Civil Disobedience* is cast within an American context, and it can be fairly said that America is still trying to accommodate these dichotomies. But the anger is universal. Sixty years earlier, Thoreau would have been the toast of the Jacobin, of Paris and Lyon, Edinburgh and Philadelphia.

But whereas Godwin knew that his cause was the cause of subversion, that democracy had to be fought for, that ideological debates had to be won, for Thoreau, and many of his generation, the cause of democracy hardly needed ideological argument. It had become a theological expression, a matter of fundamental belief, a kind of absolute truth indeed. In achieving this kind of transcendence, democracy also became synonymous with humanity.

There are few better expressions of this transcendence than Walt Whitman's *Leaves of Grass*, a text that bears a very obvious resonance with Wordsworth's *Prelude* in terms of its epic historical sweep, but which perhaps enjoys a more immediate resonance with *Walden* or *Tintern Abbey* in terms of its intense commitment to the affinity between nature and the cause of humanity. For Whitman, the very idea of the 'United States' was 'essentially the greatest poem', whilst the 'genius' of the American 'spirit' lay in the 'artistic expression' of a public philosophy, a 'new' civil 'religion' with which the people can be educated to 'think lightly of the laws'. The politics of the 'New World' will 'henceforth radiate in superior Literary, Artistic, and Religious Expressions, for more than in its Republican forms, universal suffrage, and frequent elections' ('Song of the Broad-Axe', l.115, in Whitman, 1996; also pp.741–2, 777, 780–81). The great virtues of democracy, liberalism, tolerance, all become expressions of an acute political sensibility.

It is for this reason that the greatest responsibility lies with the poet, the 'leader of leaders', the 'one complete lover' of the universe, the true 'legislator' for humanity, as Shelley put it. It is for the poet to engage humanity, and to inspire love, 'to plant companionship thick as trees along all the rivers' ('For You O Democracy', l.6, and 'By Blue Ontario's Shore', l.155, ibid.). In this way the poet can forge a peculiar democracy of compassion, of caring for others, a reverence for the 'greatness of Love and Democracy'. This will be the 'new order' which America will champion, an order in which 'every man shall be his own priest' ('Starting from Paumanock', l.133, ibid.). In many ways, there is no better definition of Enlightenment humanism than this, of a democratic politics of innate compassion and respect, of the 'romance of endless diversity', a democracy of 'effusion'. The aspiration of a romantic politics, which for Whitman was the politics which defined America itself and also its missionary duty, is to do nothing more than reduce 'unnecessary suffering' and to permit the flourishing of human 'love'. For 'underneath all', as Whitman emphasized, 'is the Expression of love for men and women' ('By Blue Ontario's Shore', st.16, ibid.).

It is a humanism which undercuts the pretensions of any supposedly deeper philosophy or ideology, the humanism of a 'vast elemental sympathy' ('A Song of Songs', l.23, ibid.). As Whitman concludes in *The Base of All Metaphysics*:

> Yet underneath Socrates clearly see, and underneath Christ
> the divine I see,
> The dear love of man for his comrade, that attraction of
> friend to friend,
> Of the well-married husband and wife, of children
> and their parents,
> Of city for city and land for land.
> (*The Base of All Metaphysics*, ll.12–15, ibid.)

Leaves of Grass is the confession of a nation, and a belief. If Wordsworth's *Prelude* is an autobiography of the delusions of ideology, *Leaves of Grass* is an autobiography of the struggles of a nation, and a humanity, to translate dreams into reality. In this sense it is very obviously part of the same utopian tradition which found an expression in Godwin's *Enquiry* and Shelley's *Prometheus*, and, of course, Thoreau's *Walden*. It assumes the unarguable case for democracy, and it projects hope from that case. Implicit is the assumption that the future well-being of the 'new' world lies in the cause of democracy. It projects democracy, indeed, as the 'new' humanism.

This idea that democracy personalizes politics finds perhaps its most obvious expression in Alexis de Tocqueville's *Democracy in America*. Written, as Charles Taylor has argued, as a 'romantic' counter to the incipient alliance between the emergent nation-state and the particular jurisprudence of legal positivism, *Democracy in America* was an encomium to the 'irresistible and universal spread of democracy', as well, of course, as being a comparative commentary on the relative successes and failures of the 1776 and 1789 revolutions (Taylor, 1989, p.414).

The virtue of American democracy, Tocqueville asserted, lay in its constituent communities. It is here, he suggested, that the 'strength of a free people resides', that the pulse of democracy is most vigorous. It is not simply a matter of recommending forms of 'civil association' and participatory self-government as a matter of democratic principle. At the heart of Tocqueville's account is the suggestion that strong community government energizes the 'spirit' of democracy, nurturing a 'superabundant force, and energy never found elsewhere', fostering a vital sense of 'common enterprise' amongst its citizens. A healthy community is one in which people feel that they have a measure of self-government, where 'each man in his sphere takes an active part in the government of society' (Tocqueville, 1994, pp.12, 62–3, 189–95, 235–7, 242–4).

But democracy is more than this. It is a 'politics of sentiment' too. True democracy is felt, for 'Feelings and ideas are renewed, the heart enlarged, and the understanding developed only by the reciprocal action of men one upon another.' Political interaction binds a community because it binds the hearts of its citizens. It is when 'people become like one another', enjoining the same 'spirit' of democracy and self-government, that 'they show themselves reciprocally more compassionate'. Genuine and free democracy reflects the 'very nature of the human heart' (ibid., pp.310, 395–6, 503–4, 515–17, 680–82). It makes people human. What de Tocqueville thought he saw in mid-nineteenth-century America was the proper balance between sense and sensibility, between Voltaire and Rousseau, between Bentham and Coleridge perhaps. And, he concluded, it was the ability to facilitate this balance that distinguished the apparent success of the American revolution from the apparent failure of the French. In Europe the 'cult of sensibility' had been crushed. In America it had been recast as democracy.

This, ultimately, is what, in their rather different ways, Tocqueville, Whitman and Thoreau all appreciated. Certainly, democracy should secure certain rights in established constitutions. But a healthy democracy must also do rather more. People should respect the laws, as Whitman implied in *Leaves of Grass*, but they should also 'think lightly' of them. A century and a half later, however, as we have already noted, we think rather more heavily of laws. The modern sciences of law and politics are defined in terms of rights and duties, rather than compassion and radical democracy. An unbound Prometheus still terrifies those who aspire to govern. It is the spirit of Bentham rather than that of Coleridge, or Godwin or Rousseau or Whitman, that holds dominion over the psyche of modern politics. Those who seek to invoke these latter spirits are cast to the edges of modern political debate. The confessional tradition, the tradition of humanity indeed, remains the subversive tradition.

The rhetoric of 1789, the appeal for 'Liberty, Equality, Fraternity', still carries a certain ideological purchase. So does the American 'dream'. But, as we also saw earlier, both worlds, the 'new' and the 'old', are populated by angry, discontented and disillusioned peoples. And the prospect of a new 'new' world order barely alleviates this discontent. Somehow the promise of Enlightenment has been lost. The sheer optimism and sheer humanity of Rousseau, of Godwin and Whitman, appear to have been crushed. If the new century that beckons, and the 'new' new world order which it heralds, are to project a brighter future for us all, they will need to somehow reinvest this optimism and humanity. They will need to retrieve the accommodation of sense and sensibility which underpinned the ideas of democracy and liberty, and which inspired, at least briefly, so much hope in so many.

In his poem *The Mystic Trumpeter*, Whitman seized once again on the need for hope which only a genuine democracy, that is a democracy of humanism and compassion, can furnish:

> Now trumpeter for thy close,
> Vouchsafe a higher strain than any yet,
> Sing to my soul, renew its languishing faith and hope,
> Rouse up my slow belief, give me some vision of the future,
> Give me for once its prophesy and joy. (Whitman, 1996, ll.60–64)

The poem was written in the context of the kind of human suffering that would subsequently engulf the twentieth century, the slaughter of the American civil war. Whitman hoped for something better, for 'new combinations', and for the 'solidarity of races' ('Years of the Modern', l.4, ibid.). A century or more later, we are still hoping.

PART II

3 A New World Order

A Big Idea

In his 1991 State of the Union speech, US President George Bush announced a 'big idea', a 'new world order' which had as its ambition 'to achieve the universal aspirations of mankind', or at least American perception of mankind, and these were 'peace and security, freedom and the rule of law'. The sentiment seemed to fit. It resonated with the end of the Gulf War, the immediate trigger for Bush's musings on a 'new world order', and with the end of the Cold War too, with the tearing down of the Berlin Wall, and with the equally important, if rather less symbolic, tearing down of trade barriers. Bush's successor, President Clinton, declared that, 'For the first time in history, more people on the planet live under democracy than dictatorship' (Schlesinger, 1997, p.2). For a moment, it seemed that the ideal of a 'perpetual peace' – one of Enlightenment's greatest promises – might indeed be realized.

Bush's 'big idea' carried a very obvious resonance with Francis Fukuyama's provocative suggestion that history had come to an 'end'. At the heart of Fukuyama's thesis was the assertion that there was a 'remarkable consensus' that the 'ideal' of liberal democracy could not be 'improved on' (Fukuyama, 1992, pp.xi–ii, 13–18, 31). The promise of Enlightenment was about to be realized. But, as he also noted, there was a critical ambiguity. For, along with liberal democracy has come liberal economics, the seemingly irresistible march of the free markets. And we, or at least many millions of us, are not as happy as we should be. The mindset which appears to have secured the triumph of radical liberalism, the mindset of 'cold calculation', has denuded humanity. Denied his 'desire for recognition', denied the solace of compassion and empathy, of human relations indeed, the 'last man' is a sad and miserable soul (ibid., pp.57–66, 77–9, 108, 112, 214, 289–92, 314–15, 325).

The idea of a 'new world order' is not, then, one that can be embraced with impunity. There is much to fear. There is, most immediately, a new spectre, that of globalization. According to George Soros, globalization announces a new kind of 'totalitarianism', representing a greater threat to the 'open society' that anything that Marxism or Nazism could throw up (Barber, 2000, p.299). On these terms, the much-vaunted 'end of history' is simply an attempt to provide an intellectual sheen to an otherwise brutal experience, to prescribe for the collective imagination what has been termed a 'global dream' or, rather more prosaically, a 'global consciousness' (Rosow, 2000, p.40; Lipschutz, 1992, p.399). In the final analysis, history defies the suggestion that we have reached the 'end of history'. The 'spectres' of modernity, as Jacques Derrida terms them, defy such a simple and such a complacent conclusion. Globalization is merely the most recent and the most mischievous of poltergeists, the harbinger of 'violence, inequality, exclusion, famine' (Derrida, 1994a, pp.56–75, 85).

The implication is, once again, clear. Despite all the euphoria of a decade ago, all the bluff and bluster, as we herald the arrival of a new millennium, we have never been further from securing a 'perpetual peace' in this world. The last decade of the twentieth century turned out to be a decade of the deepest disillusion. Our task in this chapter is to chronicle this disillusion; to try to work out what has gone wrong. Alongside this is a collateral task: to reflect on what might be done to adjust the 'new' world order, so that it appears to be one which serves the principles of justice and compassion, rather than exploitation and grotesque inhumanity. The idea of a 'new world order' inheres both the potential for the renaissance of humanism and the potential for its further annihilation.

Our first task must be to investigate further the experience of globalization. Precise definitions are elusive, but most operate within a broadly economic framework. Whilst its impact can be cultural, political, jurisprudential indeed, globalization is generally seen to be most immediately an economic experience. The global 'village', it is suggested, has been constructed 'from the economic ground up' (Rosow, 2000, p.29). According to the founding director-general of the World Trade Organisation, the 'new world order' was finally given birth in December 1993, with the completion of the Uruguay Round of the GATT (Dunkley, 2000, p.7). Before then, it was just so much hot air.

Money does, it seems, make the world go round. In his populist bestseller, *The Lexus and the Olive Tree*, Thomas Friedman recounts the events triggered by the collapse of the Thai Bhat in 1997, events which led first to a recession in the south-east Asian economy, to be followed by a slump in oil prices, the collapse of the Russian economy and then the south American, and finally the collapse of US interest rates, as panicked investors buried their money in US Treasury bonds. The tale is intended to impress upon us the extraordinary nature of the global economy, and its extraordinary capacity for destructiveness (Friedman, 2000, pp.xi–xiv).

This sense of constriction, of the disruption of received senses of time and space, is echoed by many commentators. Describing an essentially post-modern experience, Boaventure Santos has spoken of an overlapping relation of the global and the local, of 'globalized localism', meaning the globalization of local phenomena, and 'localized globalism', meaning changes in local conditions in response to global pressures (Santos, 1995, p.263). International relations scholars have coined the phrase 'glocalism' in order to give this rather bewildering experience a shorthand expression. It is intended to account for the fact that only a tiny fraction of those who wear replica Manchester United football shirts have ever visited the UK, to explain why the people of Tehran can sip their Cokes while listening to their leaders denounce the US president as the 'son of Satan'. The world is suddenly a lot smaller place, and a lot more ambiguous.

In a controversial article published in 1992, Benjamin Barber prophesied that this tension would lead to an inevitable fragmentation. Globalization, he suggested, was haunted by two 'specters':

> The first is a retribalization of large swaths of humankind by war and bloodshed: a threatened Lebanonization of national states in which culture is pitted against culture, people against people, tribe against tribe – a Jihad in the name of a hundred narrowly conceived faiths against every kind of interdependence, every kind of artificial social cooperation and civic mutuality. The second is being borne in on us by the onrush of economic and ecological forces that demand integration and uniformity and that mesmerize the world with fast music, fast computers, and fast food – with MTV, Macintosh, and McDonald's, pressing nations into one commercially homogenous global network: one McWorld tied together by technology, ecology, communications, and commerce. The planet is falling precipitantly apart and coming reluctantly together at the very same moment. (Barber, 1992, p.53)

The image is compelling.

There is certainly much support for the notion that the most serious challenge of globalization is directed against traditional national identities; something which was only too obvious in the Balkan wars. In pronouncing the collateral 'end of the nation-state', Keniche Ohmae advised that, 'in terms of the global economy, nation-states have become little more than bit actors', their power now dispersed amongst consumers and transnational corporations, global institutions and regional 'states'. The 'old world', he concluded, has quite simply 'fallen apart' (Ohmae, 1996, pp.7, 12, 15–16, 80–85).

The idea of a countervailing process of global integration and disintegration is further reinforced by cold statistics. In 1975, for example, total foreign investments worldwide amounted to just $23bn. By 1997, that figure was $644bn. By the end of the 1990s, daily currency exchanges amounted to around $1.5 trillion; a vast 'virtual economy' that exists only in the minds of its currency trading junkies. There is no doubt that we are all rather more economically dependent upon one another than we immediately realize.

The statistics that chart the downside of this process are just as stark. The 1999 UN Human Development Report stated that around one-fifth of the highest income countries control 82 per cent of the world export markets, 86 per cent of world gross domestic product, 68 per cent of foreign direct investments and 74 per cent of world telephone lines. The bottom one-fifth controls barely 1 per cent of any of these. The wealthiest one-fifth consume 45 per cent of meat and fish that is eaten. The poorest one-fifth consumes less than 5 per cent. The UNICEF report, *Development Goals and Strategies*, noted over 45 per cent of children in developing countries suffer 'critical poverty', while 250 000 die every week of malnutrition. 'Death on this scale,' the report concluded, 'is simply no longer necessary; it is therefore no longer acceptable'. In its 1993 report, *The State of the World's Children*, it noted that $25 million per year would suffice to eradicate such death rates. Each year, it was noted, European Union citizens spend far more than this on buying wine (Gray, 1998, pp.61–2; Falk, 1995, pp.55–8, 190; Friedman, 2000, p.9, 319–20; Castells, 2000, pp.54–6, 66).

And the gap, as the South Commission, in its report, *The Challenge to the South*, affirms, is widening year by year. If the impulse is primarily economic, the implications of globalization, unadulterated poverty and exploitation, are intensely social and political, and cruel too. Robert Falk refers to an environment of 'global apartheid' and 'inhumanity' (Falk, 1995, pp.49–55). It is an accusation that was implied by the *New York Times* a decade ago, when it reflected on President Bush's proud pronouncement of a 'new world order'. Adding up figures that almost defy comprehension, it concluded that, whilst 3.1 billion did indeed live in democracies, 2.6 billion did not, and one billion of the latter lived in absolute poverty. The ratios have barely altered. At present, a billion or more have insufficient food and water, half of Africa is submerged in absolute poverty, 14 million children die of starvation every year. The consequences of globalization continue to beggar the imagination.

*

According to Pierre Bourdieu, neoliberal globalization is merely a 'very smart and very modern repackaging of the oldest ideas of the oldest capitalists'. There is nothing very new about a politics that is founded on the exploitation of the weakest, and which devotes itself to maximizing the wealth of the privileged few. In this analysis, globalization is not homogenization at all; 'on the contrary, it is the extension of the hold of a small number of dominant nations over the whole set of national financial markets' (Bourdieu, 1998, pp.vii, 29–30, 34, 38). In the final analysis, as Will Hutton suggests, globalization is just another form of politics, an 'exercise of raw power' (Giddens and Hutton, 2000, p.41). Noam Chomsky has repeatedly argued that the much-vaunted 'new world order' is really a cover for a very familiar western, particularly American, economic imperialism. The imperialist charge is difficult to refute. A 1994 UN development report confirmed that 'industrial countries, by violating the principles of free trade, are costing the developing countries an estimated $50bn a year' (Chomsky, 1999, pp.20–28, 37–9, 111–12).

Familiar though it may be, there is no denying the debilitating nature of the virus. Globalization has bred an acute sense of disillusion, despair and apathy. The essential problem is succinctly expressed by Richard Barnet and John Cavanagh at the opening of their book, *Global Dreams*. 'We are all,' they opine, 'participants in one way or another in an unprecedented political and economic happening, but we cannot make sense of it. We know that we are supposed to think globally, but it is hard to wrap the mind even around a city block, much less a planet' (Barnet and Cavanagh, 1994, pp.13–14). The essential problem with globalization is that it does not really mean anything, and yet it seems to govern all aspects of our lives (Rosow, 2000, pp.29–30; Sjolander, 1996).

In the face of this dynamic, the ordinary mortal is left with a feeling of utter helplessness. The fact that far more of us have invested in the economic bubble, have dabbled in a few shares or units, have our pensions riding on the success or failure of a few mutual funds, does not mean that we have any greater control of our fates. It just means that we are more than ever dependent upon the continuing health of a process over which no one seems to have any real control. There is, of course, any number of bond-traders and stockjobbers scattered around various trading-floors, and lots more paper millionaires and dot.com. companies rising and falling. But there is nothing that we seem to be able to do about securing our own futures. With each passing moment, we seem to have less and less control over the decisions that define our lives.

And, above all, there is the sheer irresistibility of globalization. According to Friedman, 'All politics is now global. Not every country may feel itself part of the globalization system, but every country is directly or indirectly being shaped and affected by this system' (Friedman, 2000, p.76). In similar vein, Stephen Gill refers to a pervasive, malignant spirit of 'commodification' (Gill, 1995, pp.402–10). Philip Allott puts it eloquently: 'With the globalization of mass culture, the many of humanity are adrift in a sea of collective fantasy, sleepwalking in a waking dream, formed and manipulated by the few who manage the great systems of mental production, the mass reality industry' (Allott, 1992, p.233).

More and more, we find our lives propelled by external dynamics, by the myriad forces of globalization, forces over which we appear to have limited democratic control. The fact is well appreciated by Benjamin Barber:

> Ripped from the juridical and legislative box of regulatory institutions and civic institutions, markets spin freely into hyper-space, generating a 'wild' capitalism that looks like anarchy and that is corrosive not only to the national democracy on which it once relied, but to its own operation as a competition-based economic system. (Barber, 2000, p.275)

Prophecies of impending doom are plentiful. Arthur Schlesinger projects a future in which the prospects of individual nihilism and social fragmentation loom ever larger (Schlesinger, 1997). Robert Falk suggests that the tyranny of 'inhumane governance' can only result in 'a new world disorder', one in which 'strife, extremism, despair abound' (Falk, 1995, p.25). According to John Gray, the 'era' of 'hallucinatory vistas' of imagined 'new world orders' is over, and reassurance for the future remains evasive. Instead, we peer anxiously over a precipice, dimly perceiving before us a 'tragic epoch' of 'deepening international anarchy'. The 'inherent instability of global markets', he further prophesies, will ultimately crush a soporific, politically disengaged, humanity. The great success of neoliberalism is the 'euthanasia of bourgeois life' (Gray, 1998, pp.3, 22–4, 72–4, 205–8). We appear to have lost interest in the possibility of determining our own fates. Apparently operating in an extralegal anarchy, globalization appears to be a force beyond our control, and so instead we resign ourselves to the tyrannies and inequities of modern life, apparently persuaded that there is nothing that we can do to alleviate them.

The pervasive anxieties of modern life cannot be distinguished from the global experience. In an article entitled 'Brave New World', the Marxist commentator, Stuart Hall, suggested that the global expression of liberalism was in the process of destroying residual bases of social and political identity. The 'self', he argued, is now 'experienced as more fragmented and incomplete, composed of multiple selves or identities'. It is not a condition with which we are happy:

> More and more our everyday lives are caught up with these forms of power, and their lines of intersection. Far from there being no resistance to the system, there has been a proliferation of new points of antagonism, new social movements of resistance organized around them, and, consequently, a generalization of 'politics' to spheres which hitherto the left assumed to be apolitical. (Hall, 1991, p.63)

The German sociologist Ulrich Beck has similarly emphasized the global context of our present malaise. Increasingly, he affirms, people today 'struggle to live their own lives in a world that increasingly and more evidently escapes their grasp, one that is irrevocably and globally networked'. So now we are expected to live 'our lives with the most diverse and contradictory transnational and personal identities and risks'. Our received identities have been undermined. We are not comfortable with the 'multi-local transnationality' that has been foisted upon us, any more than we are happy reflecting upon the possibilities of multiple identities, multiple *demoi*, or 'multilayered democracy'. The lack of a clear identity may seem to be a primarily cultural misfortune, but it has very definite political implications, for we have lost our ability to gain access to a 'public realm'. Life is no longer a question of 'solidarity or obligation but of conflictual coexistence' (Beck, 2000a, pp.168–73). Retrieving that 'public space', the space so enthusiastically proclaimed by the likes of Godwin and Shelley, Tocqueville and Whitman, is our most pressing political concern.

The Case for Global Democracy

For most of the twentieth century, international relations theory was defined by the 'realists', who described a world of struggling international institutions trying to broker between bickering superpowers and their client nation-states. The realist world order was cast in the image of Hobbes' 'state of nature', the threat of anarchy never more than a border dispute away (Waltz, 1959, 1979). Realists feasted on the experiences of the Cold War. Against them could be found various kinds of 'liberals', the most influential of whom have also tended towards the pragmatic as opposed to utopian. The idea that international order is described by a series of institutions operating as media for the transmission of classical liberal ideology has been argued by the likes of John Ruggie, who famously described this model as 'embedded liberalism' (Ruggie, 1998, pp.47, 62–84).

The two discourses conversed in a common language, that of international relations, the language deployed by the likes of Grotius and Kant, for whom 'perpetual peace' was always designed to be a peace between nations. The classical institutions of international law and order have been cast in this mould: the World Bank, the IMF, the ILO, in time the GATT and the WTO (Fox, 1999). The WTO, in particular, in the words of one critic 'part rule-maker, part judge, part policeman', has become a focus of criticism that speaks not just to its imperialistic function as a paradigm of liberal free-trade ideology, but also to its apparent lack of juridical responsibility; whilst nation-states might be hauled before WTO, there is no-one before whom the WTO can be hauled (Dunkley, 2000, p.279; Chomsky, 1999, pp.68–77).

Similarly, whilst institutions such as the World Bank might proudly proclaim its affinity with the principle of democracy, even promising to promote democracy and to 'raise concerns about human rights', it is not itself democratic or answerable before any human rights court – no matter how many millions starve to death each year because their governments are unable to meet the terms of World Bank loans. The problem of legitimacy is one that haunts the 'new world order'. In jurisprudential terms, and as a matter of political morality, the process of globalization seems to be devoid of legitimacy (Anghie, 2000).

Legitimacy is the critical issue. It has even been suggested that the institutions of international commerce actually militate against the ethical and juridical aspirations articulated in documents such as the UN Declaration. The dynamics of globalization have crushed the pretences of international public law (Baxi, 1998, pp.163–4). Transnational corporations do not appear to leave buildings burning in the snow. But the degree of misfortune visited on vast swathes of the world's population, invariably exacerbated by the desire of one part of the world to exploit the poverty of another, is no less heinous, no less a denial of humanity and compassion. For this reason, the establishment of certain institutions in order to regulate international trade and commerce does become a matter of more than mere efficiency. It becomes a matter of moral responsibility too.

This idea of moral responsibility joins that of legitimacy and asks considerable questions of the so-called 'new world order'. Who, in short, is governing? Who is taking responsibility? Even as committed a free-marketeer as Charles Fried has argued that something must be done to address these kinds of questions. The need to establish measures to regulate 'tyrant capitalism' is compelling. It is demanded by efficiency and it is demanded by democracy (Fried, 2000).

Classical liberal theory has always proffered a sort of answer: international law, which reinforces the relations, not just between nation-states, but between nation-states and international institutions. But the dynamics that are currently reshaping international order are also reshaping international law, which leads us to another critical question: has classical international law passed its sell-by date (Schachter, 1997)?

The more cautious, such as Harold Koh or Anne-Marie Slaughter, argue not, preferring instead the idea of cross-fertilization between domestic law and emergent features of the new international order. Koh acknowledges an 'epochal transformation of international law', one in which the idea of law has been destabilized by the emergence of various alternative forms of 'soft' law, of dispute resolution, NGOs, informal regimes and networks. What has emerged is a distinctively 'transnational legal process' that locates 'reasons for compliance' at a 'transactional level', one of 'interaction, interpretation, and internalization of international norms into domestic structures' (Koh, 1997, pp.2604, 2630–31, 2648–9, 2655–9). Slaughter similarly describes an emergent dynamic of 'transgovernmentalism' which has constructed a 'global community of law' (Slaughter, 1997). In these visions of the future, national and international institutions provide forms of mutual support and sustenance, forms which can then be redetermined as transnational or transgovernmental.

Others are rather less convinced that the dynamic will lead naturally to a coherent reconstruction of international law. The proliferation of international legal institutions during the last decade or so has led many commentators to suggest that there is an acute danger of 'fragmentation' in international law and order. George Abi-Saab hazards the thought that such a process announces a 'post-post-modern' age (Abi-Saab, 1999, p.933; Romano, 1999; Dupuy, 1999). According to these critics the dynamic of transgovernmentalism is anything but passive, still less benign. For some, of course, such as Martti Koskenniemi, this incipient institutional anarchy is to be welcomed, not least because it can act to finally dismantle the 'inherited ideal of a World Order based on the Rule of Law' but which only 'thinly hides from sight the fact that social conflict must still be solved by political means' (Koskenniemi, 1990, p.7).

Philip Allott is even more vitriolic in announcing the destruction of a jurisprudence which 'uses the term self-determination' but which 'cannot conceive of nations, peoples, ethnic groups, and minorities except as inherently anomalous in relation to the supposedly unproblematic self of the state', of a theory of 'human rights' which 'cannot conceive of individual human beings except as anomalous in relation to the true and original right-holders, namely states', of an 'international system of trade relations' which can only operate in terms of 'relations between state-systems', which 'cannot systematically integrate those whose willed action is the economy of the world, except through fictions of nationality and fictions of jurisdiction' and which 'leaves systematically anomalous and unaccountable the overwhelming power of non-governmental economic decision-making'. His conclusion is compelling; classical international law is the very antithesis of humanity, the 'deformation of all selfhoods' (Allott, 1992, pp.247–8).

The debate surrounding the suitability of existing international institutions describes a similar dichotomy of opinion. For some, the practical solution is to reform existing institutions so as to make them better suited to the demands of the 'new world order'. Thus it is suggested that the 'conjunction' of the WTO, the IMF and the World Bank already describes an 'embryonic economic world government', one which can be deployed in order to oversee 'managed', rather than 'free', trade (Dunkley, 2000, pp.237–50, 263). Billionaire financier George Soros prefers this approach, declaring, 'I now fear that the untrammeled intensification of laissez-faire capitalism and the spread of market values into all areas of life is endangering our open and democratic society.' There are, he confirms, 'intolerable equities and instability' which can only be alleviated by an active 'management' of international economic order (Soros, 2000).

Others argue for a rather more radical approach, unconvinced that existing arrangements do anything other than provide an 'illusion' of international law and order (Senarclens, 1998). One of these is Jacques Derrida, who suggests that the law of nations, like the law within nations, has no choice but to 'extend and diversify its field to include, if at least it is to be consistent with the idea of democracy and of human rights it proclaims, the worldwide economic and social field, beyond the sovereignty of states and of the phantom-States' (Derrida, 1994a, pp.84–5). This was also the conclusion implied in the 1992 *Human Development Report* that suggested that, so long as transnational financial institutions remain essentially unaccountable, there can be no genuine global democracy (Falk, 1995, pp.181, 229). Radical reconstruction of global governance is the only solution; at least it is if we adhere to the notion that justice and humanity are qualities that matter in the 'new world order'.

Such a conclusion chimes with those who argue the case for what James Rosenau famously referred to as the emergent process of transnational 'governance without government' (Rosenau, 1992, pp.3–4). Some of the most enthusiastic supporters of this idea of global governance can be found amongst those who argue the case for some kind of 'third way' in national and transnational governance. Antony Giddens calls for a reinvigorated transnational 'regulation', one that will 'build up a global civil society and a framework of law' and which will encourage us to think 'about possible forms of transnational democracy' (Giddens and Hutton, 2000, pp.23, 38–9, 45). John Gray similarly argues that a 'regime of global governance is needed in which world markets are managed so as to promote the cohesion of societies and the integrity of states'. The future of humanity depends upon such a construction, for 'only a framework of global regulation' can 'enable the creativity of the world economy to be harnessed in the service of human needs' (Gray, 1998, p.199).

*

There is a pressing affinity between the advocacy of new forms of global governance, and collateral arguments for global democracy and global citizenship. David Held argues that the 'circumstances' of globalization 'present significant opportunities for the establishment of an international order based upon the principles of constitutionality and democracy'. The future of democracy, indeed, depends upon fashioning an 'international cosmopolitan' model, wherein internal democracy 'within' communities can be reinforced by 'regional and international agencies' that are located 'outside' (Held, 1995, pp.ix, 22–3, 236, 267, 270–78).

Of course, the call for principles of constitutionality speaks the language of classical liberalism. But it is, more appropriately, a call for the realization of Enlightenment's promise, for the fulfilment of an intellectual commitment which has been lost for two centuries or more. There is, as Susan Marks has observed, a tangible 'millenarian' excitement abroad. More particularly, she suggests that the central dynamic for reconstitution is a renewed interest in the idea of political democracy; for 'If politics has become global, then so too must democracy' (Marks, 1997, pp.451–60, 467–75; 2000, pp.1–7, 83).

Most extravagantly of all, Bruce Ackerman proclaims that 'Enlightenment hope in written constitutions is sweeping the world' (Ackerman, 1997, p.773). The claim may be overstated, but there is more than a grain of truth, as well as hope, here. Few would argue against the virtues of democracy and citizenship, even if they argue over what these concepts may mean. The 'ideal' of democracy, as the former UN Secretary-General Boutros Boutros-Ghali, has declared, is one 'that belongs to all humanity' (Boutros-Ghali, 1995, p.1).

As an expression of constitutionality, the argument for global democracy militates inexorably towards the idea of rights. Democracy is not merely an aspiration. It is an entitlement: the entitlement, indeed, which defines a humane politics. Writing in 1992, Thomas Franck claimed that a universal 'emerging right to democratic governance' was 'becoming a requirement of international law, applicable to all and implemented through global standards, with the help of regional and international organizations'. The 'universally celebrated' right to democracy, he concluded, 'portends to a new global political culture supported by common rules and communitarian implementing institutions' (Franck, 1992, pp.46–7, 79–80, 90). The issue, as ever, is one of balance; of the need to deploy legalism in order to enhance rather than constrict the causes of democracy and humanity.

One of the most common defences of globalization is that it democratizes communities, regardless of the extent of their internal constitutional structures. The market empowers citizens, even if governments do not. This line is most commonly taken by Hayekians such as former US Deputy Secretary of State, Strobe Talbott, who champions the 'close linkage between democratic politics and free-market economics' (Shaw and Abide, 1995, p.15). It finds an original statement in John Stuart Mill's observation, a century ago, that 'It is commerce which is rapidly rendering war obsolete, by strengthening and multiplying the personal interests which are in natural opposition to it' (Thompson, 1992, p.5).

In other words, we are all becoming just too interdependent to countenance doing violence to one another. We may or may not like our neighbour, but we need him or her more than ever. The bare statistics of another century and half of grotesque inhumanity suggests that Mill might have been rather overoptimistic. And yet, there is some truth in this thesis. The financial markets of the world do indeed prefer to invest in liberal democracies. They favour governments that are both stable and reasonably transparent. Transnational corporations want their accountants to feel safe, and to know what is going on. They also crave the predictable. As a 1981 World Bank memo solemnly noted, 'human rights violations' can have 'broader implications' relating to a country's 'prospective credit-worthiness'. In a very real sense, therefore, today's crusade is not to spread the Word of God, but to persuade people to accept common principles of accounting (Friedman, 2000, pp.172–4).

But the idea of a fundamental revolution in the practice of democracy goes further than this. For one thing, globalization has indeed encouraged greater interdependence, both moral and intellectual, as well as material. Anecdotal evidence suggests a newly invigorated kind of democracy, examples of which include the public campaign to stop the Internet bookseller Amazon selling Hitler's works in Germany. By using the Internet itself, campaigners fought fire with fire, using the dynamics of global interdependency to counter the kind of cultural irresponsibility which globalization all too commonly appears to facilitate. Other commonly cited examples here include the various environmental campaigns of Greenpeace and other related NGOs ((Friedman, 2000, pp.11, 37, 47–69, 209, 237, 406–7).

Such strategies take us into the increasingly complex world of extraconstitutional democracy, something that was emphasized in the report of the Commission on Global Governance, *Our Global Neighbourhood*, which stated:

> Governance is the sum of the many ways individuals and institutions, public and private, manage their common affairs. It is a continuing process through which conflicting or diverse interests may be accommodated and co-operative action taken. It includes formal institutions and regimes empowered to enforce compliance, as well as informal arrangements that people and institutions either have agreed to or perceive to be in their interest.

It went on, in more precise terms:

> At the global level, governance has been viewed primarily as an intergovernmental relationship, but it must now be understood as also involving non-governmental organizations, citizens' movements, multi-national corporations, and the global capital market. Interacting with these are global mass media of dramatically enlarged influence. (Commission on Global Governance, 1995, pp.2–3)

Not only is 'global governance' conceptualized outwith the nation-state, but so too can it be imagined at a radically decentralized level. Global governance is not merely described in terms of a supranational accretion of power. The arguments for a complementary decentralization of power are compelling, particularly from the standpoint of reinvesting democracy. Robert Falk argues that 'governance structures should be as decentralized and localized as possible' (Falk, 1995, p.16). Marie-Claude Smouts refers to the 'interaction of fragmented subsystems' (Smouts, 1998, p.87).

The idea of decentralized governance, of 'fragmented subsystems', relates not merely to regional democracy, but to interest-group democracy too. The rise of the NGO has been one of the most striking developments in late twentieth-century international relations; most particularly, perhaps, the success of environmental groups. Robert Cox suggests that an emergent 'civil society' constituted by a myriad of interest groups provides the basis for an 'alternative world order', one that expresses the potentially revolutionary claims of the those 'disadvantaged' by globalization (Cox, 1999, pp.10–11). Taken further still, interest-group democracy can refer to informal opinion-generating associations, to the kind of 'kitchen-table' democracy described by Julie Mertus (Mertus, 2000, pp.538–44).

The argument that globalization has already forced a localization of power is a popular one. Keniche Ohmae suggests that regional autonomy is the essential 'lever for taking advantage of the global economy to the benefit of all citizens and residents' (Ohmae, 1996, p.119). Similarly, according to Fukuyama, 'decentralized decision making' is an inevitability in the modern world. In terms of practice, 'modern' citizenship is 'best exercised' through 'mediating institutions', such as political parties, churches, school boards, literary societies, and so on. It is in such 'associations' that the 'spontaneous sociability', which was once the defining characteristic of American public life, can be regenerated, and exported around the world. Communitarianism becomes a global crusade, though one driven as much by the demands of efficiency and market forces as by principle. The 'complexities of modern economics' have rendered efficient decision making 'beyond the capabilities of centralized bureaucracies', and in this context only democratically empowered communities can counter the potentially destructive forces of globalization and consumerism (Fukuyama, 1992, pp.92–3, 322–7; 1996, pp.26–7, 355–62).

The epidemic of popular protests at WTO conferences and the like provides a vivid illustration of this kind of emergent radical democracy. For the thousands who have recently taken to the streets of Seattle and Stockholm and Genoa, the point has been reached at which the lack of democratic legitimacy in global government is no longer acceptable. As Mary Kaldor rightly observes, such protests are less 'against' globalization than 'for' its democratization (Kaldor, 2000). If there is anarchy abroad, as is so often argued in the media, then it is very much of the rational democratic kind, rather than the nihilistic, more Godwin than Nietzsche. Indeed, as Benjamin Barber has emphasized, if there is anarchy in modern international politics, it is the anarchy of unregulated neoliberalism (Barber, 2000, pp.283–91). Commenting on the events of late 1999, Stephen Gill refers to the 'collective will' of an 'emerging civil society', a 'new set of democratic identities that are global, but based in diversity and rooted in local conditions, problems, and opportunities' (Gill, 2000, pp.131–40).

Cosmopolitanism and Humanity

What is clear, above all else, is the fact that globalization demands that we should radically rethink our politics: the way in which we engage with one another, the way in which we can translate our feelings, our beliefs, our interests. We need to take a fresh look at the institutions which act as transmission belts for our sentiments and ideals, at the legal systems which are supposed to be an expression of them, and at the jurisprudential conceptions within which we clothe these same sentiments and ideals.

It was suggested earlier that the experience of globalization is as much one of fear as it is of exhilaration. And we are right to be fearful of economic apartheid, of the tyranny of forces and, most obviously, perhaps, of the markets and institutions which seek to promote this tyranny. We are particularly right to be wary of a jurisprudence which seeks to provide this tyranny with a veneer of legitimacy. Law, it should always be remembered, is as potent in its absence as in its presence. The mere fact that the free market claims to be free does not make it so. International order is policed by laws, both in their presence and in their absence.

But at the same time, while displaying a healthy scepticism of the more exploitative aspects of the so-called 'new world order' and its economic instruments, there is also a case for welcoming the opportunity to reconfigure international, or perhaps transnational, order. At the heart of this book is the argument that the promise of Enlightenment has been lost, the balance of sense and sensibility sacrificed to the voracious appetite of the overweening nation-state, and its concomitant jurisprudential fantasies, of sovereignty, of limited democracy, of the rule of law.

The experience of globalization has cast these fantasies into question, and for this it must be welcomed. In the following chapters we will, in turn, take a closer look at the extent to which the reality of the European Union has further torn away the illusions of liberal constitutionalism, at the changing perceptions of what the idea of human rights should mean, and at the possibilities described by alternative ideas of 'restorative' justice in South Africa. There is a bonfire of constitutional vanities abroad, and nothing has poured more oil on the flames that the proclamation of a 'new world order' and the experience of globalization.

It is for this reason that some of the most trenchant critics of classical liberal theories of international order are amongst those who welcome the opportunities which its apparent demise offers. According to Philip Allott, therefore, at 'the end of a century and of a millennium' humanity now 'has the possibility of reconstituting itself as society, the international society of the whole human race, the society of all societies' (Allott, 1992, p.223). This resolution is also reached by the likes of Peter Spiro, who enthusiastically recommends the 'sweeping away of foundations that had been in place if not for a millennium then at least for several centuries', and the 'mapping', in their place, of a distinctively 'postnational' law (Spiro, 2000, pp.567–76).

Precisely the same metaphor is used by William Twining in his recently published *Globalisation and Legal Theory*. Recognizing that we live today in a 'global neighbourhood', in an increasingly 'cosmopolitan' world in which reality remains 'elusive' and political identity uncertain, Twining urges a remapping of law, one that will better enable us to accommodate the 'complexities' of our present existence. What the experience of globalization has taught us, if we did not already suspect so much all along, is the fact that positivist claims to scientific clarity in the law are untenable. In reality, 'legal orders are made up of complexes of social relations, ideas, ideologies, norms, concepts, institutions, people, techniques and traditions'. We must chart the 'mental map' of law anew, and simple one-dimensional sketches will no longer suffice. What we need instead is a map that properly 'emphasises the complexities and elusiveness of reality, the difficulties of grasping it, and the value of imagination and multiple perspectives in facing these difficulties' (Twining, 2000, pp.140, 152, 172–4, 243).

The solution is to embrace once again the classical idea of a *ius humanitatis*. As the age of 'particular' jurisprudence is passed, we must now instead reach out, or perhaps reach back, to the idea of 'general' jurisprudence. Such a jurisprudence, Twining perceptively suggests, can be found in the ethical utilitarianism of jurists such as Jeremy Bentham. An equally good candidate, indeed perhaps a better one, would be Adam Smith. For what both men appreciated was the fact that a general jurisprudence is one of balance, of reason and sentiment. And it is for this reason, as Twining rightly affirms, that the 'modern Benthamite' can properly claim an affinity with the modern 'citizen of the world' (ibid., 3–4, 14–29, 65–6, 91–107).

The reinvestment of a *ius humanitatis* carries an irreducible connotation, both for the idea of positive law itself, and for ideas of international or cosmopolitan order. On the one hand, the whole basis of positive law is founded on the idea of the Hobbesian or Austinian sovereign. Without a sovereign body, it becomes increasingly difficult to conceive of positive law. On the other hand is the complementary fact that the very idea of *ius humanitatis* is anyway necessarily cosmopolitan. It describes a conception of law that is, in Twining's words, able to 'transcend jurisdictions and cultures, so far as that is feasible and appropriate, and which can address issues about law from a global and transnational perspective' (ibid., pp.49, 189, 243). In essence it describes a legal humanism that is based on 'general' principles, and which uses humanity, rather than the pretended jurisdictions of nation-states or international institutions, as its essential point of reference.

The idea of *ius humanitatis* also carries an immediately ethical import. In *Justice and World Order*, Janna Thompson argues that the reinvestment of an ethical cosmopolitanism can overcome the criticism commonly levelled against some of the more utopian idylls of global governance. The kind of intensely humanistic 'world order' envisaged by Thompson is one that recasts the Rawlsian idea of an 'overlapping consensus' as an 'interlocking network' of federations, states and NGOs (Thompson, 1992, pp.92–9). The key, once again, is to reconcile, even embrace, a complexity of legal and political relations. Indeed, it is the recognition of complexity that confirms the ethical component of any political model.

As we all become increasingly interdependent, we all come to appreciate diversity. We become more tolerant of others. There is, in this view, a kind of genetic determination to tolerance; one that seems capable, indeed, of reinvesting the promise of an Enlightenment ethics. Thompson refers to our natural 'predisposition' to peace, something that carries an obvious resonance with Kant's assertion of our 'moral disposition' to an ultimate state of 'perpetual peace'. What is necessary, and what can perhaps already be detected, is a critical 'change of political and social consciousness'. It is no surprise that Thompson repeatedly seeks recourse to the Kantian idea of cosmopolitanism which we encountered before (ibid., pp.44–61, 102, 171–2). The nexus between the ideas of humanism and cosmopolitanism, global democracy and the ultimate ideal of a just transnational or international order, is irreducible. The problem which faces the 'new world order' today is every bit as much an ethical as a political or economic one.

Ultimately, then, when we talk about a new *ius humanitatis*, about cosmopolitanism, about global democracy indeed, we are led inexorably to questions of global ethics. It is a conclusion that chimes with the call at the end of the 1995 Commission of Global Governance report, *Our Global Neighbourhood*, to a common responsibility to nurture a 'Global Civic Ethic'. International regulation can make markets work. Only principles of cosmopolitan ethics, of global democracy, can make them work justly. A world in which 250 000 children die each week from malnutrition and easily preventable illnesses is not a just one.

And neither is it democratic. The fate of humanity is tied to the various, but related, ideas of cosmopolitan ethics and global governance, the ability to give voice to a global citizenry that will be morally aware and responsible. Robert Falk deploys the resonant phrase 'citizen pilgrim' to describe someone who is committed to 'an imagined community of the future that embodies nonviolence, social justice, ecological balance and participatory democracy in all arenas of policy and decision' (Falk, 1995, p.95). His conclusion is compelling:

> Only by reconstructing intimate relations on a humane basis can the world move toward the wider public and collective realities of human community. This reconstruction, starting at home, is a critical precondition for the emergence of the sort of global polity that could inspire trust and have a reasonable prospect of providing humane governance for a democratically constituted global civil society. (Ibid., p.69)

It is a sentiment which can be found in documents such as *Agenda 21*, adopted at the Earth Summit in Brazil in 1992, which recognized that the future well-being of everyone on this earth depends upon a willingness to 'engage in a continuous and constructive dialogue, inspired by the need to achieve a more efficient and equitable world economy', and moreover, that it remained essential 'to overcome confrontation and to foster a climate of genuine cooperation and solidarity' (Held, 1995, p.106).

There are two conclusions that can be drawn from such a statement. The first is that the need for a more equitable world economy is central to any credible idea of cosmopolitan justice. Some form of distributive justice is an essential component of any cosmopolitan ethic. The starving do not become good citizens. Logic dictates that the wider interests of any good society, cosmopolitan or otherwise, depend upon addressing the needs of the marginalized and disadvantaged. As Janna Thompson concludes, the realization of some form of genuinely just 'world order', to whatever degree it is cosmopolitan in tone, will certainly be better equipped to 'distribute goods and services' from community to community, and because of their interdependent 'association' will be more likely to do so 'as a matter of justice'. 'Communities' in this 'interlocking society' will be better 'able to make legitimate demands on each other which will be taken seriously and judged according to just procedures' (Thompson, 1992, pp.80–82, 186–7).

The second, obviously related, conclusion is that justice depends upon democracy. This is not to denigrate the role of human rights, which, as we shall see in due course, provides a necessary complement. But when we talk about any form of 'apartheid', global or otherwise, we are talking primarily about the denial of democracy, which, in turn, is the denial of humanity. If democracy is defined as the capacity to participate in the politics of a 'good society', to lead a life of responsibility, both to yourself and to others, then the material capacity to do so becomes essential.

As John Kenneth Galbraith emphasizes, without food, notional rights are quite useless. 'Nothing,' he rightly asserts, 'so comprehensively denies the liberties of the individual as a total absence of money.' In *The Good Society*, Galbraith has recently reaffirmed that the ultimate aspiration of such a society must be 'peace' between nations. Moreover, and once again the echoes of a Kantian idea of cosmopolitan right are striking, the 'good society cannot allow itself to be identified with the nation-states alone'. Rather 'it must recognize and support the larger international forces to which the individual country is subject'. Such a commitment, he concludes, 'is not a matter of choice; it is the modern imperative' (Galbraith, 1996, pp.4–5, 120).

In the final passages of *The Good Society*, Galbraith focuses on the critical alignment of democracy and humanity. The 'decisive step toward a good society,' he affirms, 'is to make democracy genuine, inclusive' (ibid., p.139). His ultimate conclusion is eloquent and compelling:

> Let there be a coalition of the concerned and the compassionate and those now outside the political system, and for the good society there would be a bright and wholly practical prospect. The affluent would still be affluent, the comfortable still comfortable, but the poor would be part of the political system. Their needs would be heard, as would the other goals of the good society. Aspirants for public office would listen. The votes would be there and would be pursued. As now with the safety net, health care, the environment and especially the military power, the good society fails where democracy fails. With true democracy, the good society would succeed, would even have an aspect of inevitability. (Ibid., p.143)

Democracy, moreover, is a self-nourishing conception. The process of free discussion nurtures the political imagination necessary for its reconception. Thus Arjun Appadurai talks of a new global 'culture' of democracy which can help us adjust to living in the multiplicity of 'imagined worlds' which make up the 'new world order' (Appadurai, 1996, pp.32–3). Stephen Rosow similarly suggests that, whereas classical liberalism actually serves to 'depoliticize democratic politics', by removing citizens from decision-making forums, a 'deterritorialized' conception of politics can 'focus on the active side of democratic citizenship and practice, on questions of civic virtue, of responsibility, of the ethical requirements of being a democratic citizen'. At the heart of this ideal is the belief that individuals can identify with different political communities. Accordingly, whilst there is no particular need to prise citizens away from immediate national or even regional affinities, there is a determination to undermine the exclusionary tendencies inherent within modern, particularly ethnic, nationalism. Such is 'differentiated' or 'contextual' citizenship (Rosow, 2000, pp.39–45). Such arguments align with distinctive 'post-national' conceptions of democratic citizenship, of the kind articulated by Linda Bosniak, who defines the 'world citizen' as someone, in possession of a 'cosmopolitan outlook', who 'expresses loyalty and moral commitment to humanity at large, rather than any particular community of persons' (Bosniak, 2000, p.448).

*

No one has better understood the present dilemmas that beset the 'new world order' than Czech president, Vaclav Havel, whose various writings describe a moral and political philosophy that is unashamedly humanist, that resonates indeed with the kind of idealism pronounced by Kant. They speak of sentiment as well as reason or right, of morality and spirituality, of a commonalty described by the very nature of humanity, of human experience, and human relatedness. At the end of the twentieth century, it was clear that our salvation does not lie in political ideologies, liberal, communist or whatever; the 'salvation of this human world lies nowhere else than in the human heart, in the human power to reflect, in human modesty, and in human responsibility' (Havel, 1998, pp.18–19). This sense of responsibility is critical. We are not atomized individuals. Politics presumes relatedness and responsibility. As he cautioned the Czech nation amidst the euphoria of early 1990, 'Freedom and democracy require participation and therefore responsible action from all of us' (ibid., p.5).

In an address to the assembled leaders of globalization at Davos in 1992, Havel affirmed that the intellectual pretensions of past ages can no longer be readily accepted. Neither law nor science nor theology nor ideology can 'perfect' humanity, human knowledge or human experience. The fact that humanity denies 'perfectibility' is the central insight of globalization. The fact that there are neither theological nor scientific truths is not a reason for despair. On the contrary, for 'those who believe, in all modesty, in the mysterious power of their own Being, which mediates between them and the mysterious power of the world's Being, have no reason to despair at all' (ibid., pp.89–94).

It is, as Havel has asserted elsewhere, an irreducibly 'metaphysical' conclusion (ibid., pp.112–13), and it is one to which he returns again and again; to the thought that communities are not built by laws, or certainly not built only by laws, but by a nurtured 'moral sensitivity' to others, by a matured 'ability to reflect critically on oneself, on genuine responsibility, on taste and tact, on the capacity to empathize with others, on a sense of moderation, on humility'. The politics of tomorrow is a 'job for modest people', for men and women who are both sensitive and sensible. It is, indeed, a job for all of us. The idea that modernity has 'dehumanized' politics, that politics must be returned to the people, is common in Havel's writings. The myth that politics is somehow a science rather than an 'artform', something that can be perfected by superior knowledge rather than improved by human endeavour, has led to the dominion of an intellectually detached and emotionally illiterate professional political elite, one that is wholly wedded to the emaciated belief that political communities can be supported by nothing more than rules, regulations and rights (ibid., pp.74, 100–101, 125–7, 166–9).

Any truly democratic 'civil society', whether it be Czech, European or even global, must overcome the tyranny of the lawyer–politician. It must 'offer citizens a colorful array of ways to become involved' in the decisions that determine their own 'civic coexistence, solidarity, and participation' (ibid., pp.147–8). As we have already noted, Havel has made much of the pervasive popular 'distrust' of democracy, the reason for which lies in 'the limited ability of today's democratic world' to 'address humanity in a genuinely universal way'. Rather than being seen 'as an open system that is best able to respond to people's basic needs', democracy today is 'seen as something given, finished, and complete', something 'that the more enlightened purchase and the less enlightened do not' (ibid., p.179).

Globalization threatens to dismantle so much, to tear humanity from its rootings. But it also offers the prospect of a revitalized humanism. As Havel observed, 'We live on a planet now – for the first time in its history – embraced by a single human civilization. Within this civilization, the destinies of billions of people and hundreds of nations are so interknit that they merge together in a single destiny.' He continued by emphasizing the need for such a civilization to appreciate the possibilities that such a global experience offers, to root out a fundamental shared appreciation of what it is to be human:

> It is my belief that, if there is a bond uniting the diverse religious and cultural worlds that make up our civilization today, it can only be their unwavering certainty that the key to solid human coexistence, and to a life that does not become a hell on earth, lies in respect for what I call the miracle of Being. True goodness, true responsibility, true justice, a true sense of things – all these grow from roots that go much deeper that the world of our transitory earthly schemes. This is a message that speaks to us from the very heart of human religiosity. (Ibid., pp.240–42)

It is the presence of the 'human' that is critical. For what Havel is appealing for is a humanist religiosity, of the kind which so appealed to Mill and Eliot a century and a half ago, one that can reject the banalities of Nietzschean nihilism and institutional political theology with an equal vigour. He was, he emphasized, 'speaking of something slightly different', of the 'need to grasp and articulate anew humanity's essential, fundamental spiritual experience and to infuse the spirit of this experience into the creation of a new world order, one that would allow us all to live and work together in peace without forcing anyone to give up his cultural autonomy' (ibid.).

Speaking on the particular subject of human rights, Havel has elsewhere emphasized the extent to which a culture of rights must be founded upon something altogether deeper:

> Politicians at international forums may reiterate a thousand times that the basis of a the new world order must be universal respect for human rights, but it will mean nothing as long as this imperative does not derive from respect for the miracle of Being, the miracle of the universe, the miracle of nature, the miracle of our own existence.

In the post-modern global world, a new humanism must be 'rooted in self-transcendence', in 'transcendence as a hand reaching out to those close to us, to foreigners, to the human community, to all living creatures, to nature, to the universe' (ibid., pp.171–2).

There is no doubt that a sense of 'moral obligation', of 'duty' and 'reciprocity', are necessary to the proper functioning of the 'good society'. But so too is compassion. We need to feel a sense of obligation, certainly. But we also need to care, and we need to know that such care is reciprocated, just as much as any moral obligation might be. This is what Havel means by 'transcendence', by the ability to overcome the Nietzschean self. A politics that is compassionate, that is founded on sensibility, even love, does not have to replace a politics based on law and rights. But a politics that makes claims to justice must be compassionate. It is justice, as we mentioned before, that is 'out of joint' today; or, more precisely, it is the appreciation that justice should be a concept that balances sense and sensibility, reason and passion. The idea of humanity, of humanism indeed, cannot be divorced from compassion.

And so, as ever, we come full circle. There is no need to strain for new intellectual models. There is a familiar resonance in the call for justice and humanity, as commentators such as Ronnie Lipschutz have noted. The investment of an ethical component in the idea of 'civil society' describes a pre-Westphalian humanism. According to Lipschutz, the 'newly dominant operating system in global politics – liberalism with the individual at its core – has come to fill a role similar to the system of rules and rule promulgated by the Church prior to Westphalia'. The idea of global 'civil society', he perceptively concludes, bears its greatest resemblance to the classical *ius civile* (Lipschutz, 1992, pp.340–47).

The Kantian conception of 'cosmopolitan right' of 'universal hospitality', the ultimate expression of a mature, rational jurisprudence, is compelling. Writing in 1795, Kant suggested:

> The peoples of the earth have thus entered in varying degrees into a universal community, and it has developed to a point where a violation of rights in one part of the world is felt everywhere. The idea of a cosmopolitan right is therefore not fantastic and overstrained; it is a necessary complement to an unwritten code of political and international right, transforming it into a universal right of humanity. Only under this condition can we flatter ourselves that we are continually advancing towards a perpetual peace. (Kant, 1991c, pp.107–8)

At this point, of course, the ideas of humanity and global citizenship become inextricably linked with that of rights, an affinity to which we shall turn in the next two chapters.

Kant's conclusion, therefore, takes us a step further. The establishment of a condition of 'perpetual peace' depends upon nurturing a sensibility for violations of fellow human beings. This, ultimately, is what democracy is supposed to facilitate. It is why the future of humanity, in a world that is now irreducibly global, depends upon the security of an appropriately global conception of democratic citizenship. The global citizen can only function properly, and sensitively, in a regime of democratic global governance.

The case for democratic global governance, regardless of the extent to which it is founded on cosmopolitan or international precepts, is unarguable. If the much-vaunted 'new world order' is not to continue to disappoint, the ideal will have to become reality. To date, the case remains largely one of theoretical persuasion. However, as we shall now see, there are two rather more concrete examples which may, or indeed may not, give rise to greater expectations: the reformation of the 'new' Europe and the reinvestment of inter- or transnational human rights. It is to the first of these, to the 'new' Europe, that we should now turn.

4 The Peoples of Europe

Everyone's Europe

In an address to the European Parliament in February 2000, the President of the Commission, Romano Prodi, prophesied a 'decade of Europe', a decade of 'outstanding achievement and success'. 'If we act boldly and decisively together,' he declared, 'we can shape the new Europe our citizens want and that we owe to future generations.' This will be a 'just, humane, inclusive Europe', an 'exciting, energetic, enterprising Europe'. It will, indeed, be 'Everyone's Europe'.

It is not the first time that Europe's leaders have projected a decade of unparalleled success. It had been predicted that the 1990s would be one of the great defining decades of European integration; the decade when the European 'project' was to evolve from being a glorified free trade zone into a full-blown political union. In 1992, a draft Treaty of the European Union had actually aspired to forging a 'federal' Europe. Domestic politics within certain member states, most particularly the UK, precluded such an idyll. So instead the final Treaty projected an 'ever closer union' amongst the 'peoples of Europe'.

We in Europe are supposed to be able to make sense of this. It is supposed to inspire us. We are supposed to know what Europe is, and to identify with it. And yet it is quite clear that rather too many of us do not, that the idea of an integrated Europe has struggled to win a place in our hearts. As Prodi went on to admit, at present 'Europe's citizens are disenchanted and anxious', ever more 'sceptical' that institutions which seem so 'remote' will be able to 'deliver the kind of society they want' (Prodi, 2000).

This ambivalence may be stronger in some places than others. The UK and Denmark, for example, have long nurtured a reputation for being 'Eurosceptic'. It was the UK which crushed the federal aspirations of the draft Union Treaty. In an initial referendum, the Danes actually rejected the same Treaty in its entirety. The same country has recently rejected the possibility of joining the single currency. But even amongst the so-called 'inner core' of member states there are clearly considerable popular doubts.

When put to the test of a referendum, the French barely approved the Union Treaty. Eurobarometers reveal a steadily declining enthusiasm for the very idea of a 'new' Europe, while various far right parties in various member states continue to attract considerable popular support with virulently anti-European political rhetoric.

In some ways this is rather odd. The 'new' Europe inherited certain ready identities, geographical, historical, even cultural. But closer inspection reveals that these primordial identities are neither particularly stable nor terribly convincing. In geographical terms, it is just as true today that there are various Europes about, each dependent upon where the cartographer chooses to draw the line. For a long time, the boundary of the 'new' Europe stopped at the West German border. Today it has moved a little further to the east. In years to come it might stretch as far as the borders of Russia and the Ukraine. The historical and cultural identities might seem to be a little more promising, and there is certainly a particular tradition of European humanism that may furnish a more convincing sense of commonality or identity. But, once again, this is far from settled. We shall return to these questions of identity throughout this chapter, for they go to the very heart of the 'new' Europe's present crisis. And we shall revisit this particular humanist tradition, too, for it might just present the most compelling and inspiring way forward into the new millennium.

The idea of a unified Europe has been with us for some time. The force of commercial necessity impelled Kant to recommend a European confederation in his *Metaphysics of Morals*. As we have already seen, for Kant the striving for some kind of 'perpetual peace' in Europe was more than a mere aspiration. It was a 'duty' (Kant, 1991c, pp.158–60). A similar idea had been presented nearly a century before in Callieres' classic study of diplomacy, *On the Manner of Negotiating with Princes*, which stated that:

> we must think of the states of which Europe is composed as being joined together by all kinds of necessary commerce, in such a way that they may be regarded as members of one Republic, and that no considerable change can take place in any one of them without affecting the condition or disturbing the peace of all the others. (Held, 1995, p.19)

The idea of some kind of European confederation or union is not, then, a new one. Aside from the likes of Kant and Callieres, commentators often cite the Hanseatic League, the medieval *respublica Christiana*, even the Roman Empire, as constituents of a distinctive 'European' intellectual and political genealogy.

But what is interesting about the most recent attempt to effect some kind of European political union is the immediate context of globalization. For, in some ways, the 'new' Europe could be seen, as Martin Shapiro has suggested, as providing a 'microcosm' of 'global dynamics' (Shapiro, 1993, p.52). In similar vein, Brigitte Stern has suggested that the European Union represents the most developed model of a new world order that must now be described in terms of legally defined 'regions' (Stern, 1999, pp.264–5). In this sense, it might represent the coming to fruition of the Enlightenment project, and perhaps a movement beyond too. An enthusiastic Antony Giddens opines that the Union 'is the most important and promising experiment in transnational governance going on', a critical example of the kind of 'cosmopolitan democracy' which might ultimately emerge at a global level (Giddens and Hutton, 2000, p.51; Giddens, 1998, pp.141–7). Prodi, too, has spoken of the 'new' Europe's responsibility as a 'global civil power at the service of a sustainable global development' (Prodi, 2000).

Alternatively, it might represent its 'end', a politics that is distinctively post-modern, that lies beyond the international order described by sovereign nation-states. The German foreign minister, Joschka Fischer, has suggested that the 'old European state system' has now passed, a semiotic for the demise of the '*anciens régimes*'. This may well be so. It chimes with the still lingering euphoria for a new world order. There again, as his French counterpart, Jean-Pierre Chevènement, responded, it might just be a product of Germany's fascination with the possibility of reinvesting the Holy Roman Empire (Fischer and Chevènement, 2000). The creation of the 'new' Europe could, of course, be both, representing a return to a catholic Europe which can still provide a model for a new regime of transnational governance, for alternative, revitalized ideas of democracy and citizenship. This is the most intriguing possibility.

Either way, the fate of the 'new' Europe, its history since the inception of the Community in 1958, its present travails and its future prospects, provide a testing ground for possible transition from the politics of modernity, of the *anciens régimes*, to a politics of post-modernity, of democracy, compassion and sensibility. If we are to perceive a new form of politics for the new millennium, no matter how dimly, perhaps it can be found in the reconstitution of Europe?

*

The fate of the nation-state lies at the heart of the European question. It has become increasingly popular to talk about a Europe of 'variable geometry', one in which the sovereignty of each nation-state is 'pooled'. It is intended to describe a situation in which individual nation-states relinquish a degree of political sovereignty in return for gaining a notional measure of influence over other member states. It is a rather more elevated version of the more prosaic truth that in today's world, like it or not, nation-states are no longer self-sufficient or self-sustaining. No nation-state enjoys sovereign authority over its citizens or subjects. One pretence, absolute or parliamentary sovereignty, is replaced by another, 'pooled' sovereignty.

This process asks a further, deeper question, for whilst the demise of sovereignty may not itself matter so much, the collateral demise of democracy does. The idea of sovereignty is an essentially illusory one, a mythology described by history in order to delude the masses into thinking that they may enjoy some reified political or constitutional authority. But democracy is real, or it can be. It is democracy that matters to the European citizen, not sovereignty. To this extent, once again, the European experience is symptomatic of the essential challenge of globalization; the need to locate within these intense dynamics a space for democratic participation and expression (Verhoeven, 1998a, p.231).

Anxieties regarding democracy, and the so-called 'democratic deficit' in the 'new' Europe, have grown apace during the 1990s, most particularly following the arrival of the Union Treaty. This anxiety works at different levels. On the one hand, there is the feeling amongst many that the loss of practical political power enjoyed by nation-states and their democratic assemblies has not been properly compensated at a European level. The European Parliament remains a largely emasculated entity, one that enjoys far less power and influence than either the Commission or the Council, in the words of the French foreign minister, an essentially 'illusory' institution (Fischer and Chevènement, 2000).

At a different level, there is an added anxiety regarding the blatantly undemocratic nature of the new Union. Article 6 section 1 of the Union Treaty proudly proclaims that 'The Union is founded on the principles of liberty, democracy, respect for human rights and fundamental freedoms, and the rule of law, principles which are common to the Member States.' Section 2 added that the 'Union shall respect fundamental rights, as guaranteed by the European Convention', and 'as they result from the constitutional traditions common to the Member States' and as 'general principles' of Community law.

We shall take a closer look at the nature of Community 'rights' in due course. But it is interesting to note for now the assumed alignment of rights, the rule of law and democracy. All are meant to be central to the new Europe, yet none of them actually apply to the Union itself; for, whilst the Union might 'respect' all manner of things, it is legally answerable to no one. The rule of law is an aspiration to be achieved by all the member states but not by the Union itself. And precisely the same is true of democracy. Michael Zuern puts it succinctly, observing that, 'If the EU were to apply for membership in the EU, it would not qualify because of the inadequate democratic content of its constitution' (Zuern, 2000, p.183).

The fact that classical conceptions of democracy appear to be so inadequate in the context of the 'new' Europe has nurtured a vigorous debate about the meaning of democracy, and most particularly of *demos*. Can the ballot-box alone really fulfil the democratic yearnings of 372 million people? The European citizen, it seems, thinks not. The turnout for the last set of European Parliamentary elections fell to as low as 15 per cent in certain parts of the Community. Zuern emphasizes that a healthy conception of democracy depends upon the presence of a 'potential for democratic self-governance'. The constituents of a *demos*, all of which are absent or critically abbreviated in today's Europe, include rights to 'personal self-fulfilment', trust, 'solidarity', a public spirit as an expression of collective identity, and a 'capacity to communicate publicly' (ibid., pp.191, 195–200).

Juergen Habermas has likewise argued that the resolution of the deficit will require a bold venture into alternative ideas of democracy, into the opening up of 'public spaces'. The construction of the new Europe, he suggests, encapsulates the immanent 'tension' that exists between 'capitalism and democracy'. The solution is to reconceptualize the 'constitutional principles of human rights and democracy' in terms of an ability to facilitate the creation of a 'communicative' and 'freedom-valuing political culture' (Habermas, 1996a, pp.3–6, 183–93, 287–328, 501–7; 1996b, pp.133–7). In these terms, the new Europe would indeed chart the way towards a new democratic politics in a new world order.

Another who has argued that a revitalized conception of democracy in Europe can only be founded on the construction of a genuine *demos* is Joseph Weiler, for whom the increasing disparity between the 'empowerment' of the 'legal consumer' and the 'disempowerment' of the 'political citizen' has been the defining characteristic of European integration over the last decades of the twentieth century. At the heart of Weiler's analysis is a double condemnation. On the one hand, democracy in the Union is deficient on its own terms, the Community's Parliament being devoid of meaningful powers. On the other hand, such a form of democracy is itself wholly inadequate when it comes to contemplating how to construct an effective *demos*. Weiler's solution is a form of 'consociational' democracy; one which can 'enhance legitimacy in its inclusiveness and the broadening of ultimate consent to government' (Weiler, 1999, pp.xi, 266–9, 279–82).

Questions of democracy are indeed inseparable from those of legitimacy, and of course citizenship. As we have already noted, in a post-Westphalian world, one in which nation-states can no longer pretend to govern their citizenry, or at least not exclusively, legitimacy emerges as an essential question. Neil MacCormick convincingly argues that, without a genuine and meaningful conception of citizenship, it is impossible to envisage a genuine 'European civic *demos*', or indeed any kind of 'civic identity' (MacCormick,

1999, pp.144–5). Citizenship seals political affinity, and inscribes it, to use Habermas's resonant phrase, on the 'collective memory'. As Weiler suggests, the great facility of citizenship is its ability to bridge between an emaciated jurisprudence of legal right and the potentially more inspiring politics of cultural identity. It satiates, at least to some degree, 'our existential yearning' for 'meaning' (Weiler, 1998, pp.226–31, 246).

Back in 1992, the announcement of a European 'citizenship' was intended to be one of the great symbolic moments. 'Citizenship of the Union is hereby established,' the Union Treaty affirmed. And then some of the gloss was removed. 'Every person holding the nationality of a Member State,' it whispered, 'shall be a citizen of the Union', and not anybody else. And then another rather sad little sub-clause: 'Citizenship of the Union shall complement and not replace national citizenship.' Nothing more vividly describes the anguished tension that currently exists between the declining *anciens régimes* and the infant to which they long ago gave birth, but which now threatens to swallow them up.

According to the Spanish premier, Felipe Gonzalez, citizenship was 'aimed at convincing Europe's men and women that what we were doing only made sense if we viewed Europe as belonging to its citizens'. The juxtaposition of 'we' and the European 'citizen' speaks volumes. 'We meant,' Gonzales urges, 'to add it as a bonus', but to what is not entirely clear (Gonzalez, 1999, p.30). In the end, as Weiler has suggested, it is difficult to argue down the conclusion that Union citizenship is nothing more than a 'trite and banal' device for 'placating an alienated populace' (Weiler, 1999, pp.324, 336). French Foreign Minister Chevènement is more prosaic still: in its present form, the 'idea of European citizenship is a joke' (Fischer and Chevènement, 2000).

*

The conclusion is inescapable. If the carving out of a genuine political *demos* is a necessary constituent of a legitimate political community, then logic dictates that the 'new' Europe is politically illegitimate. But does this matter? Tony Blair suggests not. According to Blair, 'we can spend hours on end trying to devise a perfect form of European democracy and get nowhere'. More encouraging, perhaps even inspiring, is Prodi's recent acknowledgment that the presence of 'democratically legitimate institutions' is essential if the new Europe is to engage once again the affinity of its citizenry. 'People,' Prodi argues, 'want a much more participatory, "hands-on" democracy. They will not support the European project unless they are fully involved in setting goals, making policy and evaluating progress.' 'They are,' moreover, 'right' (Prodi, 2000).

Indeed so. But sadly little has changed since 1992. The bizarre construction of the Union, with only one justiciable 'pillar', continues to militate against genuine democracy and accountability. The more prosaic aspects of the democratic 'deficit' remain unresolved. The European Parliament remains emasculated. Despite the piecemeal reforms of the 1990s, in essence the power of legislative initiative remains with the Council, whilst the authority to draft legislation remains with the Commission. The absence of transnational political parties in Europe speaks volumes for an assembly that no one can be bothered to take too seriously (Weiler, 1999, pp.266–7).

In this respect, in the matter of establishing democratic legitimacy, the first decade of the Union has been an unambiguous failure. The founding Treaty of Union was roundly condemned, and rightly. Academic commentators, such as Deirdre Curtin, castigated a Treaty of 'bits and pieces', with its different 'pillars', its piecemeal institutional reforms, its various protocols by which different countries opted out of different things (Curtin, 1993, p.67). In the wake of the Maastricht Treaty, Weiler argued that the very idea of European integration had suddenly become constestable again (Weiler, 1999, pp.3, 256–60). Academic doubts translated into popular hostility. The British Parliament, reflecting a mood of uncertainty in the country, barely approved legislation designed to incorporate the Union Treaty in national law. As we have already noted, when the Treaty was put to a referendum in France, it was approved by less than 1 per cent, while in Denmark it was first rejected, and only staggered through following a hastily convened second referendum.

A barely chastened President of the Commission, Jacques Delors, muttered darkly about a 'two-tier' Europe: an inner core of committed countries, and an outer core of the less committed, whose politicians and citizens demanded their various opt-outs. By 1993, the whole idea of a Europe moving forward together, an *acquis communautaire*, was rapidly unravelling. By the 1997 Amsterdam Treaty, the talk was firmly of 'flexibility', of a Europe of 'variable geometry', of a Europe, in essence, in which the member states should feel rather more free to pick and choose which bits they want to be a part of it, and which bits they do not think they can 'sell' to their domestic electorates (Weiler, 1998, pp.224–31; Shaw, 1998; Ehlermann, 1998).

Apparently incapable of arguing from principle, seemingly stunned by popular and academic reactions against the Maastricht Treaty, Europe's leaders have spent much of the 1990s in a catatonic trance. By the end of the decade, with the corrupted Santer Commission cast out, and with Euroscepticism gaining in strength across much of the continent, power in the new Europe appears to have swung back to the nation-states. Unsurprisingly, there has been little enthusiasm for submitting any further

Treaty amendments to popular approval. On the rare occasion when such approval was sought, as in the recent Danish vote on joining the single currency, it was denied. As the century closed, it was clear that the euphoria which surrounded the completion of the '1992 project' had been spent.

If the idyll of an 'ever closer union' is to be revived, the architects of the 'new' Europe will have to come up with something rather fresher and rather more enticing. The challenge, as Deirdre Curtin puts it, of 're-imagining', not just democracy in Europe, but Europe itself, remains (Curtin, 1997, p.3). It will not go away, no matter how many political compromises Europe's leaders can cobble together as they limp from one treaty to another.

The Limits of Legalism

The root of the legitimacy problem, the genesis of the notorious and much-debated 'democratic deficit', lies back in 1958, with the inception of the European Community. The Community envisaged in the Rome Treaty of that year was intended to be a 'common market', a superannuated free trade zone. The possibility of collateral developments was never ruled out, but neither were they prescribed. As Jean Monnet, the President of the High Authority and the man often accredited with the soubriquet 'father' of the new Europe, admitted, 'the Community we have created is not an end in itself'. Instead, the establishment of the Community instituted a 'process'. 'I have never doubted,' he concluded, 'that one day this process might lead us to the United States of Europe; but I see no point in trying to imagine today what political form it will take' (Monnet, 1978, pp.522–3). The 'new' Europe has never had a clear idea of where it is going.

It is only too easy to appreciate Altiero Spinelli's famous comment, that Monnet had 'the great merit of having built Europe, and the great responsibility to have built it badly' (Ward, 1996, p.16). Without a cause or a vision, it is desperately difficult to launch a crusade. Where there should be rhetoric of inspiration, there is instead Article 2, which describes the 'task' of the Community Treaty, its objectives: a motley set of aspirations which include 'a harmonious, balanced and sustainable development of economic activities', 'sustainable and non-inflationary growth' and a 'high degree of competitiveness'. Admittedly, it concludes with the hope that the market may raise the 'standard of living and the quality of life', but there is little here that can really grab the popular imagination.

Instead of nourishing a popular dynamic of support, the founders of the Community decided to put their faith in institutions, in the neofunctionalist idea of 'spillover'; once an institutional framework is in place, and an aspiration programmed into the system, then the process of political and economic integration would take on an irreversible dynamic. An integrated Europe would become a self-fulfilling prophecy. Instead it has become a nightmare.

The byzantine world of Community and Union government has long fascinated the Eurosceptic. It goes to the very heart of the question of 'democratic deficit'. The Union all too easily fulfils the Orwellian fantasies of oppressive and corrupted bureaucracy. A largely bewildered public is fed a daily diet of apparent absurdities by an often hostile press, tales of spurious subsidies, of millions of Euros of humanitarian aid lost en route to the Balkans, and of the apparently endless desire to build grander and grander buildings for a political elite that seems to be ever more detached, not just from the citizenry of Europe, but from reality. Not content with one Parliament building costing £345 million situated in Strasbourg, the Parliament duly voted itself a further £825 million with which to build another in Brussels, a vast cavernous nothing, inhabited for most of its time only by roaming tourists. It appears that Europe's administrative and political elite simply does not care what the citizenry thinks.

The problem of excessive bureaucracy, or more importantly the appearance of excessive bureaucracy, stems from a pervasive belief in the neofunctionalist idea of integration through institutional 'process'. There is little notice here of democratic legitimacy. The problem is only exacerbated by the complementary belief in the integrationist potential of law. From its very inception, it was clear that the primary dynamic of integration in the new European Community would be geared, not by citizens, or even politicians, but by lawyers. In some ways, this legalistic faith has proved to be well-founded. But in other ways, as time has moved on, the limits of legalism have become all too apparent.

According to certain judges at the European Court, such as Federico Mancini, the responsibility of the Court to promote European legal and political integration was 'genetically coded' in the Rome Treaty, incited by such as Article 5, which vests in the Court the responsibility to 'ensure the fulfilment' of the Treaty's 'obligations' (Mancini, 1991, pp.177–94). This may be so, but it does nothing to lift the burden of democratic illegitimacy. Citizens, not lawyers, should build political communities.

The effects of such a process are only too plain. Where there should be a public philosophy, a political morality, there is instead a morass of legal doctrines and case law. The 'history' of European legal integration describes the incremental creation of a vast jurisprudential empire, as the Court of Justice first moved from establishing certain core principles of constitutional law to the 'convergence' of administrative law principles. Today, lawyers chatter about the merits of a European 'common law', with common commercial, criminal and contract codes. The prospect of a 'regime of academic lawyers' reconstructing a 'great' European 'legal family' excites applause (Legrand, 1996, p.52).

One striking example of this aspiration is provided by the emergent process of fashioning a European family law. The Commission has recently noted that Europeans do not seem to be breeding as they should. Europe, it seems, may run out of 'peoples'. The family, according to the Commission, is a primary source for raising 'future producers', as well as being a vital 'unit of consumption'. Optimal fertility rates are vital for the maximum efficiency of the market. The bizarre idea that the Community might promote some kind of model family has bounced around for some years. The Court has happily leant its support, defining the European family as something constituted by married heterosexual couples, the children of which are to be cared for in terms of primarily maternal responsibilities. Such a unit, it has reasoned, is most likely to run at maximum economic efficiency (McGlynn, 2000, pp.29–44). The assertion would be almost comical, if it was not so deeply offensive and so morally vacuous.

There can be no doubt that the European Court of Justice has provided the critical dynamic in the process of European political integration. It is therefore unsurprising that the Community that it has shaped has emerged as a legalistic empire *par excellence*, the epitome of liberal legalism. As ever, it not the presence of laws that matters. And it is not the commitment to the rule of law either; such a commitment is necessary for any political community that aspires to ideals of liberty, equality and justice. It is the over-reliance on law which is troublesome.

*

The extent to which the Community, and more particularly its Court of Justice, should promote human rights has long engaged controversy, leading some of the more condemnatory to suggest that neither the Community nor the Court has taken 'rights seriously'. Of course, Community human rights law is troubled by all the definitional problems that invariably haunt any such jurisprudence. At times it has been suggested that the European citizen enjoys 'fundamental rights' to travel abroad for an abortion, to enjoy fair labour conditions, even to fish. There is also the undoubted fact that the Court has become increasingly chary when it comes to translating fundamental rights into 'human rights'. Within the context of a Community Treaty, the primary ambition of which is clearly to refine a common market, the Court has repeatedly emphasized that any 'fundamental' rights must be 'balanced', compromised by 'certain limits justified by the overall objectives pursued by the Community': in other words, the overriding desire to make money (Coppel and O'Neill, 1992; de Burca, 1993).

It is rather easier to justify this 'balance' when talking about certain 'fundamental' Community rights. The idea that 'human rights', with all the ethical and universalistic baggage that such a phrase carries, might be compromised in order to make the market a little more efficient would be altogether more difficult to defend. When the Court was faced with the clear dilemma of ranking a market right to free movement against an alleged right to life, in the *Grogan* case in 1991, it ran into serious criticism, both from those who supported the right to move abroad for such a 'service', and those who opposed the elevation of such a right over the stipulated right to life enshrined in the Irish constitution (Phelan, 1992, p.670).

Despite these problems, or perhaps because of them, after a decade of agonized debate, the Union decided to declare a new Union Charter of Fundamental Rights at the Nice intergovernmental conference in December 2000. The Charter proudly proclaimed that 'The peoples of Europe, in creating an ever closer union among them, are resolved to share a peaceful future based on common values.' Although the discernment of certain 'common values' has proved to be rather elusive since 1958, and arguably throughout the previous two thousand years, the Charter hazarded the thought that 'Conscious of its spiritual and moral heritage, the Union is founded on the indivisible, universal values of human dignity, freedom, equality and solidarity.' The Charter then went on to list fifty-four articles, ranging from the inviolability of 'human dignity' to the 'right to life', and the 'right' to a 'private and family life', to the 'right' to contact ombudsmen; the deepest of ethical and political imponderables jostle with administrative pedantry for a place in the jurisprudential sun.

The idea that there might be a Charter of rights gained ground in the wake of the Maastricht Treaty. It was given official blessing at the Cologne Council meeting in spring 1999. Academies duly buzzed, as draft after draft had appeared on the Council web-site. In the autumn of 1998, the French president, Jacques Chirac, had appealed to the memory of the 'genius of a few visionaries', to the cause of an 'empire forged for intellectual reason', one which seeks the 'collective promotion of shared values' (Chirac, *The Independent*, 3/9/98). Grand rhetoric indeed. But, when he got to Nice, Chirac spent his time squabbling over Council voting procedures, countering Chancellor Schroeder's argument that there were more Germans than Frenchmen and women with the puerile observation that France at least had a nuclear capacity. The 'genius of a few visionaries' was long forgotten. And so was the Union Charter. Intended to be the high point of the Nice conference, to be the instrument that would finally reinvigorate the moribund Union, the Charter was treated with virtual contempt, dispensed with in the first couple of hours.

The citizenry of Europe, who were supposed to be inspired by their new panoply of rights, were curtly informed that it would only be a 'declaration' after all, and thus of no legal force. A non-justiciable Charter of rights; a wonderful jurisprudential perversity. The European Parliament condemned a Charter that fell 'far short' of what is needed to 'strengthen the Union's capability for enlargement and democratic legitimacy'. As ever, the idea of a 'new' Europe has been hamstrung by squabbling politicians, its credibility as a community founded on a rule of law actually diminished rather than enhanced (Ward, 2001).

The predicament of today's Europe, encapsulated perhaps by the fate of its Charter, epitomizes the limits of liberal legalism. As Vaclav Havel has rightly observed, 'The best laws will not in themselves guarantee legality or freedom or human rights' unless they are 'underpinned by certain human and social values', by a 'real moral awareness'. The time has come for Europe's leaders to recognize that 'a legal relationship or legal order must be preceded by a connection to or an order from the realm of morality, because only a moral commitment imbues the legal arrangements with meaning and makes them truly valid' (Havel, 1992, pp.12–20; 1998, pp.68, 247–8).

*

We return, once again, to the essential problem, that of democracy. According to Weiler, the 1990s have witnessed a popular 'rebellion against the image of constitutionalism' in the new Europe, one which all too easily translates into a fundamental 'crisis of ideals' (Weiler, 1999, pp.233–4, 238). Larry Siedentop takes a similar line, suggesting that there is a pressing need to rethink the relation between Europe's constitutional pretensions and the blatant lack of a coherent public philosophy. Europe's crisis is an expression of liberalism's crisis; of the rise of 'economism', of the interests of the consumer against those of the citizen. Where liberalism was once a philosophy of 'human flourishing' and of 'passion', it is now one of human alienation and competition. Today's Europe is a symbol of this impoverished and 'distorted' liberalism. There is much to be done if this demise is to be reversed, and if Europe is indeed to become 'truly self-governing' (Siedentop, 2000, pp.28–40, 230–31).

The criticism goes to the very heart of the Community's *raison d'être*. It is always easy to forget the obvious, and what is too often forgotten about the new Europe is that it was created in order to make money. When Monnet and his fellow 'saints' got together half a century ago, their primary concern was to rebuild Europe's economic infrastructure. It was for this reason that the question of democracy seemed to be so utterly irrelevant, and it was for this reason that the brand of neoliberalism employed was so little concerned with 'human flourishing'.

The limits of such an approach have become only too clear. The 1991 Report of the Second European Poverty Programme concluded that 'two different societies' were currently emerging in the Community, 'one of them active, well-paid, well-protected socially, and with an employment-conditioned structure; the other poor, deprived of rights and devalued by inactivity'. Little has changed in the intervening decade. And, so long as the Commission remains preoccupied by the illusory lures of pure competition and unfettered trade, nor will it. Markets, as Schumpeter long ago advised, tend towards exclusion; competition thrives on disadvantage (Holland, 1993, p.125).

And all the predictable forms of disadvantage are present. The high-blown rhetoric of Article 2 of the Community Treaty, of an anticipated 'harmonious development' and a 'balanced expansion', has proved to be fatuous. The poorer regions of the Community are still poorer. Regional policy remains largely unrealized. Funds are more commonly spent on preserving ancient temples than on building hospitals (Scott, 1995, pp.44–9, 65–70). The poorer citizens remain poorer: those that are black, those that are immigrant, those that are female (Geddes, 1995, pp.200–202). The role of the Court of Justice in perpetuating the social disadvantage of such groups is undoubted. Its treatment of gender inequalities is only the most notorious example. Eighty per cent of part-time workers in the Community are female. Part-time work, the Court has adjudged, is not proper work. And neither is care work or charity work, or any of the other kinds of work generally done by women. Those that devote their lives to the compassionate relief of others do not conform to the rational economic actor model beloved of the neoliberal and, it seems, the European Court of Justice (Scheiwe, 1994, p.243).

The governing sentiment is irreducibly economic. It is the market that counts, efficiency, competition, the free movement of capital, goods and services. It is the furtherance of these goals which has driven the Court, and thus the process of European integration; all shrouded in the pervasive myths of modernity, of irreversible progress towards some kind of rationalist, scientifically determinate *telos*. And neither the politicians nor the other institutions of the Community have seen fit to alter this mindset. Instead, they have simply tinkered with occasional gestures, drafted Treaty Preambles wistfully declaring all manner of aspirations, desperately trying to reinforce ever less credible mythologies, promising any number of reforms tomorrow. There is always, it seems, another treaty on the way; it is just a matter of being patient.

Europe's current predicament is indeed schizophrenic. It wants to be a common market, but with a bit of politics thrown in; an element of democracy so long as it does not sacrifice the idylls of efficiency. So it has constructed a peculiar constitutional edifice, with a strong Community pillar, with an extravagant array of legal and economic instruments, to which has been added a series of political institutions, concepts and aspirations, all scattered around a grand Union Treaty; an emaciated Parliament, an impoverished notion of citizenship, a non-justiciable Charter of so-called 'fundamental' rights and freedoms.

It is simply not good enough. If the new Europe is to flourish in the new millennium, if it is indeed to carry the banner at the vanguard of a new world order, it will need to take a deeper look at the nature of political and legal integration. It will need to chart a future which is very different from its recent past; for, in the final analysis, the citizens of Europe deserve better.

In Search of a European Ethos

So what does the future hold? The primary concern, fear indeed, is what to do with the 'other' Europe.

As he visited a rapidly disintegrating Balkans in 1991, the Luxembourg prime minister, Jacques Poos, could announce that 'The hour of Europe has dawned' (Garton Ash, 2000, p.211). Pictures of the Berlin Wall being torn down, of crowds milling in Wenceslas Square, of the Ceaucescus being placed before a wall in Bucharest and shot; all contributed to the thrill. Commentators aligned events with the prophetic 'end' of history and the triumph of liberal democracy. The fate of the former Eastern 'bloc' could be said to be a semiotic for the conjoined fates of the 'new' Europe and the 'new' world order.

Ten years later and 250 000 have died in a European war; a war that the grand new European Union was clearly unable to do much about. And the spectres of nationalism are still not laid. Still people rape and murder one another along the Union's borders. If the 1990s have taught us anything, it is that the fate of central and eastern Europe is very much dependent upon the endeavour of its more prosperous neighbours, their generosity and their willingness to sponsor the reconstruction of democracy and humanity. So far, the Union's attempt to ameliorate the suffering of those rather less fortunate Europeans has been less than convincing. As Timothy Garton Ash observes, looking back to 1992, 'We fiddled at Maastricht whilst Sarajevo began to burn' (ibid., pp.22–7, 180–89, 327). The Union, as Prodi admits, now faces a 'credibility' problem in south-eastern Europe. Redressing it will be the 'acid test' of its foreign policy over the next decade. The commitment will be 'long and costly', but a failure to commit will condemn the rhetoric of enlargement to a justifiable contempt (Prodi, 2000).

The intergovernmental conferences (IGCs) come and go, the prospects of enlargement tantalize. The Commission has warned of the 'unique challenge' which would be posed by integrating the 'wealth of different histories and cultures' that come along with 105 million more Union citizens. But it is not really the wealth of cultures that matters. It is a rather different sort of wealth that matters, the more prosaic wealth, of money. Whilst the Agenda 2000 programme has given rise to a certain cautious optimism, it remains wedded to the need for a visible economic 'track record' first established at the 1993 Copenhagen IGC. Such a 'track record' requires evidence of 'the irreversible, sustained and verifiable implementation of reforms and policies for a long enough period to allow for a permanent change in the expectations and behaviour of economic agents and for judging that achievements will be lasting' (European Commission, 2001).

In October 2000, Tony Blair told the assembled bankers and businessmen of Poland, the only audience that seemed to be worth addressing, that the Union's 'greatest opportunity' is an 'economic one'; an odd inversion of the received wisdom that the Union should add a political, perhaps even ethical, dimension to the completed market of the Community. 'Nobody,' he cheered himself, 'who considers the role that open markets have played in generating wealth and prosperity in the European Union can doubt the benefits of creating a market of half a billion consumers.' But there was still much to be done, for economic 'reform', he sternly reminded his hosts, 'is the only entry ticket' (Blair, 2000).

So much for the 'new' Europe. The prospective experience of enlargement speaks to one of the essential questions which currently faces the new Europe, that of identity. What precisely is the 'new' Europe supposed to be, and what makes it 'new'? The Commission has hazarded the thought that the idea of Europe 'combines geographical, historical and cultural elements which all contribute to the European identity' (European Commission, 1992). At various times over the past couple of decades, the Commission has sponsored all manner of trinkets designed to somehow enhance a European identity; from cycle races and orchestras to flags, hymns and space stations. But there will have to be something more convincing than this. The problem, as Gerard Delanty has emphasized, is that the idea of Europe lacks 'emotional value' (Delanty, 1995, p.132). It struggles to inspire.

Intellectuals chatter endlessly about what a 'European' identity might mean. André Malraux famously observed 'There is no Europe. There never was one.' There are instead merely various ideas of 'what Asia is not'. Malraux gestured towards the mythic 'other', a favoured recourse of the contemporary post-modernist (Fitzpatrick, 1998, pp.31–3). Delanty suggests that Europe remains 'an idea as much as a reality', a 'fantasy homeland that goes hand in hand with a retrospective invention of history' (Delanty,

1995, pp.1, 8). Garton Ash similarly suggests that there are two Europes, a real geopolitical Europe and an imagined Europe, a 'dream', a 'progress towards some visionary goal'. It is the latter which finds voice in the crusading rhetoric of an 'ever closer union' (Garton Ash, 2000, pp.316, 328–9).

In *The Other Heading: Reflections on Today's Europe*, Jacques Derrida aligned the question of identity with that of unity and diversity. Europe, Derrida suggests, has forgotten its past, its history. Today's 'crisis' is one of 'memory'. That history is a history of heterogeneity, of a toleration of 'others', of an appreciation of essential cultural difference. As he affirms in *Specters of Marx*, what defines Europe, what provides it with a cultural as well as geopolitical identity, is an appreciation of justice as a toleration of fundamental difference, of the very essence of what it is to be human, indeed. In contrast, today's Europe has been possessed of a determination to homogenize, to erase cultural, moral and intellectual distinctions. It is a determination that is as debilitating and alienating as it is ultimately futile and divisive (Derrida, 1994a, pp.3–5, 10–12, 24–6, 72–5; 1994b, pp.4–5, 62–4).

Back in late 1957, on the very eve before the dawning of the European Community, Albert Camus wrote:

> Unity and diversity, and never one without the other – isn't that the very secret of our Europe? Europe has lived on its contradictions, flourished on its differences, and, constantly transcending itself thereby, has created a civilization on which the whole world depends even when rejecting it. This is why I do not believe in a Europe unified under the weight of an ideology or of a technocracy that would overlook these differences. Any more than I believe in a Europe left to its differences alone – in other words, left to an anarchy of enemy nationalisms. (Camus, 1974, pp.234–5)

Europe, Camus added, is 'neatly balanced between the sword and the spirit' (ibid., p.25).

The sentiment has echoed down the decades. It has found a recent expression in President Prodi's speech at Lublin University in March 2001, in which he advised:

> Let us enrich Europe through its great diversity. After all, Europe has always been about diverse peoples with varied cultures and religions learning to live together because they share a common destiny. In doing so, we discover shared values, a shared sense of identity and European citizenship. (Prodi, 2001)

The reality of a Commission president speaking the language of Derridean deconstruction is intriguing. The reason lies in the fact that the politics of deconstruction is intensely humanist politics. At the heart of *The Other Heading* are the complementary and related concepts of 'capital' and 'capitale', of economic dominion and cultural dominion (Derrida, 1994b, pp.47–55). Dominion negates humanity. It denies the essential truth, that a genuine democracy is a democracy of diversity and tolerance and inclusion. According to the president of the Bundesbank, the future of Europe depends upon securing the 'long-term confidence of the investor' (Bourdieu, 1998, p.47). Nothing could be further from the truth. It is the obsession with completing markets and establishing legal empires that lies at the root of Europe's present crisis. The future of Europe depends, not upon the confidence of investors, but upon the affinity of its citizens.

The striving for balance is never easy, as the history of European integration over the previous half-century reveals. Indeed, as Prodi admits, the governing sentiment of the previous decades has been that of homogeneity. Integration is invariably seen to be a one-way process, to an 'ever closer union'. A willingness to talk rather more about diversity is to be welcomed; the reality of the new world order, the countervailing forces of convergence and fragmentation to which it has given birth, makes such debate essential. Yet, in the context of an integrative mindset, translating rhetoric into practice might prove to be rather more difficult. Prodi has called for a 'radical decentralization' (Prodi, 2000). Whether the process of incremental integration is capable of accommodating such an aspiration remains dubious.

The balancing of diffusion and concentration invites consideration of one particular concept, subsidiarity. For it may be that subsidiarity, or some revised version of it, can emerge as the keystone of the newly constructed Europe. That was certainly an intention in 1992, when subsidiarity first emerged blinking into the political light in Article 3B of the Community Treaty, which stated that the Community would only 'take action' in 'areas' which did not fall 'within its exclusive competence' if the 'objectives of the proposed action' could not be 'sufficiently achieved' by the member state and could therefore, 'by reason of the scale or effects of the proposed action, be better achieved by the Community'.

Some commentators, such as Neil MacCormick, have welcomed subsidiarity as a conceptual mechanism which might help to reinvest democracy and a sense of civic identity. The 'emergent picture of Europe,' he suggests, is 'of a Europe as a confederation of federations' within which there is an array of semi-autonomous regions. Such a picture, he adds, 'squares well' with subsidiarity, even if it does resemble a rather 'strange commonwealth' (MacCormick, 1999, pp.192–3). Most recently, Prodi has suggested that it might be revised in terms of a kind of 'networking arrangement, with all levels of governance shaping, proposing, implementing, and monitoring policy together' (Prodi, 2000). Such a radical, progressive idea of politics is innately evolutionary.

Moreover, as Prodi further suggests, such an understanding of subsidiarity would support the institution of 'new, more democratic form of partnership between the different levels of governance in Europe' (ibid.). So, once again, we return to the same essential questions. Subsidiarity demands that we revisit our conceptions of democracy, the complementary determination of *demos* and *ethos*.

*

There has been much recent talk that the 'new' Europe, and the institution of subsidiarity, might describe the foundations of a 'third way' in transnational or international politics. Paul Spicker has noted the congruence between recent 'third way' ideology and social democratic political thought within a number of member states (Spicker, 2000). For Ulrich Beck, the 'hopes of a Europe of the Third Way' coincide with the revival of social democratic politics in a number of member states, most obviously Germany. Such a politics, he maintains, encompassing the reinvigoration of 'democratic families, local communities, cosmopolitan nations', will 'allow people and economy to creatively renew themselves'. It will define a new public philosophy, most importantly one that marries reason with sensibility; for the Europe of the future 'needs a new alternative centre of inclusion – citizen work combined with citizen income as condition *sine qua non* for a political republic of individuals who create a sense of compassion and cohesion through public commitment' (Beck, 2000b, pp.177–81).

The possible affinity between the politics of the 'third way' and subsidiarity has been noted by Anthony Giddens, who argues that the future of Europe will depend upon 'treating subsidiarity as more than a doctrinal term', and as a principle which can describe an entirely new public philosophy. The stakes, moreover, are high; for if subsidiarity does emerge as the essential gear to European integration, it could be then deployed as an example for other forms of putative 'global governance'. According to Giddens, the relation between the nation-state and any number of international and transnational institutions, from the UN to the WTO, could similarly be regulated by the principle of subsidiarity, in conjunction with a 'world assembly' and supervening International Court which would be entrusted with the responsibility to refine competences (Giddens, 1998, pp.73, 141–7).

Once again, it seems, the respective fates of the 'new' Europe and the 'new' world order seem to be entwined. In this case, they appear to coalesce around the emergence of a 'third way' of civil governance. But there are alternative reconceptualizations which also speak to both the European and the global experiences. Deirdre Curtin suggests that both demand a fundamental and radical 're-imagining' of democratic politics, one that can conceive of a politics that is 'fragmented and fluid'. Reconciliation to such a politics, she affirms, will confirm the new Europe as the first truly 'post-national', even 'post-modern', polity in the new world order (Curtin, 1997, p.16). The idea that the post-national might gesture towards the post-modern has gained momentum. Concentrating further on the need to reconceptualize democracy, Jo Shaw describes a 'post-national constitutionalism' the strength of which is gauged by the vigour of its 'continuing conversation' (Shaw, 2000, pp.19–24). There is a very immediate affinity here with the kinds of radical democracy ventured by advocates of a new global citizenship.

There is a case to be mounted for both prophecies, the 'third way' and the post-national or post-modern. But the overriding criterion must be the reassertion of humanist values of justice, of what Pierre Bourdieu refers to as 'a higher degree of universalisation', an intellectual tradition of 'humanism' which is definitively European in sentiment (Bourdieu, 1998, pp.9, 40–41). It is to such an *ethos* that Prodi alluded in his address to the European Parliament in February 2000:

> Europe needs a sense of meaning and purpose. We Europeans are the heirs of a civilisation deeply rooted in religious and civic values. Our civilisation today is being enriched by its openness to other cultures. What we need now is a humanistic perspective. Daily and systematically, our economic and social system must recognise the primacy of human dignity. It must ensure that all our citizens have genuine access to liberty, inter-personal communication, culture and spiritual life. (Prodi, 2000)

It is a sentiment which has surfaced in a number of Prodi's most recent speeches. At Lublin University in March 2001, he spoke of a 'humanist tradition of tolerance and intellectual openness', one which could nourish an active *demos* (Prodi, 2001).

Such an imagining of Europe is ambitious indeed. It demands an intellectual suppleness that can accommodate the postmodern 'paradox of paradoxes', the ability to reconcile uniformity and diversity. But it is a necessary endeavour. Europe needs a new imagining. What Prodi's words share with those of Derrida or Bourdieu is a determination that the idea of Europe should symbolize a renewed humanism, a revitalized sense that liberty lies in an appreciation of diversity and tolerance and freedom and justice. The reinvestment of 'humanistic perspective', most especially one that recognizes the 'primacy of human dignity', becomes more a necessity than a mere aspiration. If the Europe that Prodi's predecessors designed half a century ago is to reach any kind of settlement, these words will need to find a genuine political expression. Europe's future depends upon reinvigorating an increasingly disillusioned and recalcitrant citizenry, and it will only do so if it can project a vision, a public philosophy which can inspire.

There is an undoubted irony in the fact that one of the most compelling advocates of a revitalized European humanism should be the leader of one of the countries that has not yet been permitted to join the 'new' Europe. In a series of essays and speeches, Vaclav Havel has repeatedly argued the case for a public philosophy that can underpin the process of pan-European political integration. As we noted in the last chapter, Havel's political philosophy is rooted in classical humanist conceptions of the relation between citizen and state. The language of Smith and Kant, of morality, right and virtue, is resonant. As we also noted, at the heart of Havel's vision for a 'new world order' is a re-balancing between the role of the law and the power of the democratic participant. Any credible form of global governance must 'offer citizens a colorful array of ways to become involved' in the decisions which determine their own lives (Havel, 1998, pp.147–8).

It is a suggestion that enjoys a particular, and very obvious, resonance in a Europe which has been almost exclusively integrated by lawyers and bureaucrats. Havel is fully aware that the new Europe appears to lack 'heart'. At root, Europe today seems unable to inspire its all too obviously disengaged and disenchanted citizenry. Inspiration depends upon the revitalization of the political imagination. As he advised the Council of Europe as long ago as 1990, 'We shall never build a better Europe, if we cannot dream of a better Europe' (ibid., p.46).

It is this inability to inspire which is, once again, so tragic. In a 1993 address to the same Council, Havel affirmed that all Europeans, not just those who happen to reside within the boundaries of the self-proclaimed 'European' Union, share an inheritance that is defined by certain 'values and ideals', amongst which are the 'principles of civil society and the rule of law', as well as a 'respect' for 'the notion of unity in diversity'. The 'discrepancy' between possibility and reality can be traced to the essential failing, to the related absence of *demos* and *ethos*. 'We argue about quotas, tariffs and interest rates', but not about the facility for human expression, about the possibility of providing the 'framework of a broad civil society':

> To put it more succinctly, Europe today lacks an ethos; it lacks imagination, it lacks generosity, it lacks the ability to see beyond the horizon of its own particular interests, be they partisan or otherwise, and to resist pressure from various lobbying groups. It lacks a genuine identification with the meaning and purpose of integration. Europe appears not to have achieved a genuine and profound sense of responsibility for itself for as a whole, and thus for the future of all those who live in it. (Ibid., pp.129–30)

Moreover, the 'European question' does indeed speak to the wider question of the 'new world order'. It is, irreducibly, the 'human and global question as well'. The 'new' Europe gestures towards a 'new world spirit'. It is a 'metaphysical' question, one that elevates Europe's peculiar 'responsibility' to encourage the 'general mobilization of human consciousness'. What the 'new' Europe needs is a public philosophy which can infuse its politics with a 'climate of solidarity, creativity, cooperation, tolerance', to a 'deepening' sense of 'civic responsibility', leading to a 'sense' of 'compassion' indeed (ibid., pp.114, 184–5, 246–8; 1992, pp.65–72, 82–4, 113–17, 158–9).

The 'question' may be freshly stated, and the context may be rather different, but it is still the same old question. It is the question that was asked three centuries ago by Gottfried Wilhelm Leibniz. And the answer is the same too. In his correspondence with the French ecclesiastic Bossuet, Leibniz advised a threefold strategy for the reinvestment of a common European public philosophy. The first 'means' towards 'regaining the common good' in Europe is 'exposition'. Agreement depends upon the forging of a common understanding, and for this there must be an active, and necessarily transparent, process of dialogue. The second is 'deference'. There must be an accommodation of interests, not just between states, but between 'peoples'. And for this there must be a 'consensus', not just a consensus as to the establishment of certain legal rules, but a consensus forged by the common acceptance of a principle of 'justice as charity'. The third means is 'abstraction or suspension'. Where consensus is strained, there must be tolerance and respect for the preferences of others. In other words there must be a governing principle of flexibility (Leibniz, 1988, pp.188–91).

The resonance is striking. And the conclusion is clear. The success or failure of the prospective 'decade' of Europe will not lie in drafting more statutes, arguing more cases, or even making more money. If the 'decade' of Europe is actually to address the 'question' of Europe, it will have to engage once again with an intellectual tradition which champions democracy and humanity, tolerance and compassion. There is no credible alternative; and nor should there be.

5 The Battle for Humanity

Declarations of Intent

The very idea of human rights is intended to fire us with a zeal for the principles of Enlightenment, for liberty, equality and fraternity. The idea of human rights is supposed to be a central part of Enlightenment's promise, a symbol of the 'end' of history, of the triumph of 'liberal institutionalism' proclaimed by the likes of Francis Fukuyama and Anne-Marie Slaughter. It should be an expression of the much-vaunted 'new world order' so confidently proclaimed barely a decade ago. In should be an epitome. In many ways the very credibility of the Enlightenment depends upon making sense of human rights and human rights law.

Yet atrocity has piled on atrocity. The twentieth century was saturated in the blood of countless millions, a 'unique contribution' in the words of one commentator, 'to the history of inhumanity' (Finkielraut, 2001, p.4). In a recent speech given in Israel, Vaclav Havel remembered the most devastating example of all, the Holocaust. When 'faced with documents' accounting for that particular genocide, he observed:

> I feel strangely paralyzed: I know that I should say something, do something, draw conclusions, yet I feel that words would be false, inadequate, inept, or deficient. I can only stand in silence and incomprehension. I know that I must not remain silent, yet I am utterly speechless. That state of paralysis proceeds from a deep – perhaps even metaphysical – feeling of shame. I am ashamed, if I may put it this way, of the human race. I feel that it is man's disgrace, and therefore it is my crime and my disgrace, too. That paralysis allows me to perceive human guilt, and my own co-responsibility for human actions and the condition of our world, from the bottom up. As a human being, I feel responsible for humanity as such and, staring uncomprehendingly at this cruelty, I cease to understand myself – for I, too, am human. (Havel, 1998, p.75)

The idea of a silenced incomprehension is, of course, familiar. As we have already noted, it has been deployed by the likes of Lyotard and Ionesco as a metaphor for the current state of post-modern humanity. It serves, too, to define our incomprehension at all the holocausts, all the 'violence, inequality, exclusion, famine' and 'economic oppression' chronicled by Derrida (Derrida, 1994a, pp.56–75, 85).

This was not supposed to happen. The promise of Enlightenment was for quite the reverse, for an ever more acute sensibility to human pain and suffering. Something, clearly, has gone wrong. The prophets of doom seize on the stark examples of our continuing capacity for the inhuman. Thus the likes of Robert Kaplan can argue that the 'banal truth' is that 'we are not in control', and that the future will be every bit as 'cruel, painful, violent and uneven' as the past (Kaplan, 1996, pp.436–7). The 'illusions of harmony', as Samuel Huntington calls them, have been finally cast down. A renewed nationalism is at present transforming the 'new' world order into a 'tribal conflict on a global scale' (Huntington, 1997, pp.281–91).

Alain Finkielraut suggests that the 'sickness of history', or ideology, has now given way to the 'sickness of geography'. 'With the end of the cold war,' he argues, 'the great confrontation of world systems has been reduced to bitter little wars, to disagreements over borders, to a ridiculous and bloody hotch-potch of squabbles, to the tautology of identity politics' (Finkielraut, 2001, p.97). By this reckoning, the horrors of the Balkans are merely the *hors d'œuvre*. Even Tony Blair, one of those who continues to expound on the prospects of a new world order, admits that the 'battle for humanity', in the Balkans and elsewhere, is still to be fought and won (Rawnsley, 2000, p.276).

This general mood of pessimism, which underpins the idea of a new world 'disorder', has thoroughly infected the academy. Scholars such as Costas Douzinas suggest that we are now experiencing the 'end' of human rights. It was intended that human rights should represent the 'fulfilment of the Enlightenment promise', and yet chroniclers of the twentieth century are compelled to write from one holocaust to another. The idea of human rights reveals the 'hypocrisies' of modernity, whilst the emergence of human rights law represents the ultimate pretension of international law, replacing the God that Nietzsche so irrevocably pronounced to be dead, with a new kind of apparently irreproachable jurisprudence (Douzinas, 2000, pp.1–2, 116–17, 121–7).

The more particular legal academy has been troubled by this thought for some time. As we noted before, critical legal scholars have consistently railed against the myths of liberal legalism, and most particularly the greatest delusion of all, that a fair and democratic political community can be secured by the vesting of rights in subject citizens. Douzinas' anxiety is therefore familiar. And it is shared by other human rights commentators. Rolando Gaete accuses modernity of establishing an idol of human rights as a 'metanarrative' which can be used to legitimate the otherwise undemocratic and systematic abuse of 'power' (Gaete, 1991, p.149). Lindgren Alves accuses classical human rights of perpetuating economic inequality. Its reform, he challenges, can only be realized by embracing the 'anarchistic' strategies of deconstruction (Lindgren Alves, 1998, pp.528–32; 2000, pp.484–7).

At the centre of the post-modern critique lies the accusation that international human rights law carries a particular ideological baggage, one that is imperialistic in a variety of ways. Upendra Baxi worries about its inevitably 'exclusionary criteria', something which seems to be all the more threatening in a global age of rampant neocapitalism (Baxi, 1998, p.125). The argument is commonly deployed by those who accuse classical human rights of cultural imperialism, an accusation which has come to the fore in the continuing debate surrounding 'Asian values'. The claims of Enlightenment universalism were famously questioned in the Bangkok Declaration, which demanded that human rights be set within 'national and regional particularities'. Human rights, it concluded, are described in many different 'cultures' (Engle, 2000, p.291). Globalization, as has been noted elsewhere within international studies, describes a very particular paradox: that the ideals of homogeneity constantly come up against the reality of 'glocalism', of a localized reshaping of dynamics that pretend to be universal (Twining, 2000, pp.3–5, 212–14).

Another exclusionary critique attaches more particularly to questions of gender inequality. Dianne Otto has aligned the two critiques, arguing that international human rights law asserts a 'European, masculinist, heterosexual supremacy', one which 'masquerades as universal knowledge in the form of human rights law, erasing context and specificity' in a 'world of enormous diversity'. Ultimately, and this lies at the root of our present 'crisis' of international human rights, what is erased is the very essence of 'human connectedness' (Otto, 1997, pp.2–3, 14–15).

Few today deny the value of human rights as an idea. But equally, few would deny that the reality of human rights has disappointed in many ways; and it is this sense of disappointment which inspires the deeper intellectual critiques of rights, and human rights in particular. What is clear, above all, is that, if we are to reinvest our conceptions of human rights, if we are indeed to take the idea of human rights seriously, we will need to use our imagination. We will need to focus once again upon what the relation between humanity and rights should be.

*

It was in the immediate aftermath of the Second World War, a century and a half after the Declaration of the French National Assembly and Tom Paine's

Rights of Man, that the ideal of universal human rights appeared to take second wind. The opening statement of the Universal Declaration of the United Nations declared its 'recognition of the inherent dignity' and of 'the equal and inalienable rights of all members of the human family' that is 'the foundation of freedom, justice and peace in the world'. Article 1 went on to affirm that 'All human beings are born free and equal in dignity. They are endowed with reason and conscience and should act toward one another in a spirit of brotherhood.'

The forging of the United Nations and its Declaration seemed to give a certain permanence to the more ad hoc events of the Nuremberg and Tokyo trials and all the satellite war crimes trials taking place around the globe. In due course, the rebuilding of the European continent would be jurisprudentially anointed with a Convention on Fundamental Rights and Freedoms. The universal recognition of human rights, it was thought, would finally bring about a 'new' world order. The mood was perhaps best captured by Albert Camus. 'We must,' he insisted, 'mend what has been torn apart, make justice imaginable again in a world so obviously unjust, give happiness a meaning once more to peoples poisoned by the misery of the century' (Camus, 1968, pp.135–6).

Taken together with the institution of the UN itself, the UN Declaration is often said to describe the 'rudiments' of an international constitution. This was certainly the intention famously articulated by President Truman at the San Francisco Conference in 1945, and it is still the orthodox view. According to Antonio Cassese, for example, the UN remains the only 'legitimate representative' of 'the whole world community' (Petersmann, 1999, pp.754–70; Fassbender, 1998, pp.531–2, 568–84; Onuf, 1994, p.16). The less convinced tend to cast the UN as a more immediately realist entity, a forum within which nation-states might be encouraged to cooperate, but one which can be more accurately configured in terms of political jobbery rather than as a body of international government (Hoffmann, 1995, pp.317–24).

At the same time, recent events have illustrated various operational shortcomings in the UN. Following the experiences of the 1990s, there is a general consensus that its role in 'peace-keeping' and 'humanitarian' missions needs clarification. Despite the stated desire to reinvest the idea of 'collective security' in the 1992 *Agenda for Peace* package, international response to individual instances of conflict remain rather piecemeal, and essentially dependent upon the support of a handful of member states (Ruggie, 1998, pp.243–55; Koskenniemi, 1996). There are also worries regarding the constitutional status of the Security Council, and the extent to which its increased activity during the past decade is consonant with the overarching sentiments of the Declaration. Such worries correspond with criticisms about the juridical nature of UN institutional arrangements, not least the extrajudicial capacity of the Security Council, and the corresponding inability of the International Court of Justice to impose its authority over constituent institutions (Koskenniemi, 1995; 1996, pp.481–8; Herdegen, 1994).

Yet, despite these problems, there is an obvious consonance between the institution of the UN, and its Declaration, and the idea of a 'new' world order. Suddenly, half a century after its inauguration, the idea of a UN seems to be apposite. And this seems to be particularly so with regard to the idea of an international human rights capacity. It has been suggested that the United Nations Human Rights Committee could play an enhanced role in any emergent forms of global governance. The same has been said of the particular European experience, with its various courts of human rights and of justice.

In fact, as we saw in the last chapter, the 'new' Europe has rather struggled to make sense of this particular responsibility. But that should not detract from the idea that any credible form of global governance should be founded on a common acceptance of certain fundamental principles of human rights. It is, as Helfer and Slaughter suggest, 'in the spirit of the times' (Helfer and Slaughter, 1997, p.390). The problem, as ever, will be the provision of rights that will be acceptable across all cultures. There is only one solution; the founding of rights on core principles of humanity, of liberty, equality, tolerance and dignity; principles moreover which must not be compromised by any spurious claims to cultural, ethnic or theological distinction.

This leads us to consideration of the critical weakness in the current provision of international human rights, and for this the very term 'United Nations Declaration' is instructive for at least two reasons. First, it reveals that it is indeed a declaration, and thus a form of primary rather than secondary legislation. In crude terms, it hopes to persuade rather than seeks to enforce. For this reason it is often suggested that what really distinguishes the UN as a 'constitutional' body is its dependence upon 'consensus' (Fassbender, 1998, pp.546–51).

Second, it is a declaration of 'nations'. It is dependent upon the continued goodwill, or political whim, of its constituent subjects. The perception that international order (and international law) is nothing more than the ordering of relations between nation-states has taken firm root. It is the language of the Westphalian world-view, of the *ius cogens* of the Vienna Convention on the Law of Treaties. It finds an obviously juridical expression in the establishment of the International Court of Justice, under Article 92 of the UN Charter. The only bodies to enjoy standing before the ICJ are nation-states and, as we have already noted, the configuration of the 'new world order' renders this particular demarcation of international order archane.

But it is still the dominant mindset, both in general international law and more particularly in international human rights law. The effect is acutely schizophrenic. Human rights are secured in various international charters, and then, in addition, in a majority of domestic constitutions. Even the most patently undemocratic and brutal regimes tend to pay lip-service to the protection of human rights. In turn, classical human rights law tries to legitimate these sensitivities with notional principles such as the 'margin of appreciation'. According to this particular principle, nation-states enjoy a certain latitude in how they, and their courts, choose to interpret certain obligations to which they might be bound in international human rights law. In such a world there is no such thing as fundamental universal human rights. There are merely various rights incorporated into various national and international documents, all interpreted in various ways by various governments and their courts.

One very recent, and not terribly impressive, example of this process is the enactment of the UK's Human Rights Act. Historically, few nation-states have been more suspicious of human rights than the UK. 'Nonsense on stilts', Jeremy Bentham famously observed, on hearing Sir William Blackstone expound his theory of natural rights in a London lecture hall (Bentham, 1982, pp.xxxvii). However, from October 2000, much of the European Convention on Human Rights has been incorporated into domestic law. The influence of the European Convention, and indeed the Community, is undoubted. Commentators go further still. Helena Kennedy suggests that the arrival of the Act marks 'a different *Zeitgeist*, a shift in the legal tectonic', while Francesca Klug refers to a 'new spirit of the age' (Klug, 2000, pp.xi, 6–7). Perhaps so. Perhaps the British no longer distrust rights. According to Conor Gearty, the campaign for the incorporation of the European Convention in UK law has 'grown from an eccentric liberal side-show into a central part of our contemporary political culture' (Gearty, 1999, pp.169–70).

Yet, in reality, the Act is rather mean-spirited in a number of ways. Not least perhaps, is the refusal to incorporate the Preamble to the Convention. For some reason, the British government is none too keen to reaffirm an explicit and 'profound belief in those fundamental freedoms which are the foundations of justice and peace in the world'. More important still is the failure to incorporate Article 13 of the Convention and thus provide for 'effective' remedies. Section 3.1 of the Act, meanwhile, merely empowers domestic courts to interpret legislation to be compatible 'so far as it is possible to do so'. If this is not possible, judges can make 'declarations of incompatibility' (Ewing, 1999, pp.84–6, 91–3, 98). The delusive notion of absolute constitutional sovereignty still gears our legislative jurisprudence.

Developing familiar critiques of the idea of rights themselves, critics of the Act have rounded on these more obvious weaknesses. Allan Hutchinson suggests that the incorporation of the European Convention is a 'huge step backwards on the path to truly democratic government' (Hutchinson, 1999, p.30). It is certainly something less than it might have been. Such criticisms attach to those levelled more at the broader conception of human rights we considered at the beginning of this chapter. Yet there is little doubting the faith that the modern world has placed in the idea of human rights. Charters of rights have assumed a hugely symbolic place at the head of the much-vaunted 'new world order'. The UK Human Rights Act, like the European Convention from which it is spawned, and like the UN Declaration to which both ultimately owe their genesis, is a totem, a statement of sometimes wistful intent, of a better, more humane, future.

The Rotten Heart of Europe

On St Vitus day 2001, an anniversary steeped in Serbian history, the former president of Serbia was smuggled out of Belgrade by government officials, and sent to the International Criminal Tribunal for Yugoslavia (ICTY) sitting at the Hague. He had been purchased for $1.3 billion of much-needed financial aid. The chairman of the US Senate Foreign Relations Committee championed 'events' which 'demonstrate the wisdom of our position'. Few thought to concern themselves with its morality: either of buying an alleged war criminal, or of absolving the rest of Serbia of the responsibility of trying one themselves.

Twelve years earlier, on precisely the same anniversary, Milosevic had visited Kosovo, together with around two hundred thousand of his compatriots, in order to mark the six hundredth anniversary of the destruction of an Islamic army. The battle may have been six centuries ago, but it was very much alive in the minds of Milosevic and his fellow celebrants. And there was a clear political message. A 'greater' Serbia would be secured by zeal. The Balkan wars would be crusades, their battle-lines would be regional and ethnic, and the struggle would be brutal (Akhaven, 1998, pp.758–65).

No quarter was given. No laws of international conflict seemed to apply. Crusades are rarely constrained by the injunctions of international convention. As Misha Glenny observes, it was a particular tragedy that the 'confessional detritus' of three empires, the Catholic, the Eastern Orthodox and the Islamic, should have 'collided' in Bosnia, at the 'heart' of Europe (Glenny, 1992, pp.i, 1–30). It did not take long for regional skirmishes to escalate into a full-blown intercivilizational religious war. Blair termed it a war 'between good and evil; between civilization and barbarity', a rather simplistic dichotomy, though not perhaps as facile as the suggestion of his Cabinet colleague, Clare Short, that the forces of NATO were being deployed in a war against the 'scum' of Europe (Rawnsley, 2000, p.263; Tariq Ali, 2000, p.xv).

It was certainly a war that everyone fancied a part in, whether it was in the cause of humanity, the need to strengthen transatlantic political and military ties, or simply the need to find something for NATO to do. As the surrounding powers circled like hawks above the rotting carcass in the early 1990s, a motley mix of historical, religious and cultural affinities determined presumed affinities. The Russians articulated an affinity with fellow Orthodox Serbs. Turkey and the Arabic nations sent money to Islamic Bosnia. Saudi Arabia donated around $1bn, some in humanitarian aid, some in military support. In April 1994, two thousand people gathered in Sarajevo central square waving the flags of Saudi Arabia and Turkey. The Bosnian army was already populated by recruits from across the Muslim diaspora, including Lebonese Hezbollah, trained and supplied by the Iranian Revolutionary Guards.

The Europeans, meanwhile, led by Germany, aligned with the Catholic Slovenes and Croats. In 1991, as events started to run apace, the Pope declared that Croatia was the 'rampart of Christianity', and extended diplomatic recognition with as much casual recklessness as the European Union displayed in its presumptive recognition of both Slovenia and Croatia (Glenny, 1992, pp.62–5, 98–101, 111–12, 143, 178–80; Woodward, 2000, pp.227, 230–32, 249–50). By 1993, Germany was selling Croatia fighter aircraft. Russian troops were already serving in Serbian military units, many operating their own T-55 tanks. Needless to say, in time the skies of Belgrade were full of US fighter-bombers, knocking out military installations and radio stations, along with a few unfortunate victims of 'collateral damage' (Huntington, 1997, pp.281–91). The Balkan wars were world wars in everything but name.

And they were also rather 'old-fashioned' wars, wars about national boundaries and ethnic identities. The whimsical thought that global economic and cultural interchange would render such conflicts outdated was rapidly rendered illusory. The 'Golden Arches Theory of Conflict Prevention' postulated by Thomas Friedman, that no two countries with McDonalds restaurants had gone to war with each other, lost its credibility as US fighter-bombers flew over Belgrade while McDonalds carried on serving cheeseburgers and fries (Friedman, 2000, pp.248–53).

Yet they were also 'new' wars, wars exacerbated by the peculiar state of our emergent global 'disorder'. Ours is a world in which nationalism is as virulent a force as ever, but in which the decaying nation-state is no longer able to satiate its energies. This poses particular problems. Thus, as James Wilets suggests, one of the immediate tasks must be to facilitate 'aspirations to cultural and national development while simultaneously disassociating those aspirations from the concept of statehood' (Wilets, 1999, pp.195–7, 201). It is precisely this challenge, of course, which faces the rest of Europe too. It is the defining problem of the 'new' world order.

The Balkan wars might have mixed the old with the new, but the horrors which it engendered were all too familiar. Details of the Omarksa camp presented before the ICTY during the Tadic trial ridiculed the idea that we live in an enlightened age:

> Prisoners were often forced to excrete and urinate in their rooms. There were no effective washing facilities, and men and their clothes quickly became filthy and skin diseases were prevalent, as were cases of diarrhoea and dysentery… Women who were held at Omarksa were routinely called out of their rooms and raped. One witness testified that she was taken out five times and raped and after each rape she was beaten… The white house was a place of particular horror. One room in it was reserved for brutal assaults on prisoners, who were often stripped, beaten and kicked and otherwise abused. Many died as a result of these repeated assaults on them. Prisoners who were forced to clean up after these beatings reported finding blood, teeth and skin of victims on the floor. Dead bodies of prisoners, lying in heaps on grass near the white house, were not an infrequent sight. (Akhaven, 1998, p.789)

And the nature and degree of such horrors is not restricted to formal court submissions and documents. It was presented before the grand jury of the world, or at least western, public opinion. The Balkan 'tragedy' was a piece of political theatre to which everyone, or at least everyone who had regular access to a television set, was invited, a performance played out before a public audience that enjoyed unprecedented access to the action. On his visit to Kosovo, Tony Blair affirmed what everyone back home in their sitting rooms already knew, the countless instances 'Of women raped. Children seeing their fathers dragged away to be shot. Thousands executed, tens of thousands beaten, 100 000 men missing.' Across the Balkans as a whole, the figure is nearer to 250 000 missing, with, according to the UN Commission on Refugees, approximately 3.5 million forceably expelled, deported or 'ethnically cleansed' (Rawnsley, 2000, pp.267–8, 272–3, 276, 283; Stiglmayer, 1994a, pp.16–22).

Testaments of horror abound, the numbers almost defy comprehension, the varieties of torture are numbing. Eight thousand were led away to fields outside Srebrinica and executed by Bosnian Serb troops; the single most shuddering example of inhumanity in Europe since 1945. Untold thousands were raped; the European Union estimates around 20 000 rape victims, the Bosnian Ministry of the Interior suggests at least 50 000 Muslim women alone. Given the number of resultant pregnancies, suggested by the same Ministry to be about 35 000, it has been calculated that the number of individual instances of rape probably runs into the millions. Accounts that have emerged from established 'rape-camps' reveal a ritualized sadism: violation, mutilation, humiliation, then cold-blooded murder, often committed, as a number of testaments reveal, by former 'friends and neighbours' (Niarchos, 1995, pp.654–9; Salzman, 1998, pp.348–66; Stiglmayer, 1994b; MacKinnon, 1994a). This particular example of ritualized and brutalized mysogyny is not made to smell any better by the establishment of brothels in Kosovo and elsewhere for the benefit of UN 'peacekeepers' (MacKinnon, 1994b, pp.192–3).

The indictment issued against Milosevic in 1999 related solely to Kosovo, and cited, in breach of Article 5 of the Court's Statute, the deportation of 740 000 and the deaths of 340 identified Albanians. The UN indictment suggested that Milosevic had 'planned, committed or otherwise aided and abetted in a campaign of terror and violence directed at Kosovo Albanian civilians'. But so, it was clear, had many others. Dozens had planned, thousands had committed, millions had directly or indirectly abetted violence; and not just Serbians. Over half of the 200 000 Serbs resident in Kosovo were driven out by the combined force of KLA paramilitaries and NATO aircraft. It is estimated that at least a thousand were killed.

*

The most immediate problem which faced the international community was to somehow bring the wars to an end. The most immediate solution was to ask the USA and one or two of its allies to donate the use of its airforce. But this could only ever be an interim solution. The bombing into submission of a recalcitrant Serbia would not itself bring peace to the region, as indeed subsequent events in Macedonia and elsewhere have revealed. There needs to be more.

Economic assistance is a very obvious, and a very pressing, necessity. So, too, is the establishment of political institutions which are set within a constitutional settlement which itself promotes a culture of civil and human rights. The new constitution for Bosnia and Herzegovina is often cited as an exemplar (Yee, 1996). But it must be seen to work, and for this there needs to be both carrots and sticks. For all the shattered nation-states in the region, the lure of European Union membership will help to concentrate the minds. Membership of the Union, as well as that of the international community as a whole, will be dependent upon a clear commitment to nurturing a culture of civil and human rights.

In the final analysis, of course, political and constitutional settlement is predicated upon the restoration of a sense of justice. This is the most pressing problem of all; what can be done to somehow address the various injustices suffered by so many for so much of the decade?

The mooted juridical solution is, once again, familiar; the institution of a war crimes trial in which the defeated, or so many of the defeated who can be persuaded, or indeed forced, to attend, will be called to account. The specific International Criminal Tribunal for Yugoslavia was established in 1993 by the UN Security Council under its Article 29, and more distantly authorized by Article 92 of the UN Charter. Accordingly, if the UN is indeed the constitutional authority of the 'world community', then the ICTY can claim a certain genetic legitimacy. But it needs more than this, for if the solution is familiar, so too are the problems with such institutions.

Such problems fall into two broad categories. There are problems of principle and there are problems of practice. The problems of principle relate to two of the most treasured concepts of liberal jurisprudence, the rule of law and the independence of the judiciary. International courts such as ICTY conduct their business to the echo of Hermann Goering's famous charge at Nuremberg: that such trials are invariably trials of the vanquished by the victors, regardless of the legal veracity of the regime within which the vanquished operated. In an address to the UN Security Council, US Secretary of State Madeleine Albright attempted to pre-empt the inevitable criticism. 'This,' she tried to assure everybody, including herself, 'will be no victor's tribunal.' The 'only victor', she added, will be 'the truth' (Akhaven, 1998, p.781). But the charge is not dismissed by such simple verbosity.

There are, in turn, two constituent, and related, problems which must be addressed here. The first is the theoretical argument surrounding the substance of law, the kind of argument famously discussed at length in the Hart–Fuller debate in the wake of the Second World War and the institution of various war crimes tribunals and courts. According to Herbert Hart, one of the foremost positivists of his generation, whilst we might find the legal regime under which Nazi Germany operated repugnant, that did not detract from the formal quality of its constituent law. It merely made it bad law. The clear implication from this argument is that alleged war 'criminals' can only be punished on the grounds of the immorality of their acts, not their breach of any supposed law, domestic or international. The counter-argument was presented by Lon Fuller, an equally renowned natural lawyer, who argued that the substance of Nazi law fell so far short of a minimum content of morality that it could not be properly called law. Accordingly, the perpetrators of such gross acts of inhumanity could never claim that they had operated within the law (Hart, 1958; Fuller, 1958).

The arguments projected in the Hart–Fuller debate are irreducible. Their value lies less in any particular resolution than in confirming our belief that neither of these essentially esoteric, and to a degree archane, theories of law, positivist and natural, can actually assist us in addressing the critical questions surrounding the relation of law, justice and humanity.

The second constituent problem also relates to the principle of the rule of law. Regardless of whether the definitions of law pronounced by Hart or

Fuller seem to be more compelling, there is a critical issue of consistency. If criminal acts are to be punished in international courts, and legitimated by appeal to certain universal principles, either of form or of content, the same rules should apply to everyone. If it was painfully obvious that the Nuremberg trials infringed this principle, it is even clearer that ICTY does, for there is no comparable consensus as to the ultimate responsibility for the Balkan wars themselves. At least the international mood broadly supported the Nuremberg trials. There is no such support for ICTY. Moreover, the mere fact that Bosnian and Croat soldiers appear in the same dock as Serbians does not detract from the basic infringement of the principle of the rule of law; for, in their different ways, all three communities were vanquished.

The unwarranted murder of any individual in the name of the state, it might well be argued, is a crime against humanity. Just as the devastation of Dresden and Tokyo was no less a crime against humanity than the devastation of Coventry, so too the needless slaughter of the citizens of Belgrade is no less reprehensible than the wanton murder of the citizens of Srebrenica. According to a UN report, the damage caused by NATO aircraft in the former Yugoslavia was not merely excessive, and thereby in large part unnecessary, but 'near apocalyptic' (Falk, 1995, p.23). It was also, quite possibly, unlawful (Sofaer, 2000, pp.2–8). Though they are happy to provide the finance, donate judges and draw up indictments, the forces of 'civilization' do not themselves seem inclined to answer before their own tribunal. The former president of ICTY, Antonio Cassesse, explains this in terms of taking 'into account the exigencies and tempo of the international community'; which means the ability of the victors to treat the idea that they too should be answerable before humanity with utter contempt (*Guardian*, 2/8/2001).

Such contempt is not so surprising, for the self-proclaimed heralds of the 'new world order' have long refused to accede to the authority of international law. Following the notorious *Nicaragua* case in 1986, the USA blocked a UN Security Council resolution calling upon all states to observe international law. The 'new world order' envisaged in Washington does not appear to be one described by law. As Secretary of State Albright informed the Security Council, the USA will 'behave, with others, multilaterally when we can and unilaterally when we must' (Chomsky, 1999, p.76). The subsequent refusal of the USA to approve the text of a treaty creating a permanent International Criminal Court in 1998 further adds to the impression that, despite its earlier rhetoric regarding the 'new world order', the most important player in current international affairs remains the one least inclined to take seriously the idea of an international rule of law.

The second and third problems with such tribunals are more immediate and prosaic. The first of these is the problem identified by Hannah Arendt in her commentary on the trial of Adolf Eichmann, *Eichmann in Jerusalem*. Despite all the grand theatre that the show trial of such figures might present, at the end of the day their achievement tends to be rather anti-climactic. When all was said and done, the conclusion was remarkably simple, 'banal' as Arendt affirmed. What Eichmann did was simply evil. There was no great insight here. This fact was known long before Eichmann was brought to trial. What the court could not, or would not, do is address the deeper ethical issues. It could not, or would not, investigate the moral and intellectual conditions within which one community can seek to systematically slaughter another. Flashy show trials of certain individuals merely blind us to these; worse still, they allow the rest of us to pretend that we are not ourselves in some way responsible (Arendt, 1963, pp.4–9, 26–7, 91–3, 148–50, 253–79, 290–98).

This leads to the third problem. In what way do such trials help to heal the scars inflicted by acts of gross humanity? How will it help the survivors in the Balkans to piece their lives back together again? How, in short, will it help to preclude the same thing from happening again? Arendt suggested that there was nothing about the Eichmann trial that made future comparable acts of gross inhumanity any less likely (ibid., pp.272–3). History has proved her right. Arguments that such courts can act as deterrents are refuted by the very experience of the Balkans wars themselves. The Hague tribunal was established in 1993. Hundreds of thousands were still to be deported, raped and murdered. What is needed in the Balkans is a reinvigorated sense of toleration. It is far from clear how the institution of an international war crimes trial is supposed to help this process.

It is only too easy to allow ICTY to take the strain. It allows the rest of humanity to disown the events in the Balkans, just as it was able to use the Nuremberg trials and the trial of Eichmann in order to draw some kind of line under the Holocaust. The formalities of law relieve us of the deeper ethical problems, of shared responsibility for the fate of humanity. They also relieve us of the more immediate material responsibilities too. The imprisoning of individual soldiers and politicians does not rebuild schools, hospitals and roads. It does not rebuild trust within devastated communities either. And the fact that countries that are struggling to rebuild their material infrastructure, as well as the social networks of their political community, might be held to ransom by the rest of us is distasteful. Chancellor Gerhard Schroeder termed the $1.3 billion dollar ransom for Slobodan Milosevic the 'dividend of democracy' (*Guardian*, 2/8/2001). But the idea that financial aid should be bartered for a vanquished politician diminishes us all. Compassion, and a due sense of moral responsibility, should fire our desire to help rebuild the Balkans, not a burning need to wreak vengeance on one man.

The institution of the International Criminal Tribunal, like indeed the experience of the Balkan wars themselves, seems then to be rather more sobering than exhilarating. The Tribunal remains afflicted by the same accusations of bias and illegitimacy that beset the Nuremberg trials, and potentially just the same degree of sheer futility and banality which Arendt identified in Jerusalem. The same accusations might, of course, have afflicted any comparable legal tribunal or court in Serbia; but not necessarily. There is certainly precious little evidence that the Hague tribunal is doing much to help heal the festering sense of injustice that is felt by so many in the former Yugoslavia. Those that suffered have not had the chance to participate in an immediate judicial procedure, to air their own grievances in a public forum. Those that actively participated in the war in support of Milosevic are not inclined to hate those they perceive to be their enemy any less. As the Bosnian ambassador to the UN observed, in the eyes of the overwhelming majority of residents across the Balkans, ICTY is 'a Court of cultural imperialists' (Akhaven, 1998, p.796).

The most obvious alternative would have been to permit the trial of those accused of crimes against humanity in their respective countries. Similar accusation of bias and illegitimacy might still have been levelled, but the legitimacy of such trials could hardly be any less than that which is desperately craved by ICTY. Moreover, regional trials, within or without immediate national boundaries, would have encouraged an immediate sense of corporate responsibility. With the particular example of the now indicted former president, Serbian judges would be trying a Serbian defendant indicted by a Serbian government.

The millions who repeatedly voted for Milosevic, and who fought in his armies and slaughtered his enemies, would have been denied the excuse that the indictment of their former leader is simply a matter of NATO mendacity. Ultimately, and this is perhaps most important of all, those who suffered would have been able to seek a kind of justice that was not bounded solely by legal principles. Such a justice is one which facilitates the airing of grievances, the telling of stories and the fashioning of reconciliation. In the final analysis, as Payam Akhaven has observed, 'reconciliation' in the Balkans 'requires a shared truth', something that 'appeals to a common bond of humanity transcending ethnic affinity' (ibid., p.741).

And, for all its apparent good intentions, ICTY cannot furnish this. There may be a role for international tribunals, as there undoubtedly is for international charters. But if the 'old' world order taught us anything it is that the cause of human rights depends upon something more. That something is captured in Michael Ignatieff's observation regarding the kind of 'truth' which will be needed if there is to be an emotional and intellectual reconstruction in the Balkans. 'The truth that matters to people,' he suggests, is not 'factual', or indeed legal, but 'moral'. It is a 'narrative truth', not one that merely tries to describe 'what happened' but one that 'explains why it happened and who is responsible'. What the discovery of such a truth facilitates, in the end, is the necessary 'public ritual of atonement' upon which the reconstruction of any just society depends (ibid., pp.770, 773).

Another Justice

> They were kicking me across the face, they treated me like a donkey… After being assaulted I was bleeding from my mouth and nose, but still I was hanged, left dangling from a tree… And then Tebogo, who was also very young, he raped me and cut my genitals – he cut me through from number one to number two. And then he put me in a certain room, he tied my legs apart. He tied my neck and then poured Dettol over my genitals. (Krog, 1999, pp.278–9)

Antjie Krog's harrowing account of South Africa's attempt to come to terms with its past, *Country of My Skull*, chronicles dozens of such atrocities. In her own words, 'Week after week; voice after voice; account after account. It is like travelling on a rainy night behind a huge truck – images of devastation breaking in sheets on the windscreen' (ibid., p.48).

The comparison of atrocities seems somewhat banal. Pain and suffering are common experiences, and so is the social dislocation which invariably follows when the suffering has been so traumatic and of such magnitude. But what is most striking about the South African situation, in comparison with that of the Balkans at least, is the radically different approach that has been taken in dealing with this trauma. Rather than simply establishing a particular court or tribunal with the remit to indict and punish those who are deemed to have committed the grossest acts of inhumanity, post-apartheid South Africa chose to employ a Truth and Reconciliation Commission (TRC).

The problems which post-apartheid South Africa faces are not dissimilar from those that currently afflict the Balkans. The statute which established the Commission, the Promotion of National Unity and Reconciliation Act, certainly talked the language of human rights, defining the ambit of the Commission which it established as limited to 'gross violations of human rights'. But there the similarity ends; for whereas the structure and aspiration of ICTY is rather familiar, and its shortcomings similarly predictable, the TRC is very different indeed. In large part, this difference is explained by an alternative conception of human rights. Whereas ICTY reflects the dominant mindset of liberal international jurisprudence, focusing on establishing crimes and punishing criminals, the TRC was established as part of a constitutional settlement that is designed, not merely to list a set of notional rights, but to actually nurture a 'culture' of human rights (Sarkin, 1998, pp.628–65).

Whilst the TRC did not replace the ordinary criminal jurisdiction, it did offer itself as an alternative mechanism for the effecting of a rather different idea of justice. The establishment of the Commission, of course, must be understood within a particular context: the need, as spelled out in the interim constitution, Act no.200 of 1993, to achieve 'reconciliation between the people of South Africa and the reconstruction of society'. The postscript to the Act emphasized that the redress for the gross violations of human rights experienced under apartheid 'can now be addressed on the basis that there is a need for understanding not vengeance; on reparation, not retaliation; a need for *ubuntu*, not victimisation' (de Lange, 2000; Villa-Vicencio, 2000; Rotberg, 2000).

According to Archbishop Desmond Tutu, who chaired the TRC hearings, the idea of *ubuntu* in African jurisprudence seeks the 'healing of breaches, the redressing of imbalances, the restoration of broken relationships'. It 'speaks of the very essence of being human' (Tutu, 1999, pp.34–5, 51–2). The very first hearing of the TRC opened with a Xhosa hymn, 'The forgiveness of sins makes a person whole'. *Ubuntu* enjoys a certain congruence with the idea of 'restorative' justice, something which, as Tutu emphasized, in turn resonates with Christian conceptions of confession and atonement. But this congruence evidences that there is no particular intellectual heritage. Confession and atonement, like compassion and forgiveness, are concepts that are common across cultures of various theological or secular tone. They are simply more or less familiar in different cultural guises (ibid., pp.74–5; Krog, 1999, pp.165–9; Moosa, 2000).

A willingness to contemplate 'restorative' justice opens up the possibility of promoting a very different 'culture' of human rights, one that is not simply about establishing legal or political rights, and punishing transgressors, but one that focuses upon participating in the suffering of others. When asked who would be best equipped to serve as a Commissioner, Tutu replied 'People who were once victims. The most forgiving people I have ever come across are people who have suffered – it is as if suffering has ripped them open in empathy.' Such people, he added, are 'wounded healers' (Krog, 1999, p.24).

Justice becomes more than a matter of judging guilt or innocence. It becomes a matter of entering into the dramatic life of a community. It thus becomes a necessarily democratic facility too. Law is no longer the possession of judges and jurors, but the moral and political expression of that community of sympathetic 'spectators'. Against the petrified formalism, what Arthur Chaskalson, the first president of the post-apartheid Constitutional Court, referred to as the 'impoverished' jurisprudence of legal positivism, 'restorative' justice returns to the original principles of legal humanism advanced by the likes of Adam Smith and Immanuel Kant (Dyzenhaus, 1998, p.81).

It is this ability to marry justice and democracy that distinguishes 'restorative' justice. In his opening 'welcome' to the Commission, Tutu emphasized that the 'healing of a traumatised and wounded people' could only be restored by the readiness of everyone to listen to 'stories' and to tell them (Tutu, 1999, pp.86–7). Between 1996 and 1999, the three constituent committees of the TRC received 20 000 statements and conducted 2000 public hearings. In the context of the South African Commission, Martha Minnow has emphasized the extent to which such bodies, in comparison with formal court structures, can focus more immediately on 'the voices and lives of real people', and thereby reinvest both individual and communal 'sensibilities' (Minnow, 2000, pp.238–45, 254). As Krog confirms, when it comes to choosing between the truth and reconciliation, and the strictures of the law, truth and reconciliation must win every time, for without this the law is nothing more than tyranny (Krog, 1999, p.35).

The need to open up conversation is critical. There must be a conversation, not just about rights, but about what it means to be human. As Richard Rorty has observed, human right is as much about listening to 'sad and sentimental stories' as it is agonizing about the meaning of enumerated rights (Rorty, 1989, p.186; 1993). It is this facility for telling stories which is so striking. It makes claim, not just to a new and alternative idea of justice, but also to a new and alternative idea of democracy. Indeed, it describes a justice that is impressionistic precisely because it is democratic: in Krog's words, something that is 'quilted together from hundreds of stories' (Krog, 1999, p.259). In the words of one deponent, the 'process' of the Commission 'allows me to remember but also to believe that we as human beings are all interdependent, that we can only exist through our common humanity', for 'Everyone has a story to tell' and 'People need to be given the opportunity to tell these stories, since there are different perceptions of the truth' (Henry, 2000, pp.170, 173). The ability to tell your story, to participate in the narrative construction of your society, is an essential expression of democracy.

Criticisms of 'restorative' justice remain. Many, including those who practised law, if not justice, during the apartheid regime, have been conspicuous in their half-hearted contribution to the process of reconciliation and truth. Equally, for many of those who had suffered under apartheid, and who preferred more familiar concepts of retributive justice, it was wholly inadequate (Dyzenhaus, 1998, pp.136–83).Yet, once again, the particular context is important. And, moreover, there are just as many who claim that only restorative justice could heal their wounds, could give voice to their suffering and ultimately address the restoration of their individual dignity and humanity, as well as that of their community.

The experience was summed up in one particular, and often quoted, statement given to the Commission by a young man blinded by the police. According to this particular deposition, what had 'brought my sight back, my eyesight back, is to come here and tell the story. I feel what has been making me sick all the time is the fact that I couldn't tell my story'. But now, he concluded, 'it feels like I've got my sight back by coming here and telling you the story' (Krog, 1999, pp.45–6; Tutu, 1999, pp.127–9).

*

The greatest quality of narrative democracy and restorative justice is this particular ability to reinvest individual dignity. As Smith and Kant recognized, dignity comes from knowing that people are prepared to regard you, and to listen to you. As Tutu observed, 'Our humanity is caught up in that of all others. We are human because we belong. We are made for community, for togetherness, for family, to exist in a delicate network of interdependence.' We are made to be 'respected', and we are made to be 'compassionate' (Tutu, 1999, p.155). To be dependent, to be respected, to be compassionate; it is what it means to be human, to appreciate in the truly Kantian sense that the individual is an 'end' rather than a 'means'. It was the restoration of this facility which represented the greatest virtue of the TRC. As Krog concludes, 'Against a flood crashing with the weight of a brutalizing past on to a new usurping politics, the Commission has kept alive the idea of a common humanity' (Krog, 1999, p.422).

The idea that 'dignity' should be a human right is not, of course, new. As we have already seen, the UN Declaration enshrines the principle; and all comparable ensuing human rights charters have made similar commitments. For commentators such as Jack Donnelly and Michael Freeman, the mark of a philosophy of human rights, as opposed to mere legal statement, is the appreciation that such rights are 'needed not for life but for a life of dignity, that is, for a life worthy of a human being' (Donnelly, 1989, pp.16–19, 22–3; Freeman, 1994, pp.502–3). Moreover, the particular concern with 'dignity' and democracy resonates with the present debate surrounding a 'third wave' in human rights, the idea that human rights impose obligations of mutual respect on individuals, rather than merely governing the relationship between states and citizens. According to Francesca Klug, the idea of human 'dignity' has replaced that of God as the founding concept in modern human rights theory (Klug, 2000, pp.6–10, 59–66, 98–101).

Such a conception of 'mutuality' rights nurtures a sense of 'solidarity' within political communities; something that is, of course, of particular value in those communities which have a recent history of fragmentation and violence (Wellman, 2000, p.639). This conclusion has been advanced by Alan Gewirth, who has advocated the idea of a 'community of rights' based on a principle of 'mutual sharing'. According to Gewirth:

> The concept of human rights thus entails a mutualist and egalitarian universality; each human must respect the rights of all others while having his rights respected by all others, so that there must be a mutual sharing of the benefits of rights and burdens of duties... By the effective recognition of the mutuality entailed by human rights the society becomes a community. So the antithesis between rights and community is bridged. (Gewirth, 1996, p.6)

This approach finds an influential echo in John Rawls' invocation of an emergent right of peoples, something which he explicitly relates to the Kantian idea of 'cosmopolitan right' (Rawls, 1993).

And it must not be thought that human rights, or more particularly the nurturing of a human rights culture, is of immediate importance only in states which have recent past experience of acute political fragmentation and discord. Any political community that claims to be liberal, tolerant and humane should be able to evince such a culture. Despite all its various legalistic shortcomings, it is here that the UK Human Rights Act may, after all, have something to contribute to British public life. Ushering the statute through Parliament, the home secretary, Jack Straw, suggested that its deeper purpose was indeed to 'bring about the creation of a human rights culture in Britain', something which, he later added, should be founded on universal 'considerations of common humanity' (Klug, 2000, pp.7, 49, 66). It is a sentiment shared by a former foreign secretary, Geoffrey Howe, who suggests that rights 'depend at least as much upon enlightened public opinion' as 'upon anything the law might design' (Howe, 1995, p.137).

Of course, such rhetoric can appear to be a little allusive, particularly when it is articulated on political platforms. But there is an immediate ideological context, or more particularly a consonance, here, between the 'third wave' of human rights, of rights of 'mutuality' and obligation identified by the likes of Francesca Klug, and the idea of rights pronounced by 'third way' prophets such as Tony Giddens who assure us that there can be 'no rights without responsibilities' (Giddens, 1998, pp.65–6).

And once again there is a political provenance. In a 1996 lecture, Tony Blair castigated the 'individualistic' liberalism exemplified by John Rawls' *Theory of Justice*. The 'third way' was to be defined in terms of 'families and communities', the nature of humanity 'only' through the 'moral power of personal responsibility for ourselves and each other'. Two years later he repeated the mantra: 'A decent society is not actually based on rights,' he averred. 'It is based on duty' (Klug, 2000, pp.51–3, 59–61). As Murray Hunt has concluded, it is clear that the Act is 'designed to introduce a culture of rights that is more communitarian than libertarian in its basic orientation'. In such a culture 'the individual citizen' is intended to be 'more than the mere bearer of negative rights against the state, but is a participative individual, taking an active part in the political realm' (Hunt, 1999, pp.89–90).

The ultimate fate of the Human Rights Act will depend upon judicial attitude. This may not seem to be particularly reassuring, yet recent judicial expressions of support encourage a degree of cautious optimism. Sir Stephen Sedley, for example, whilst admitting that the British judiciary might have a 'long history' of 'illiberal adjudication', has acknowledged that the courts must play a role that is more than merely 'legalistic', one that recognizes that human rights 'are by nature political, for they seek to condition how states treat individuals'. Moreover, their greater responsibility still will be to appreciate that the ultimate value of a human rights charter rests, not in the mere enumeration of laws, but in the ability to nurture, amongst both citizens and judiciary, a 'common sense of equity, an ethic of kindness, a morality of feeling', ultimately an appreciation that the realization of justice is very different indeed from the enforcement of law (Sedley, 1995, pp.386, 391).

A similarly nuanced view has been presented by Sir John Laws, who has had a still more explicit recourse to Kantian jurisprudence in order to balance claims to rights with the practical demands of constitutional sovereignty and political power. 'Ultimate sovereignty rests,' he concludes, 'in every civilised constitution, not with those who wield governmental power, but in the conditions under which they are permitted to do so.' The British constitution, accordingly, must now be understood to be itself subject to those certain 'fundamental principles' which underpin the 'imperative of democracy', and which are derived, not just from the 'sovereign autonomy of the individual', but from a 'description of the 'moral nature' of humanity itself. A 'good constitution,' Laws argues, is one in which the authority of a political institution, even a parliament, is subservient to the 'fundamental' rights which pertain to a human being. In the final instance, a human rights 'culture' is forged in the 'crucible of a life shared with others', the reflection, above all, of a 'shared morality' which defines the 'good' community (Laws, 1995, pp.81–7, 92–3).

There appears, then, to be a new sensibility to the idea of human rights as a cultural, as opposed to merely juridical, instrument. As Sedley concludes, the UK must develop its own 'juridical culture', one 'which does not imagine that the poorest citizen is made equal to the richest corporation simply by according both the same rights', one 'which perceives the role of power in determining who gets to drink first and longest at the well', and one, finally, 'which understands above all that in every society fundamental human rights, to be real, have to steer towards outcomes which invert those inequalities of power that mock the principle of equality before the law' (Sedley, 1995, p.400).

*

It might seem to be rather odd to conclude a study of human rights, and human rights law, with an endorsement of English judicial attitudes. As we noted before, the history of English public law shows scant concern for such 'nonsense'. But there is something of great importance in an understanding of human rights law that is not particularly wedded to the actual idea of law itself. A human rights culture is the necessary complement to any legalistic notion of human rights. It represents precisely the balance between sense and sensibility advocated by Smith, or that of right and virtue as advocated by Kant. As we shall see shortly, it is to this kind of culture that modern advocates of a non-foundational, perhaps even post-modern, liberalism turn. It is for this reason that the likes of Richard Rorty argue the case for a reconception of human rights that reasserts the role of sentimentality over the presumptions of pure reason, for in the final analysis 'sentimentality may be the best weapon we have' (Rorty, 1993, p.130).

And it is to this idea of 'sentiment' that Costas Douzinas, too, has recourse, speaking of the need to strengthen the position of 'passion' in our jurisprudence, to encourage the 'bonding of human nature' with a viable political conception of humanity (Douzinas, 2000, pp.253, 259). The idea of a distinctively post-modern conception of human rights rests with this invocation of acute, even passionate, subjectivity. According to Douzinas:

> The utopia projected by the human rights imaginary would be a social organisation which recognises and protects the existential integrity of people expressed in the imaginary domain. The postmodern utopian hope has ontological importance: it protects the integrity of unique beings in their existential otherness, by promoting the dynamic realisation of freedom with others. While the individual imaginary helps build an other-dependent identity, the social imaginary supports a social organisation in which human relationships will respect and promote the uniqueness of the participants. (Ibid., p.341)

The echoes of the Kantian imperative are resonant. Human rights do not vest in the self alone. They mediate between selves, patrolling the boundaries of human relatedness. This innate fluidity is their very strength. As Douzinas concludes, 'Rights are linguistic fictions that work and recognitions of a desire that never ends' (ibid., p.261).

No longer the fixed statements of a particular cultural imperialism, rights become the true possessions of humanity, fundamental statements of democratic empowerment, expressions of individual self-determination. And the key concept here is very much that of expression, the human right to express, in simple terms to tell a story. In a lecture entitled 'The Other's Rights', Jean-François Lyotard articulated the idea of human rights as a reciprocal preparedness to converse and to listen, to what he termed the 'interlocutory capacity' which by 'its association with the recursiveness and translatability of human language' cannot 'help but bind all human speakers in a speech community':

> If any human being can be an interlocutor for other human beings, he must be able to, that is, must be enabled or allowed to… Reciprocity respects not only the alterity of interlocution but the parity of the interlocutors. It thus guarantees their respective liberty and their equality before the word. These are the characteristics of justice itself. (Lyotard, 1993, p.140)

Half a century ago, as the formal institutions of international human rights law were being set up, Eleanor Roosevelt asked, 'Where, after all, do human rights begin?' The answer, she concluded, was 'In small places, close to home.' She continued, 'Unless these rights have meaning there, they have little meaning anywhere', for 'Without concerned citizen action to uphold them closer to home, we shall look in vain for progress in the larger world' (Glendon, 1998, p.1170). The insight is compelling. Human rights only have meaning within a particular setting, one which can facilitate their democratic expression. For it is only in this setting, with this facility, that they can become a felt possession, something that seems to matter to people in their everyday lives, something indeed worth cherishing.

This is what Wordsworth realized as he sat musing above Tintern Abbey in the summer of 1798. Wordsworth did not think in terms of human rights, or even democracy, but he did think in terms of feelings and sensibilities, in terms of those 'little nameless, unremembered, acts/ Of kindness and of love', of the 'warmer love' that calibrates the 'still, sad music of humanity'. To learn from Wordsworth, to approve his dismissal of abstract ideologies of legalistic rights, does not mean that we have to abandon the very idea of humanity, or even that of human rights. But it does remind us that we must embrace, once again, the deeper import of sensibility. It is for this reason that what happened in South Africa between 1996 and 1999 is so much more inspiring than what is today taking place in The Hague.

To contemplate the 'end' of human rights is not, then, to contemplate anarchy, any more than it is to contemplate a utopian world in which rights are no longer necessary. To suggest that human rights might be pluralist is not to say that the conceptions of what is good or evil must be too. It is merely to avoid the intellectual agonies which attach to a jurisprudence which is obsessed with somehow establishing certain absolute, and positive, legal truths. If the idea of human rights is to blossom in the new millennium it must, as Stephen Toope has observed, be prepared to 'listen to diverse voices' (Toope, 1997, p.184). Michael Freeman reaches the same essential conclusion, urging that a 'theory of human rights that is contingent and not arbitrary should not be alarming', for a 'conception of human rights should be flexible enough to allow space for the human creativity it seeks to defend and to address the changing conditions of the world that may threaten its values' (Freeman, 1994, p.514).

The 'end' of human rights gives us the opportunity to deny the claims of positive jurisprudence, and instead to refocus on the idea of humanity itself. As Antjie Krog notes, the idea of human rights which took possession of the TRC was not so much concerned with legal conceptualizations as with the essential question, 'How is it possible that the person I loved so much lit no spark of humanity in you?' (Krog, 1999, p.67). This is the question that matters, and the only justification for a 'law' of human rights is that it might be able to assist in searching for some kind of answer.

It has been suggested that the international response to the Kosovo crisis represented 'the first war initiated in the name of human rights', that it was, indeed, a war 'fuelled', not by a concern with the idea of law or justice or even right, but by 'our moral imagination' (Klug, 2000, pp.2–3). Juergen Habermas refers glowingly to a momentous 'step on the path from the classical international law of nations towards the cosmopolitan law of a world civil society' (Callinicos, 2000, p.176). The claim might be a little overblown, but the thought that the 'battle for humanity' in the Balkans was a battle fought for the cause of compassion is a provocative one. We should hope that it is true. We should hope, too, that Archbishop Tutu's closing comments at the end of the final sitting of the TRC are true: 'We have survived the ordeal and we are realising that we can indeed transcend the conflicts of the past, we can hold hands as we realise our common humanity' (Tutu, 1999, p.91). Ultimately, the idea of human rights is itself about hope, and it is to this hope that we must now turn.

Conclusion: towards a New Humanism?

The Indifference of Humanity

As the 1990s dawned, there seemed to be good reason to hope. In Europe, the Berlin Wall had come down, a new political 'Union' was about to be born, the idea of a reformed European *respublica* captured the imagination, of some at least. The president of the United States, now unchallenged as the single global superpower, could talk of a 'new world order', of an age of democracy and liberty and human rights. Populist intellectuals such as Francis Fukuyama suggested that the 'ideal' of liberal democracy could not be 'improved on' (Fukuyama, 1992, pp.xi–xii, 13–18, 31).

But, as we have seen, by the end of the decade, such proclamations no longer seem so credible. Even if liberal democracy has triumphed, the idea that political ideology cannot be 'improved on' seems to be dubious in the extreme. In its gross exacerbation of existing social and economic inequalities, the 'new' world order seems to bear all the least endearing aspects of the 'old'. The 'new' Europe seems beset by intractable difficulties, quite unwilling to embrace the kind of radical conceptions of democracy and citizenship that might give it a second wind. And, whilst we are possessed of more and more rights, in more and more charters, nothing it seems can prevent the systematic exercise of the most gruesome acts of inhumanity across the globe. So much for a new world order.

The 1990s, it seems, was a decade just like any other; one in which bankers bickered and the starving starved, where thousands raped and murdered their neighbours, where politicians continued to posture, and electorates stayed at home. The much-vaunted age of reason, of technology and progress, has given way to an age of disillusion, apathy, even disgust. As Derrida affirms, 'never' before 'have violence, inequality, exclusion, famine, and thus economic oppression affected as many human beings in the history of the earth and of humanity' (Derrida, 1994a, p.85). Our illusions have been shattered. The 'utopian spirit', as Russell Jacoby termed it, has 'vanished' (Jacoby, 1999, pp.xi–xii).

At the very beginning of this book, we noted a pervasive spirit of intellectual pessimism. It can only reinforce our present disillusionment. Four decades ago, George Steiner observed:

> we find ourselves in a culture in which the methodological use of torture towards political ends is widely established. We come immediately after a stage of history in which millions of men, women and children were made to ash. Currently, in different parts of the earth, communities are again being incinerated, tortured, deported. There is hardly a methodology of abjection and of pain which is not being applied somewhere, at this moment, to individuals and groups of beings. (Steiner, 1971, p.43)

Nothing has changed.

Indeed, whilst pronouncing the triumph of liberalism, Fukuyama readily admits that the 'last man', trapped within a world of 'bureaucratic organization', is not a happy soul. The drive of 'cold calculation', of the 'demand for rationality', denies humanity. It unsettles the 'last man' and makes him a potential rebel. Something, he senses, is lacking: the Nietzschean insight that humanity must be satisfied in its 'desire for recognition'. Unless we can somehow overcome the 'contradiction', between the advance of reason and the suppression of sympathy and respect, the 'end' of history may well prove to be cataclysmic (Fukuyama, 1992, pp.77–9, 112, 214, 289–92, 314–15, 325).

There is, as we have seen, little doubting the nature of our present crisis, or indeed the extent of our anxiety. Moreover, whilst the 'end of history' thesis speaks to grand theories of global construction, its impact is felt by real individuals in their rather more immediate worlds. This is one of the many paradoxes of globalization. People live their lives in rather more limited spheres. The advance of the 'new' world order compounds the festering decay of the 'old'. Two recent examples of this decay, one from the USA and one from the UK, are instructive.

The first is that provided by the convicted and executed Oklahoma bomber, Timothy McVeigh. In a letter to the *Lockport Union Sun and Journal*, McVeigh wrote that 'The American Dream of the middle classes has all but disappeared, substituted with people struggling just to buy next weeks groceries.' Alluding to what right-wing extremists refer to as 'Patriot's Day', to the famous dumping of tea in Boston Harbour in 1776, he concluded, 'We have no proverbial tea to dump. Should we instead sink a ship full of Japanese imports? Is a civil war imminent? Do we have to shed blood to reform the current system? I hope it doesn't come to that. But it might' (Esler, 1998, pp.229–30).

Such rantings cannot be treated in isolation. One in five Americans approved the evangelist Pat Buchanan's assertion that Washington is 'involved in a conspiracy' against the American people. According to Buchanan, there is currently a 'religious' and 'cultural war' going on for the 'soul of America', one that is 'as critical to the kind of nation we will one day be as the cold war itself' (ibid., p.173). In similar vein, Robert Bork talks in apocalyptic terms of a 'decline' that 'runs across our entire culture'. As 'we approach' the 'desolate and sordid precincts' inhabited by the 'barbarians of modern liberalism,' he cheerfully confides, 'the pessimism of the intellect tells us that Gomorrah is our probable destination' (Bork, 1996, pp.342–3). In his populist bestseller, *The Spirit of Community*, Amitai Etzioni joined the wailing chorus, advising that Americans currently 'live in a state of increasing moral confusion and social anarchy'. What is needed, he advises, is a renewed 'moral voice', one which speaks, predominantly, the language of traditional family values (Etzioni, 1995, pp.11–12, 72–88, 249, 255, 266–7).

Millions of Americans, it seems, share McVeigh's concerns. It was these Americans who secured the presidency of George Bush junior in November 2000. Indeed, anxious to tap their anxieties, the new president rapidly announced a series of 'initiatives' to promote 'compassionate conservativism'. The use of the rhetoric of compassion is intriguing. Unfortunately, however, it is a rather different compassion from that which might have attracted Wordsworth or Whitman. For Bush's compassion will be a deeply institutionalized compassion, one directed through various religious bodies. Compassion, it appears, cannot be left to individuals. It will not be the kind of compassion that draws its strength from liberty or democracy. And whether it will make America ever less angry remains doubtful. The mentally unhinged will still be inclined to blow up Federal buildings, while the emotionally illiterate will greedily indulge their need for vengeance in the macabre rituals of judicial murder. This is not the kind of compassion that we need.

The second of our events is very different in character. In September 1997, the death of a princess reduced the United Kingdom to the edge of hysteria. Thousands gathered in the streets of London to mourn for someone they had never met, but with whom they felt a deep personal attachment. The more disturbed excitedly described cloud formations which appeared to resemble the profile of their lost princess. Mysticism and mania swept the nation. Commentators such as Paul Johnson in the *Daily Mail* advised his readers: 'I am reminded of the Blessed Virgin who, told of her destiny answered with proud modesty "I am the handmaiden of the Lord".' The 'surge of feeling,' he concluded, 'has been a spontaneous collective religious act by the Nation'. Fifty million pounds' worth of flowers banked up outside the gates of Kensington Palace. Shrines to Diana popped up alongside. 'The People are suffering grievously,' The *Mirror* proclaimed. Some had clearly lost their senses. Psychiatrists are still dealing with what has become know as the 'Diana syndrome' (Campbell, 1998, pp.3–8).

The Britain in which Diana lived is clearly little happier than the America within which McVeigh was put to death. 'Families are falling apart, religion's discredited. So where does our sense of identity come from? What holds this country together? Not bloody much!' So says Roy Strong. Andrew Marr describes a country that has become a 'shabby, jerry-built and generally provisional suburb of the rest of the world'. As a recent withering editorial in *Le Monde* concluded, 'You never hear debates about ethics or morals here, just about saving money, no wonder the place is falling apart' (Paxman, 1998, pp.17, 232–66; Marr, 1995, pp.8–9, 336–46).

In a notorious interview, Diana had claimed to represent a 'constituency of the rejected'. If this was the case, it was clearly a very big constituency. It was a suspicion articulated by the playwright David Edgar, who observed that the thousands who waited for hours to sign the forty-three books of condolence at St James's Palace, were doing so in order 'to record their anger and their love'. There is a critical alignment here, between the politics of exclusion, the craving to express love and the recourse to a quasi-theological humanism. People did not just love Diana; they worshipped her. Many of the mourners who watched her cortege trundle through the streets of London compared themselves to pilgrims at Lourdes. Critics had coined the phrase 'Diolatry' long before her death. Diana had satiated a craving for worship that established institutions of religion could only dream of satisfying. As Sarah Benton observes, 'Among the mass of people' who engaged in the 'virtual reality' of her televised funeral were millions 'who saw Diana as representing their own martyrdom and exile' (Benton, 1998, p.98).

Diana had also claimed that she wanted to be known as the 'Queen of Hearts' (Campbell, 1998, pp.202–3, 250). Ever the leader of fashion, Diana brought emotion back into vogue. Ever the follower of fashion, Prime Minister Blair was quick to sense the moment, and opine that 'Diana's power is born out of emotion and there's nothing wrong with that' (Rawnsley, 2000, pp.60–62). Indeed there is not. But the moment did not last. The sudden expression of yearning, for tolerance, for inclusion and for compassion, has been rather forgotten. Britain has returned to its melancholy, its inner city riots, its railway accidents, its institutionalized racism, its contempt for the poor. Commentators continue to treat the idea that sentiment might have a place in our politics with a haughty disdain (Humphreys, 1999, pp.50–56). The fear of an unbound Prometheus causes just as much fear amongst our ruling elites today as it did two centuries ago.

*

These two examples, of the McVeigh case and of the reaction to Diana's death, are deeply revealing. They are descriptive of the failure of Enlightenment's promise. They are reactions against an obsessive rationalism, against the seemingly irreversible march of science and bureaucracy, against a world devoid of ethical debate. In their different ways, too, they are appeals to compassion. They describe individuals who feel emotionally disconnected, perpetrators, victims and spectators alike.

In part this disconnection can indeed be placed at the door of the 'new' world order, and the economic forces of globalization that appear to drive it. As Arthur Schlesinger observes, the 'law of acceleration' now 'hurtles us into a new age', one in which not too many of us are sure that we want to reside (Schlesinger, 1997, pp.2–12). It seems that the promise of untold riches cannot be separated from the threat of individual nihilism and social fragmentation. All the prophecies of Nietzsche and Heidegger seem to be true. And so does that of Shelley. The 'end' of history, like the 'triumph of life', appears to be a delusion. All that we can really perceive are the masks of anarchy.

The problem is well documented in Richard Sennett's influential book, *The Corrosion of Character*. According to Sennett, at all levels of governance, in all aspects of working lives, we have been destabilized by the march of 'flexible capitalism'. We are both driven and governed by the 'fear' that we 'are on the edge of losing control of our lives'. Such a fear can only lead to the disturbance of our 'emotional lives outside the workplace'. What is missing, he shrewdly surmises, is 'narrative', a way of giving our lives a sense of cohesion, purpose even. It is a weakness that lies at the very heart of the Enlightenment project. It is the weakness anticipated by the likes of Smith and Eliot and Mill, amongst many (Sennett, 1998, pp.9, 19–23, 30, 118, 134–5).

The psychologist Oliver James has similarly suggested that our present and pervasive anxieties have been fostered by a philosophy of 'spurious individualism'. As such humanity has been infected by an 'epidemic of irritability and aggression, of depression and paranoia, of obsessions, panics, addictions, compulsions, relationships that are not working, careers that dissatisfy, an outbreak of living in the future and pathological re-enactment of the past' (James, 1997, pp.x–xi). James suggests that our problems are sociobiological. Society has vastly increased the stresses under which we live, and our bodies are no longer equipped to ameliorate them.

This may well be so. But the root of our ailment does not lie in biology. It lies in politics, in the society in which we live and which makes so many of us so miserable so much. It is this salutary truth that lay behind Erich Fromm's seminal study of the human condition, *Man for Himself*. Writing in 1949, Fromm suggested that the root of the 'profound confusion and despair' which characterized our 'contemporary human crisis', and which manifested itself in our 'retreat from the hopes and ideas of the Enlightenment', is at once both psychological and political. Humanity, he suggested, has detached the capacity to care from the capacity to reason, and the prospect of a better future is dependent upon retrieving this essential sensibility, on resuscitating the politics of 'love and decency', and balancing them against the prevailing obsession with scientific reason. Rather than seeking a 'science of man', Fromm advocated reconceptualizing the politics of 'living' as an 'art' (Fromm, 1990, pp.4–5, 17–18, 81, 198, 207).

In conclusion, he observed:

> Our moral problem is man's indifference to himself. It lies in the fact that we have lost the sense of the significance and uniqueness of the individual, that we have made ourselves into instruments for purposes outside ourselves, that we experience and treat ourselves as commodities, and that our own powers have become alienated from ourselves. We have become things and our neighbors have become things. The result is that we feel powerless and despise ourselves for our impotence. Since we do not trust our own power, we have no faith in man, no faith in ourselves or in what our own powers can create. We have no conscience in the humanistic sense, since we do not dare to trust our judgment. We are a herd believing that the road we follow must lead to a goal since we see everybody else on the same road. We are in the dark and keep up our courage because we hear everybody else whistle as we do. (Ibid., p.248)

Once again, whether or not we have truly reached the 'end of history', there is little here that is not just as apposite today. There is no doubting the extent of our present anxieties. The 1990s have disappointed. The 'new' world order has failed to deliver freedom and equality for all, or, indeed, for that many. It has done little to promote either the cause or the principle of humanity. What we need, more than anything, as Fromm noted half a century ago, is a reinvested sense of humanity. What we need, in short, is a new humanism.

The New Humanism

The idea of a 'new' humanism is perhaps rather misleading, for their is no new philosophy to be had. And there is no need of one either. What we need to do is to retrieve the core principles of a humanist, and humanitarian, political philosophy, the kind of philosophy recommended by Portia, and then Leibniz, and which was later reforged in the intellectual crucible of the Enlightenment, in Coleridge's 'rage' of metaphysics.

We have repeatedly argued that a genuine humanism is one that balances politics with passion, sense with sensibility. In the first chapter, we explored the attempts of Smith and Kant to fashion such a balanced public philosophy. In the second chapter, we examined some of the more extreme attempts to infuse modernity with a measure of undiluted romanticism, the most striking examples of which were the 'cult of sensibility' associated with Jean-Jacques Rousseau, and the varieties of radical democracy recommended by the likes of Godwin and Shelley, Whitman and Thoreau.

In their different ways, each was reminding us that politics is as much about compassion as it is about rules and regulations, ideas and ideologies. As John Stuart Mill came to realize, a progressive politics is as dependent upon the Jeremy Benthams of the world as it is upon the Samuel Taylor Coleridges. And the same is true of a progressive conception of law. Modernity, as we have noted, has made much of law. It is for this reason that the greatest critics of modernity, such as Kafka and Camus, have striven so hard to undermine its jurisprudential pretensions. A new humanism must then also provide for a new jurisprudence. It must, in short, provide a complementary realignment, so that, alongside the balance of sense and sensibility, there must be a concomitant rebalancing of law and justice.

The idea of a 'universal' jurisprudence has been out of fashion for two centuries. The age of positivism has crushed any wistful remembrances of an 'age of gold'. Now, however, there is a discernible sense that the time for recollection has arrived, the time, perhaps, for a renaissance in legal and political humanism. And there can be little doubt that the experiences of the twentieth century, and more particularly its final decade, have played a large part in refining this sensation. For whilst there is nothing that we can do to reverse the march of the 'new' world order, and perhaps nothing that we should anyway wish to do, there is much that we can do to shape a future that is more democratic, more liberating, more humane and indeed more hopeful too.

It is to this kind of future that the likes of Vaclav Havel and Desmond Tutu have appealed, a future in which the claims of ideology cannot be allowed to shroud the more primal appeals to a sense of common humanity. Such an idea of humanity cuts across the pretensions of time and progress. As Wordsworth appreciated, the appeal to humanity, to a 'warmer love', exists outwith any ideology. We must never allow the grandiose claims to the 'new' world order or the 'new' Europe to blind us to this salutory truth. The cause of humanity is simple. It is the cause of compassion, of justice and of democracy. It is not something that needs to be legitimated by any science or any ideology.

The great contribution of radical Enlightenment political thought was to make the principles of democracy and justice, as well as those of liberty, equality and fraternity, more than merely ideological concepts. For men like Rousseau, Godwin and Whitman, democracy was a kind of secular theology, a matter of belief, something indeed that is determinative of the human condition. And the same is true of justice, and of liberty, equality and fraternity. The accommodation of sense and sensibility finds its most compelling expression in this determination. Democracy is no longer a kind of politics. Rather, it underpins the politics of humanity. Of necessity, it secures liberty, it ensures an equality of respect, and it binds compassionate political communities.

Without democracy, then, there can be no justice. And without both, there can be no flourishing sense of humanity. There is, once again, nothing new in this insight. It is not a new philosophy. But it is an ideal that has proved to be elusive. Enlightenment promised all of this, liberty, equality and fraternity, democracy, justice and compassion. But the promise is still to be delivered. The cause of humanity has been sold short. We are still striving for liberty and equality, for democracy and justice. Above all, perhaps, we still yearn for a politics of compassion.

*

To a certain extent this call for a reinvested humanism bears some similarity to more familiar communitarian appeals for the imaginative reinvigoration of the 'good society'. A classic and influential example of this thesis is provided in the writings of Alasdair MacIntyre, who sets his appeal for a return to classical values of individual 'virtue' within the context of a perceived 'disorder' which defines the 'post-Enlightenment' condition. According to MacIntyre, this crisis is the result of the inevitable failure of Enlightenment, the schism between a residual concern for community and the overpowering fascination in the 'invented' individual (MacIntyre, 1985, pp.2–7, 50–62, 80–87; 1988, pp.393–5). As MacIntyre emphasizes, this failure has particular implications for jurisprudence; for only those who are themselves possessed of an understanding of virtue and the 'good society' can properly appreciate the concept of justice. Justice is always exercised in the particular, but its principles are always drawn from something more universal, an intrinsic sense of humanity that binds any political community. This, he alleges, is the essential foundation of an Aristotelian jurisprudence (MacIntyre, 1985, pp.146–64, 237, 344; 1988, pp. 103–23, 162–3).

At the heart of the communitarian case is the need to reawaken the political imagination. MacIntyre invokes the idea of 'narrative selfhood'. So too does Michael Sandel, who refers anxiously to our declining 'capacity for narrative' and to the pressing need to 'rebel against the drift to storylessness' (Sandel, 1966, pp.350–51). According to Charles Taylor, we can only 'find a sense of life through articulating it', through the 'narrative understanding' with which we construct our self-identities, and the processes of democratic 'conversation' which define the politics of the 'good society'. It is the 'assurance' that we are 'turned towards this good', Taylor affirms, that 'gives' us all a 'sense of wholeness, of fitness of being as a person or self, that nothing else can'. It is also, Taylor warns, this 'sense' that has been lost in the centuries following Shakespeare, Leibniz and his contemporaries (Taylor, 1989, pp.18, 34–8, 63, 275–7).

There is, then, an obvious affinity between the kind of political philosophy articulated in their different ways by Leibniz or Smith, or even Godwin or Whitman, and that which is currently advocated by communitarians such as MacIntyre and Taylor. But there is also a critical difference. For, whilst the contemporary communitarian deals in contingencies, for the likes of Leibniz and Smith, or indeed Kant or Coleridge, the 'quality of mercy' does indeed 'droppeth' on everyone. Or so it should.

This sense of innate universalism is, of course, stronger amongst classical liberals, particularly those who have developed Kantian conceptions of the 'good society'. A good example, here is John Rawls, whose famous *Theory of Justice* explicitly demanded a return to Aristotelian and Kantian principles of social and moral good. Driven by the common desire to perfect the critically reflective moral self, Rawls held that 'free and equal persons' would necessarily 'arrive' at a common appreciation of the 'need for principles of justice' (Rawls, 1971, pp.251–2). Justice, in this sense, becomes an expression of morality, and more particularly of the moral self. Invoking the Aristotelian 'principle of motivation', Rawls suggested that every person has a rational plan. Every community, accordingly, is constituted by an array of persons, each possessed of such plans or 'motivations'. It is for this reason that the rationality by which every community operates is collective, the product of constructive communication. Every community will construct an 'end', a vision of the 'good'. This is a universal imperative. But there should be no assumption that the substantive visions of the 'good' will be the same (ibid., p.395–8, 404–9, 416–41).

The final passages of the *Theory of Justice* emphasized Rawls' particular affinity with the Kantian *sensus communis* (ibid., pp.523–9). This affinity became clearer still in his later writings. In 'Kantian Constructivism in Moral Theory', Rawls asserted, quite simply, that 'there are no moral facts'. The idea of 'justice as fairness,' he impressed, 'takes deep and unresolvable differences on matters of fundamental significances as a permanent condition of human life' (Rawls, 1980, pp.516–19, 525, 537–42). As Kant had originally noted, it is difference which defines the human. But it does not uproot morality itself. There can be morality without the need for a moral truth. The responsibility of such a political morality is to provide the 'framework for deliberation' (ibid., pp.560–61, 570–72). Thus morality might constrain choice, but it does not seek to determine it. Here, then, there is a critical translation, from the metaphysical language of the free-will and the moral self to the political language of democracy and civil and human rights. Constructivism makes Kantian moral philosophy practical in terms of law and politics. It makes it relevant in today's world.

In his most recent work, on the 'Law of Peoples', Rawls argued that this principle of Kantian constructivism can be deployed as a mechanism for mediating between political communities while also setting minimal standards of mutual respect. In doing so, moreover, constructivism presents itself as an alternative to universalism. Here Rawls consciously aligns this kind of inter-community constructivism with Kant's 'cosmopolitanism'. The 'Law of Peoples' becomes a 'law of democratic peoples', one that respects difference while demanding, as an expression of the categorical imperative, that such respect is reciprocated. Respect for fellow human beings, and their dignity, becomes a fundamental duty for all world citizens. Human rights, therefore, do not need to be founded on any 'comprehensive moral doctrine', but merely on a common understanding that justice is the aspiration of all moral selves. The pursuit of justice is, indeed, the defining characteristic of humanity (Rawls, 1993).

Another recent example of this attempt to develop the Kantian critique of the 'good society' is Ronald Dworkin's *Sovereign Virtue*. The need to realize such a society, Dworkin asserts, is a 'matter of justice that should be accepted by everyone because it is right'. It is significant that Dworkin should seek to accommodate the classical principle of liberty with a conception of equality as 'equality of resources'. Such an accommodation describes 'mutually reflecting aspects of a single humanist ideal', the 'ideal of political association' (Dworkin, 2000, pp.7, 23, 120–22, 134, 181–3).

The Aristotelian overtones are compounded when Dworkin deploys the Kantian imperative in order to affirm that a 'political community has that ethical primacy over our individual lives'. The 'integrated' liberal, the liberal who subscribes to the Aristotelian ideal of the good society, is one who recognizes an ethical responsibility to others. An 'integrated citizen accepts that the value of his own life depends on the success of his community in treating everyone with equal concern'. This, Dworkin affirms, means that such a citizen recognizes that the cause of justice is as much a cause of ethics, as it is of right. There is a very obvious resonance. The justice which underpins the good society is as dependent upon realizing the 'duties' of Kant's second Doctrine as it is on realizing those described in his first (ibid., pp.231–6, 282–4).

Dworkin's *Sovereign Virtue* betrays a tangible anger, most particularly against the 'disgrace' of modern American politics (ibid., pp.318, 351), but it is an anger which can also be attached to the wider failure of Enlightenment's promise. It is the anger which finds an expression in John Kenneth Galbraith's invocation of the classical idea of the 'good society' in order to moderate our present acute political, social and economic inequalities. The need to ameliorate the 'human suffering' which currently disfigures so much of the globe, as Galbraith suggests, makes the assertion of the good society a universal imperative. Moreover, the only way in which we can approach this problem is by reinvesting the original promise of a 'genuine' and 'inclusive' democracy, rather than merely a 'democracy of the fortunate' (Galbraith, 1996, pp.2–8, 110–43).

It is this promise which must be realized. It does not require any particular vision of a good society, but it does necessitate the projection of a sense of goodness, of virtue and justice and compassion. It is to the good society, too, that Francis Fukuyama turns at the conclusion of *The End of History*, to the 'passions of the first man' (Fukuyama, 1992, pp.336–7). It is passion that is missing; or, more precisely, it is the necessary balance of reason and passion. For whilst reason might make societies progress, it is passion which makes them worth living in. Above all, what a 'good society' needs is inspiration, a sense that the human condition can improve and will improve. It implies vitality. As Charles Fried has argued, the 'good society' is 'prosperous', not because of the sum of its wealth, but because it is 'a natural expression of the active human spirit' (Fried, 2000, p.6).

It would be foolish to underestimate the many differences that distinguish the respective ideas of MacIntyre and Rawls, Dworkin and Galbraith. But it would be just as foolish to ignore their common intellectual mood. For each is seeking to realize a certain idea, that of the classical 'good society', and each is working in the aftermath of the 'rage of metaphysics', each trying to recover some conception of political morality, some reinvested sense of humanity indeed, from the intellectual carnage wrought of the struggle between sense and sensibility.

*

The idea of the 'good society' has also gained currency amongst those liberals who might be described as progressive, even poetic or romantic. A striking example of this kind of liberal is Martha Nussbaum. In *Love's Knowledge*, Nussbaum argues that the play of literature might be more effective in nurturing the idea of the 'good society' than the mere enforcement of legal and moral 'rules'. For what literature can do, unlike either law or morality, is 'support' the intensely human desire to 'love', and it can do this because it engages the reflective faculty which facilitates our ability to judge the 'particular' situation of ourselves and others (Nussbaum, 1990, pp.53, 75–6, 94–6, 165–6, 173, 184, 190–91).

In simple terms, it encourages us to translate our 'narrative emotions' into our more immediately political 'imagination'. It is perhaps no surprise that, in searching for a paradigmatic expression of this idea of 'sympathetic' judgment in Enlightenment thinking, Nussbaum alights on Adam Smith (ibid., pp.294–7, 338–45). In an eloquent passage from her more recent *Cultivating Humanity*, Nussbaum argues the importance of developing this capacity for 'narrative imagination' as an integral part of 'intelligent' liberal citizenship. 'This means,' she suggests, 'the ability to think what it might be like to be in the shoes of a person different from oneself, to be an intelligent reader of that person's story, and to understand the emotions and wishes and desires that someone so placed might have' (Nussbaum, 1997, pp.10–11).

In a second, equally compelling, passage, Nussbaum goes on to make the same essential connection as Derrida, between an ethics of sympathy and compassion, and democracy. What marks the liberal humanist, she affirms, is the appreciation

> that there is after all more joy in the kind of citizenship that questions than in the kind that simply applauds, more fascination in the study of human beings in all their real variety and complexity than in the zealous pursuit of superficial stereotypes, more genuine love and and friendship in the life of questioning and self-government than in submission to authority. (Ibid., p.84)

Nussbaum's more immediately jurisprudential essay, *Poetic Justice*, has returned to Aristotle and Kant, and most particularly to Smith and the idea of 'judicious spectator', in order to take on Walt Whitman's suggestion that good judges are those who appreciate the poetry of ordinary political life. A good judge in a 'good society' must be 'capable of fancy and sympathy', must be able to imagine pain and suffering, to understand what it means to be tortured, oppressed, excluded. Echoing the sentiments of Shelley or the young Coleridge, as well as those of Whitman, she acclaims the poet's 'democratizing mission', of 'imagination, inclusion, sympathy, and voice'. If we do indeed aspire to justice, and to the 'good society', it is not the door to the law that we must go through, but the 'doors of sympathy' that we must 'open' once again (Nussbaum, 1995, pp.73–8, 90–91, 115–20).

Another of the more romantic liberal humanists is Richard Rorty. In an eloquent passage from *Contingency, Irony, and Solidarity*, Rorty provides a sketch for a 'new' post-modern humanism:

> A liberal society is one whose ideal can be fulfilled by persuasion rather than by force, by reform rather than revolution, by the free and open encounters of present linguistic and other practices with suggestions for new practices. But

> this is to say that an ideal liberal society is one which has no purpose except freedom, no goal except a willingness to see how such encounters go and to abide by their outcome. (Rorty, 1989, pp.60–61)

Dismissing the claims to truth which have tended to characterize so much classical liberalism, Rorty has increasingly sought to marry the Nietzschean insights of 'private irony' to the democratic imperatives of 'social hope'. In many ways, as he acknowledged, the move bears certain similarities to Rawls' turn from a more foundational theory of justice to the later political liberalism (Rorty, 1991, pp.197–202).

But whereas Rawls' revised political liberalism finds its deeper roots in Kantian revisionism, Rorty's owes rather more to a mixture of American pragmatism and Derridean deconstruction. For Rorty, it is language which defeats the claims of metaphysical truth, and it is language which, accordingly, preserves the space for democratic engagement. As he asserts in *Contingency, Irony, and Solidarity*, 'The world does not speak. Only we do' (Rorty, 1989, pp.5–6). It is this commitment to liberal democracy which underpins Rorty's political writings, the democracy of 'social hope' rooted in the Nietzschean philosophy of 'private irony'.

For Rorty, the heart of any liberal democracy is the 'romance of endless diversity' that underpinned the original Deweyan description of American political culture, the 'metaphysic of the relation of man and his experience of nature'. In this vein, he specifically approves Whitman's idea of democracy as 'a poetic agon, in which jarring dialectical discords would be resolved in previously unheard harmonies' (Rorty, 1998, p.24–5). As we saw earlier, for Whitman, the very idea of the 'United States' was 'essentially the greatest poem', a celebration of the human capacity for 'love' written into cultural and constitutional form ('By Blue Ontario's Shore', st.16, Whitman, 1996).

This 'Emersonian culture of radical democracy' is, then, necessarily poetic: as Dewey affirmed, a 'narrative of freedom and hope'. It finds a compelling expression in Tocqueville's description of the democratic 'spirit' as the expression of 'feelings and ideas' by which the heart is 'enlarged' and by which its politics is rendered more 'compassionate' (Rorty, 1999, 96–7, 122). It is for this reason that Rorty approves Rawls' later turn to 'prioritize' democracy over philosophy. To do so is to champion 'accommodation and tolerance' over dogma and creed, to visualize democracy, and democratic institutions, 'as experiments in cooperation rather than as attempts to embody a universal and ahistorical order' (Rorty, 1991, pp.189–91, 196). A willingness to tolerate others is, of course, the hallmark of any humanism. Rather than pretending to a delusive sameness, we must strive to appreciate the essential difference that defines humanity, for only in this way can we marry individuality with solidarity.

Once again, then, there is no need to seek out any fantastic new philosophy. Instead, we must concentrate on somehow redressing the debilitating 'loss of faith' and 'distrust in humanity' which currently afflicts our politics. In order to do this, Rorty suggests that we must revisit the New Testament 'message of human fraternity'. The advice might seem rather incongruous. It does not seem to be at one with the Nietzschean spirit of canonical iconoclasm. But a belief in hope does not require a commitment to metaphysics. We can, as Rorty says, 'skip lightly past the predictions, and concentrate on the expressions of hope' (Rorty, 1998, pp.37–8, 84–7, 230–34; 1999, pp.204–5).

This idea of hope is pivotal. In our present intellectual and political state, a state in which the mythical 'comprehensive' theories of truth are no longer credible, the 'most one can do', indeed, is to 'substitute hope' (Rorty, 1999, p.24). It is the most that we should ever want anyone to do. Moreover, as Mill realised a century and a half ago, it is the poets who give us hope. And so it is to the 'poetry of justice' that we must turn, to the 'ultimate romantic hope' that humanity can improve itself without recourse to metaphysical truths, but by the rather simpler strategy of striving to improve the sum of human 'happiness' (ibid., pp.93–100, 212, 263, 270–77).

It is precisely in the writings of Smith and Hume, of Coleridge and Whitman, that we can relocate an 'ethics without principles', a sense of 'moral progress' that is described in terms of 'increasing sensitivity' rather than the discovery of moral 'truths'. Such an idea of moral progress, he affirms, is nothing more than a 'matter of wider and wider sympathy'. Whilst we 'cannot aim at moral perfection', there is nothing to prevent us from adhering to the simple duty of political romanticism, to take 'more people's needs into account' than we 'did previously' (ibid., pp.77–87). This struggle to retrieve the humanist insights of Enlightenment romanticism is, Rorty maintains, the common ambition of all 'antidualists' and 'antiessentialists', not just American pragmatists such as Dewey and himself, but also European 'ironists' such as Heidegger, Foucault and Derrida (ibid., pp.47–9, 63).

Once again, this might seem to be a fantastic claim. At first blush, the deconstructive urges of post-modernism appear to militate against the idealism of Enlightenment. But Rorty is not the only 'ironist' who seeks to excavate within this intellectual tradition. In his essay 'The Force of Law', Jacques Derrida has recourse to the Kantian faculty of reflective judgment in order to reinvest the idea of 'justice' as the necessary 'supplement' to the 'force of law'. It is this faculty, he rightly affirms, which preserves a respect for 'difference', different perceptions, different imaginations, different sensibilities (Derrida, 1990, pp.925–33, 945–7, 959–73). It is here, in Kant's third *Critique*, that a deconstructionist ethics can be uncovered.

In his more recent *Politics of Friendship*, Derrida has returned once again to the Kantian critique of Aristotelian justice, arguing that the 'very work of the political ... amounts to creating (to producing, to making etc) the most friendship possible'. A politics of friendship is intrinsically democratic, because, quite simply, friendship is made, not received. It is this that provides us with an 'unequaled hope'. According to Derrida, Kant's greatest contribution to modern philosophy was to make friendship, understood as 'respect', an integral part of a coherent political theory. Of course, the 'force' of the 'moral law' meant that Kant's second Doctrine defined a 'public friendship', but this can never be cleanly divorced from the 'private' qualities of 'love'. A humanist political philosophy recognizes that we all crave both 'universal' and 'particular' friendships (Derrida, 1997, pp.3–8, 22–4).

The conclusion resonates across the spectrum of modern intellectual visions. It finds an echo with MacIntyre and Taylor, as well as Nussbaum and Rorty. But the deeper echo is with Coleridge and Shelley, Godwin and Rousseau. It is here, in the reinvestment of a progressive idea of justice, in the reinvigoration of genuine democracy of tolerance and respect, that a new political humanism can be nurtured. The time for a renaissance in political romanticism has come. If we are to hope for a better future, we must first be able to imagine it.

Imagining Sisyphus

Writing in the immediate wake of the First World War, the English poet and critic Herbert Read resolved that the 'human spirit' must be retrieved from its 'attitude' of 'despair' (Read, 1974, pp.35, 109–21). He was tempted by all kinds of ideology: sydicalist, communist, socialist. But in the end he rejected them all. No ideology, he concluded, could properly account for the 'passionate' and the 'spontaneous'. It was for this reason that he shared Heidegger's fascination in the pre-Socratic philosopher, Heraclitus, and it was for this reason that he so stridently argued for a politics of rebellion. The promise of Enlightenment, he affirmed, lay in a passionate politics of indeterminate, and indeterminable, progression (ibid., pp.17, 26, 38–40, 103).

Read was convinced that the struggle for democracy was an aesthetic one. It is the capacity to create which defines humanity, whilst, conversely, the 'concretization and vitalization of ideals is one of the main tasks of the aesthetic activity in man'. Accordingly, while the 'modern artist' might look around in despair at the apparent 'wreck of the humanist tradition', it is the same artist who will be the 'pioneer of the new humanist tradition'. It was for this reason that he was so enamoured of Shelley, and most particularly his poem *Prometheus Unbound*, the 'greatest expression ever given to humanity's desire for intellectual light and spiritual liberty'. The 'evolving' political 'consciousness' of humanity is 'coeval' with the 'universal truths of romanticism' (ibid., pp.20–23, 228).

Like Shelley and Godwin, Read was committed equally to reason and sentiment. An anarchic society is not one 'without order', merely one without a 'ruler'. Anarchy is governed by the 'rule of reason', to 'live according to natural laws', a balance indeed of 'romanticism' and 'local politics'. Unsurprisingly, Read shared an abiding mistrust of representative democracy, something which he termed a democratic 'absurdity', a 'myth', a 'quite illusory delegation of power', a form of democracy designed to negate democratic participation. The oxygen of 'pure liberty' can only be found in the politics of 'small communities' (ibid., pp.15, 25, 88–9, 104–5).

Time and again, Read sought to rebut assertions that anarchy was somehow nihilistic or irrational. On the contrary, anarchy was the purest expression of human reason and justice too, the purest expression of 'mediation between persons' as opposed to the ritualistic 'absurdities' of formal law. A democratic society, and only a democratic society, is 'naturally just' precisely because it is sealed by 'a bond of mutual consideration'. The spirit of democracy, he affirmed, was inaugurated by Aristotle, pursued by Enlightenment figures such as Rousseau and Godwin, and then crushed by the legal positivists and their mythologies of institutionalized 'popular sovereignty' (ibid., pp.107–8, 129, 187–201).

Read's anxious romanticism captured the mood of a generation. Another, perhaps more famous, articulation was Albert Camus's *The Myth of Sisyphus*. Camus had already defined this mood in a series of essays in the resistance journal *Combat*. 'We live in terror,' he asserted, 'because dialogue is no longer possible, because man has surrendered himself entirely to history, because he can no longer find that part of himself, every bit as real as history, that sees beauty in the world and in human faces.' This was the dark side of Enlightenment, the side that let reason loose uncoupled from sentiment and humanity (Camus, 1991, pp.117–18).

In *Sisyphus*, Camus collapsed all the defining anxieties of the modern human condition into the 'one truly serious philosophical problem'. In a world devoid of a determinate 'future', why should we wish to live? The answer is not 'universal reason, practical or ethical'. It is not religion or ideology. The answer, the only one that can 'explain everything enough to make a decent man laugh', is 'revolt', the revolt that defines 'freedom' and 'passion' (Camus, 1975, pp.11–12, 26, 55–7, 62–3).

Camus described the fate of Sisyphus, condemned 'to ceaselessly rolling a rock to the top of a mountain, whence the stone would fall back of its own weight'. The gods 'had thought that there was no more dreadful punishment than futile and hopeless labour'. Sisyphus is 'the absurd hero', someone who lives 'as much through his passions as through his torture'. It is by living 'through his passions' that Sisyphus lives at all. A passionate man is a man who can reconcile himself to the tortures of absurdity. It is passion that makes life worth living, for it is passion that enables humanity to triumph, in the final analysis, over hopelessness. We all have 'our nights of Gethsemane', as Camus describes them. We have all shared the sense of hopelessness, when 'boundless grief is too heavy to bear' (ibid., pp.107–9). Only passion can make us descend the hill, pick up the boulder and begin the slow ascent once more.

Camus left Sisyphus 'at the foot of the mountain'. As a passionate man, who was reconciled to the absurdity of his life, but who also realized that he was saved, not by the grace of God, or by a grand ideological illusion, but merely by hope, Sisyphus found the 'universe without a master' to be 'neither sterile nor futile'. For 'Each atom of that stone, each mineral flake of that night-filled mountain, in itself forms a world', and so, accordingly, 'The struggle itself towards the heights is enough to fill a man's heart.' We 'must,' Camus urges, 'imagine Sisyphus happy' (ibid., p.111).

It is this reconciliation which defines the absurd hero, the preparedness to settle for life itself, for humanity and for passion. It is also a preparedness to search for justice, rather than merely settle for law. A concern with justice is not merely a concern with humanity, it is a concern for the 'other', a matter of taking responsibility for conversation, for seizing politics and for redefining it as something that counts, that speaks to everyone's everyday experience of life. It is here, as Camus implied, that hope really lies. It is hope that keeps Sisyphus going, and it is hope that keeps us going too: the hope that we can improve our own lives, and those who live with us, in our families, our neighbourhoods, our worlds.

*

In his 1959 essay, 'The End of Philosophy', the title of which consciously echoed Heidegger's essay of the same name, Maurice Blanchot argued that the 'culmination of metaphysics' is the 'precursor sign of another possibility', and concluded:

> This then is the sunset that from now on accompanies every thinker, a strange funereal moment which the philosophical spirit celebrates in an exaltation that is, moreover, often joyful, leading its slow funereal procession during which it expects, in one way or another, to obtain its resurrection. (Derrida, 1994a, p.36)

The possibility of 'resurrection' furnishes the human condition with hope. It is this possibility that kept Sisyphus marching up his mountain, and it is this that allows us to 'imagine' him happy. And it is this hope, aligned with justice and compassion, that defines a romantic humanism. If we are to recast a 'new' humanism, we will first need to reawaken our political sensibilities, our ability to dream, to imagine Sisyphus happy.

'To reduce the imagination to a state of slavery,' as André Breton wrote in the first manifesto of Surrealism, 'is to betray all sense of absolute justice within oneself.' It is 'Imagination alone' which provides an 'intimation of what can be' (Breton, 1972, pp.4–5). The observation echoes that of Sebastian Mercier, writing on the eve of the French Revolution, 'Let us endeavour to render this life tolerable; or, if that be too much, let us at least dream that it is so' (Jacoby, 1999, p.180). The affinity of hope and the imagination is irreducible. In *Eros and Civilization*, Herbert Marcuse argued that the exercise of the imagination is the only recourse against legalistic totalitarianism. It is the 'refusal to accept' pretended determinations, the 'refusal to forget what can be', that permits humanity to hope (Marcuse, 1966, p.136).

The ability to hope was, in the final analysis, the defining promise of Enlightenment. It is eloquently affirmed by the French historian Fernand Braudel, for whom 'Humanism is a way of hoping, or wishing men to be brothers one with another, of wishing that civilizations, each on its own account and all together, should save themselves and save us.' It 'means accepting and hoping that the doors of the present should be wide open to the future, beyond all the failures, declines, and catastrophes predicted by strange prophets' (Braudel, 1980, p.217). We have encountered many prophets in this book, perhaps none stranger or indeed more pessimistic than Martin Heidegger. But even Heidegger hoped. In a lecture on Schelling and the Enlightenment, he observed: 'According to the old saying of Heraclitus, struggle is the basic principle and moving force of being. But the greatest struggle is love – which provokes the deepest contest precisely in order to be and display itself in its reconciliation' (Dallmayr, 1993, p.128).

Whereas law, or truth, demands a tyrannical homogeneity, love thrives on difference. It is love which mediates politics, not rights or duties or laws. In *Man for Himself*, written within the pervasive intellectual context set by Heidegger, Erich Fromm searched for the traces of a 'humanistic ethics'. The decline of Enlightenment 'optimism', he concluded, was an immediate product of our failure to appreciate that the bedrock of a stable politics is the human capacity to love. The qualities of 'love and decency' have become 'signs of weakness' in modern politics, and it is this perverted appreciation of human relationships which denies us the feeling of 'security' which compassion breeds (Fromm, 1990, pp.62–3, 81).

Human existence, Fromm insists, is defined by a critical paradox. Humanity is 'alone and separated from the world', but is 'impelled to seek for relatedness and oneness'. Politics is not simply about getting along, in the Hobbesian sense of somehow preventing us from beating each other senseless. Politics is about a fundamental human craving to engage with others, to seek 'affirmation of one's own life' through the 'production' of love and compassion. Love is 'the productive form of relatedness to others and to oneself'. It 'implies responsibility, care, respect and knowledge, and the wish for the other person to grow and develop' (ibid., pp.96–7, 110–130).

In this sense, love is the essence of being human:

> To love one's neighbor is not a phenomenon transcending man; it is something inherent in and radiating from him. Love is not a higher power which descends upon man nor a duty which is imposed upon him; it is his own power by which he relates to the world and makes it truly his. (Ibid., p.14)

Like Read and Shelley, and Rorty and Whitman, Fromm was convinced that the idea of humanity is innately democratic and liberating precisely because it is about poetry and sentiment. Living, he asserted, is 'itself an art', something fashioned from humanity's innate capacities of 'self-awareness, reason, and imagination'. The balance of reason and imagination, of sense and sensibility, is once again critical, for, rather than being the 'disembodied intellect' projected by the Enlightenment rationalist, the 'most striking feature in human behavior is the tremendous intensity of passions and strivings which man displays'. We cannot understand without recourse to our sensibilities. Humanity 'comprehends the world, mentally and emotionally' both 'through love and through reason' (ibid., pp.13, 17–23, 26–9, 40–47, 97).

There is, as W.H. Auden affirmed, writing on the eve of the Second World War, no alternative: 'We must love one another or die' (Taylor, 1989, p.483). Two centuries earlier, Alexander Pope made a similar assertion in his *Essay on Man*:

> Look round our World; behold the chain of Love
> Combining all below and all above.
> See plastic Nature working to this end,
> The single atoms each to other tend,
> Attract, attracted to, the next in place
> Form'd and impell'd its neighbour to embrace…
> Self-love thus push'd to social, to divine,
> Gives thee to make thy neighbour's blessing thine.
> Is this too little for the boundless heart?
> Extend it, let thy enemies have part:
> Grasp the whole worlds of Reason, Life, and Sense,

> In one close system of Benevolence:
> Happier as kinder, in whate'er degree,
> And height of Bliss but height of Charity. (Pope, 1978, III, ll.7–12; IV ll.353–60)

Pope, like Shakespeare and Leibniz, was writing at the edge of Enlightenment. His fear was theirs, the fear that Mill later realized had come to pass, the fear that the march of reason would destroy the roots of human sensibility.

This, of course, was the essential thesis of Smith's *Theory of Moral Sentiments* and Kant's *Critique of Judgment*, of Rousseau's *Discourse* and Godwin's *Enquiry*. It found expression, too in Wordsworth's *Tintern Abbey*, Shelley's *Prometheus Unbound* and Whitman's *Leaves of Grass*. Now, more than ever, perhaps it warrants restatement. If the 'new world order' is to emerge as something to cherish, we must learn to hope once again, to imagine indeed a better world. The haughty disdain for sensibility, a disdain that characterizes so much of our current legal and political debate, must be replaced by a jurisprudence of compassion, from which can then be refined a politics of respect and responsibility for others. The only way in which this can be effected is by an opening up of political conversation, by the institution of genuine democratic engagement which will provide us with the facility to imagine the aspiration, and the fate, of others.

The appeal to a renewed sense of humanity, to a jurisprudence of compassion, of sense and sensibility, crosses the centuries. With each 'new' world order, the cry has been resurrected. But it has never been more apposite than it is today. The claims of democracy have never been more compelling, the claims of humanity never more pressing. Both claims must be addressed. Ultimately, the case for a 'new' humanism is founded upon the same 'virtue' of justice that originally inspired Aristotle and then, in time, the likes of Shakespeare and Leibniz, Smith and Kant, Tocqueville and Mill.

It is this ethical component that is absent in the 'new' world order. The absence is even more patent, as we have seen, in the 'new' Europe and in late modernity's desperate groping towards a credible idea of human rights. It is only with the final realization of Enlightenment's promise, with the institution of radical democracy and with the casting of a public philosophy that properly balances the complementary dynamics of sense and sensibility, that the 'new' world order can make claim to moral, as well as political, legitimacy.

Bibliography

Abi-Saab, G. (1999), 'Fragmentation or Unification: Some Concluding Remarks', *New York Journal of International Law*, 31, 919–33.

Ackerman, B. (1997), 'The Rise of World Constitutionalism', *Virginia Law Review*, 83, 771–97.

Akhaven, P. (1998), 'Justice in the Hague, Peace in the Former Yugoslavia? A Commentary on the United Nations War Crimes Tribunal', *Human Rights Quarterly*, 20, 758–65.

Alexander, E. (ed.) (1967), *John Stuart Mill: Literary Studies*, New York: Bobbs-Merrill.

Allott, P. (1992), 'Reconstituting Humanity – New International Law', *European Journal of International Law*, 3, 219–52.

Allott, P. (1997), 'The Crisis of European Constitutionalism: Some Reflections on the Revolution in Europe', *Common Market Law Review*, 34, 439–90.

Alston, P. (1997), 'The Myopia of Handmaidens: International Lawyers and Globalization', *European Journal of International Law*, 3, 435–48.

Althusius, J. (1995), *Politica*, Indianapolis: Liberty Press.

Anghie, A. (2000), 'Time Present and Time Past: Globalization, International Financial Institutions, and the Third World', *New York Journal of International Law and Politics*, 32, 243–90.

Appadurai, A. (1996), *Modernity at Large: Cultural Dimensions of Globalisation*, Minneapolis: University of Minnesota Press.

Arendt, H. (1963), *Eichmann in Jerusalem: A Report on the Banality of Evil*, Harmondsworth: Penguin.

Arendt, H. (1982), *Lectures on Kant's Political Philosophy*, Chicago: University of Chicago Press.

Aristotle (1976), *Ethics*, Harmondsworth: Penguin.

Austin, J. (1995), *The Province of Jurisprudence Determined*, Cambridge: Cambridge University Press.

Bacon, F. (1985), *The Essays*, Harmondsworth: Penguin.

Bagehot, W. (1963), *The English Constitution*, London: Fontana.

Barber, B. (1992), 'Jihad versus McWorld', *The Atlantic*, 53–8.

Barber, B. (2000), 'Can Democracy Survive Globalization?', *Government and Opposition*, 35, 275–301.
Barnet, R. and J. Cavanagh (1994), *Global Dreams: Imperial Corporations and the New World Order*, London: Simon and Schuster.
Bassnett, S. (1993), *Shakespeare: The Elizabethan Plays*, London: Macmillan.
Baxi, U. (1998), 'Voices of Suffering and the Future of Human Rights', *Transnational Law and Contemporary Problems*, 8, 125–69.
Beck, U. (2000a), 'Living Your Own Life in a Runaway World: Individualisation, Globalisation and Politics', in A. Giddens and W. Hutton (eds), *On the Edge: Living with Global Capitalism*, London: Jonathan Cape, pp.164–77.
Beck, U. (2000b), 'Democratization of Democracy – Third Way Policy Needs to Redefine Work', *The European Legacy*, 5, 177–81.
Benevisti, E. (1999), 'Margin of Appreciation, Consensus, and Universal Standards', *New York Journal of International Law*, 31, 843–54.
Benjamin, W. (1973), *Illuminations*, London: Fontana.
Bentham, J. (1982), *An Introduction to the Principles of Morals and Legislation*, London: Methuen.
Benton, S. (1998), 'The Princess, the People and Paranoia', in M. Merck (ed.), *After Diana: Irreverent Elegies*, London: Verso, pp.87–101.
Berger, K. (1977), 'Prospero's Art', *Shakespeare Studies*, 10, 211–22.
Blair, T. (2000), 'Speech to the Polish Stock Exchange'(*www.number-10.uk/news*), October.
Bork, R. (1996), *Slouching Towards Gomorrah: Modern Liberalism and American Decline*, New York: HarperCollins.
Bosniak, L. (2000), 'Citizenship Denationalized', *Indiana Journal of Global Legal Studies*, 7, 447–509.
Bourdieu, P. (1998), *Acts of Resistance: Against the Tyranny of the Market*, London: New Press.
Boutros-Ghali, B. (1995), 'Democracy: A Newly Recognized Imperative', *Global Governance*, 1, 1–12.
Braudel, F. (1980), *On History*, Chicago: University of Chicago Press.
Breton, A. (1972), *Manifestos of Surrealism*, Ann Arbor: Michigan University Press.
Butler, M. (1982), 'Godwin, Burke, and *Caleb Williams*', *Essays in Criticism*, 32, 237–57.
Callinicos, A. (2000), 'The Ideology of Humanitarian Intervention', in Tariq Ali (ed.), *Masters of the Universe?: NATO's Balkan Crusade*, London: Verso, pp.175–89.
Campbell, B. (1998), *Diana Princess of Wales: How Sexual Politics Shook the Monarchy*, London: Women's Press.
Camus, A. (1968), *Lyrical and Critical Essays*, New York: Knopf.

Camus, A. (1974), *Resistance, Rebellion and Death*, London: Vintage.
Camus, A. (1975), *The Myth of Sisyphus*, Harmondsworth: Penguin.
Camus, A. (1991), *Between Hell and Reason*, Hanover: Wesleyan University Press.
Cassirer, E. (1981), *Kant's Life and Thought*, Newhaven: Yale University Press.
Castells, M. (2000), 'Information Technology and Global Capitalism', in W. Hutton and A. Giddens (eds), *On the Edge: Living with Global Capitalism*, London: Jonathan Cape, pp.52–74.
Chomsky, N. (1999), *Profit Over People: Neoliberalism and Global Order*, New York: Seven Stories Press.
Coleridge, S. (1969), *Complete Poetical Works*, Oxford: Oxford University Press.
Coleridge, S. (1997), *Biographia Literaria*, London: Dent.
Commission on Global Governance (1995), *Our Global Neighbourhood*, Oxford: Oxford University Press.
Coppel, J. and A. O'Neill (1992), 'The European Court of Justice: Taking Rights Seriously?', *Legal Studies*, 12, 227–45.
Cowling, M. (1990), *Mill and Liberalism*, Cambridge: Cambridge University Press.
Cox, R. (1999), 'Civil Society at the Turn of the Millennium: Prospects for a New World Order', *Review of International Studies*, 25, 3–28.
Crowther, P. (1989), *The Kantian Sublime: From Morality to Art*, Oxford: Oxford University Press.
Curtin, D. (1993), 'The Constitutional Structure of the Union: A Europe of Bits and Pieces', *Common Market Law Review*, 30, 17–69.
Curtin, D. (1997), *Postnational Democracy: The European Union in Search of a Public Philosophy*, Dordrecht: Kluwer.
Dallmayr, F. (1993), *The Other Heidegger*, Ithaca: Cornell University Press.
Dart, G. (1999), *Rousseau, Robespierre and English Romanticism*, Cambridge: Cambridge University Press.
De Burca, G. (1993), 'Fundamental Human Rights and the Rights of EC Law', *Oxford Journal of Legal Studies*, 13, 283–319.
De Lange, J. (2000), 'The historical context, legal origins and philosophical foundation of the South African Truth and Reconciliation Commission', in C. Villa-Vicencio and W. Vervwoerd (eds), *Looking Back, Reaching Forward: Reflections on the Truth and Reconciliation Commission of South Africa*, Cape Town: University of Cape Town Press, pp.14–31.
Delanty, G. (1995), *Inventing Europe: Idea, Identity, Reality*, London: Macmillan.
Deleuze, G. (1995), *Kant's Critical Philosophy*, London: Athlone Press.

Derrida, J. (1989), *Of Spirit: Heidegger and the Question*, Chicago: University of Chicago Press.

Derrida, J. (1990). 'The Force of Law: The Mystical Foundations of Authority', *Cardozo Law Review*, 11, 921–1045.

Derrida, J. (1992), *Acts of Literature*, London: Routledge.

Derrida, J. (1994a), *Specters of Marx*, London: Routledge.

Derrida, J. (1994b), *The Other Heading: Reflections on Today's Europe*, Bloomington: Indiana University Press.

Derrida, J. (1997), *The Politics of Friendship*, London: Verso.

Doheny, J. (1998), 'Herbert Read as Literary Critic', in H. Cecil (ed.), *Herbert Read Reassessed*, Liverpool: Liverpool University Press, pp.46–69.

Donnelly, J. (1989), *Universal Human Rights in Theory and Practice*, Ithaca: Cornell University Press.

Donnelly, J. (1999), 'Human Rights, Democracy and Development', *Human Rights Quarterly*, 21, 608–32.

Douzinas, C. (2000), *The End of Human Rights: Critical Legal Thought at the Turn of the Century*, Oxford: Hart.

Dunkley, G. (2000), *The Free Trade Adventure: The WTO, the Uruguay Round and Globalism*, New York: Zed Books.

Dupuy, P. (1999), 'The Danger of Fragmentation or Unification of the International Legal System and the International Court of Justice', *New York Journal of International Law*, 31, 791–807.

Dworkin, R. (2000), *Sovereign Virtue: The Theory and Practice of Equality*, Cambridge: Harvard University Press.

Dyzenhaus, D. (1999), *Judging Judges, Judging Ourselves: Truth, Reconciliation and the Apartheid Legal Order*, Oxford: Hart.

Eagleton, T. (1986), *William Shakespeare*, Oxford: Blackwell.

Ehlermann, C. (1998), 'Differentiation, Flexibility, Closer Co-operation: The New Provisions of the Amsterdam Treaty', *European Law Journal*, 4, 246–70.

Eksteins, M. (1989), *The Rites of Spring*, Toronto: Lester and Orpen Denys.

Eliot, G. (1990), *Selected Essays, Poems and Other Writings*, Harmondsworth: Penguin.

Engle, K. (2000), 'Culture and Human Rights: The Asian Values Debate in Context', *New York Journal of International Law and Politics*, 32, 291–333.

Esler, G. (1998), *The United States of Anger*, Harmondsworth: Penguin.

Etzioni, A. (1995), *The Spirit of Community: Rights, Responsibilities and the Communitarian Agenda*, London: Fontana.

European Commission (1992), 'Europe and the Challenge of Enlargement', *Bulletin of the EC*, supplement 3/92.

European Commission (2001), 'An Unprecedented Enlargement' (*europa.eu. int/enlargement*), 13/1/01.

Ewing, K. (1999), 'The Human Rights Act and Parliamentary Democracy', *Modern Law Review*, 62, 79–99.

Falk, R. (1995), *On Humane Governance: Toward a New Global Politics*, Cambridge: Polity Press.

Fassbender, B. (1998), 'The United Nations Charter as Constitution of the International Community', *Columbia Journal of Transnational Law*, 36, 568–84.

Finkielraut, A. (2001), *In the Name of Humanity: Reflections on the Twentieth Century*, London: Pimlico.

Fischer, J. and J. Chevènement (2000), 'France v Germany: What Kind of Europe?', *Prospect*, August/September, 38–41.

Fitzgibbons, A. (1995), *Adam Smith's System of Liberty, Wealth and Virtue: The Moral and Political Foundations of the Wealth of Nations*, Oxford: Oxford University Press.

Fitzpatrick, P. (1998), 'New Europe and Old Stories: Mythology and Legality in the European Union', in P. Fitzpatrick and J. Bergeron (eds), *Europe's Other: European Law Between Modernity and Postmodernity*, Aldershot: Ashgate, pp.27–45.

Foot, P. (1990), *Shelley's Revolutionary Year*, London: Redwords.

Forsythe, D. (1997), 'The United Nations, Human Rights and Development', *Human Rights Quarterly*, 19, 334–49.

Fox, G. (1999), 'Strengthening the State', *Indiana Journal of Global Legal Studies*, 7, 35–77.

Franck, T. (1992), 'The Emerging Right to Democratic Governance', *American Journal of International Law*, 86, 46–91.

Franklin, B. (1986), *Autobiography and Other Writings*, Harmondsworth: Penguin.

Freeman, M. (1994), 'The Philosophical Foundations of Human Rights', *Human Rights Quarterly*, 16, 491–514.

Fried, C. (2000), 'Markets, Law and Democracy', *Journal of Democracy*, 11, 5–18.

Friedman, T. (2000), *The Lexus and the Olive Tree*, New York: Anchor Books.

Fromm, E. (1990), *Man for Himself*, London: Routledge.

Fukuyama, F. (1992), *The End of History and the Last Man*, London: Penguin.

Fukuyama, F. (1996), *Trust: The Social Virtues and the Creation of Prosperity*, London: Penguin.

Fuller, L. (1958), 'Positivism and Fidelity to Law – A Reply to Professor Hart', *Harvard Law Review*, 71, 630–72.

Gabel, P. and D. Kennedy (1984), 'Roll Over Beethoven', *Stanford Law Review*, 36, 1–52.
Gadamer, H. (1975), *Truth and Method*, London: Sheed and Ward.
Gaete, R. (1991), 'Postmodernism and Human Rights: Some Insidious Questions', *Law and Critique*, 2, 149–70.
Galbraith, J. (1996), *The Good Society: The Humane Agenda*, London: Sinclair-Stevenson.
Garton Ash, T. (2000), *History of the Present: Essays, Sketches and Despatches from Europe in the 1990s*, London: Penguin.
Gearty, C. (1999), 'The Human Rights Act 1998 and the Role of the Strasbourg Organs: Some Preliminary Reflections', in G. Anderson (ed.), *Rights and Democracy: Essays in UK–Canadian Constitutionalism*, London: Blackstone, pp.169–91.
Geddes, A. (1995), 'Immigrant and Ethnic Minorities and the EU's Democratic Deficit', *Journal of Common Market Studies*, 33, 197–217.
Gewirth, A. (1996), *The Community of Rights*, Chicago: University of Chicago Press.
Giddens, A. (1998), *The Third Way: The Renewal of Social Democracy*, Cambridge: Polity Press.
Giddens, A. and W. Hutton (2000), 'In Conversation', in A. Giddens and W. Hutton (eds), *On the Edge: Living with Global Capitalism*, London: Jonathan Cape, pp.1–51.
Gill, S. (1995), 'Globalisation, Market Civilization, and Disciplinary Neoliberalism', *Millennium*, 24, 399–423.
Gill, S. (2000), 'Toward a Postmodern Prince?: The Battle of Seattle as a Moment in the New Politics of Globalisation', *Millennium*, 29, 131–40.
Glendon, M. (1998), 'Knowing the Universal Declaration of Human Rights', *Notre Dame Law Review*, 73, 1153–90.
Glenny, M. (1992), *The Fall of Yugoslavia: The Third Balkan War*, London: Penguin.
Godwin, W. (1982), *Caleb Williams*, Oxford: Oxford University Press.
Godwin, W. (1985), *An Enquiry Concerning Political Justice*, Harmondsworth: Penguin.
Gonzalez, F. (1999), 'European Union and Globalization', *Foreign Policy*, summer, 28–42.
Gray, J. (1998), *False Dawn: The Delusions of Global Capitalism*, London: Granta.
Griswold, C. (1999), *Adam Smith and the Virtues of Enlightenment*, Cambridge: Cambridge University Press.
Guyer, P. (1993), *Kant and the Experience of Freedom: Essays on Aesthetics and Morality*, Cambridge: Cambridge University Press.

Haakonssen, K. (1981), *The Science of a Legislator: The Natural Jurisprudence of David Hume and Adam Smith*, Oxford: Oxford University Press.
Habermas, J. (1996a), *Between Facts and Norms: Contributions to a Discourse Theory of Law and Democracy*, Cambridge: Polity Press.
Habermas J. (1996b), 'The European Nation State. Its Achievements and its Limitations. On the Past and Future of Sovereignty and Citizenship', *Ratio Juris*, 9, 125–37.
Hall, S. (1991), 'Brave New World', *Socialist Review*, 21, 58–63.
Hart, H. (1958), 'Positivism and the Separation of Law and Morals', *Harvard Law Review*, 71, 593–629.
Havel, V. (1992), *Summer Meditations: On Politics, Morality and Civility in a Time of Transition*, London: Faber and Faber.
Havel, V. (1998), *The Art of the Impossible: Politics as Morality in Practice*, New York: Fromm International.
Hazlitt, W. (1964), *Spirit of the Age*, London: Everyman.
Hazlitt, W. (1982), *Selected Writings*, Harmondsworth: Penguin.
Heidegger, M. (1972), *Basic Writings*, ed. D. Krell, New York: Harper and Row.
Heidegger, M. (1992), *The Basic Problems of Phenomenology*, Bloomington: Indiana University Press.
Held, D. (1995), *Democracy and Global Order: From the Modern State to Cosmopolitan Governance*, Cambridge: Polity Press.
Helfer, L. and A. Slaughter (1997), 'Toward a Theory of Effective Supranational Adjudication', *Yale Law Journal*, 107, 282–391.
Henry, Y. (2000), 'Where healing begins', in C. Villa-Vicencio and W. Verwoerd (eds), *Looking Back, Reaching Forward: Reflections on the Truth and Reconciliation Commission of South Africa*, Cape Town: University of Cape Town Press, pp.166–73.
Herdegen, M. (1994), 'The Constitutionalization of the UN Security System', *Vanderbilt Journal of Transnational Law*, 27, 135–59.
Hoffmann, S. (1995), 'Thoughts on the UN at Fifty', *European Journal of International Law*, 6, 317–24.
Holland, S. (1993), *The European Imperative: Economic and Social Cohesion in the 1990s*, London: Spokesman.
Holmes, R. (1995), *Shelley: The Pursuit*, London: Flamingo.
Holmes, R. (1998), *Coleridge: Darker Reflections*, London: HarperCollins.
Hooker, R. (1989), *Of the Laws of Ecclesiastical Polity*, Cambridge: Cambridge University Press.
Howe, G. (1995), 'Sovereignty, Democracy and Human Rights', *Political Quarterly*, 66, 127–37.
Hume, D. (1966), *An Enquiry Concerning the Principles of Morals*, London: Open Court.

Hume, D. (1978), *A Treatise of Human Nature*, Oxford: Oxford University Press.
Humphreys, J. (1999), *Devil's Advocate*, London: Hutchinson.
Hunt, M. (1999), 'The Human Rights Act and Legal Culture: The Judiciary and the Legal Profession', *Journal of Law and Society*, 26, 86–102.
Huntington, S. (1997), *The Clash of Civilizations and the Remaking of World Order*, New York: Simon and Schuster.
Hutchinson, A. (1999), 'Supreme Court Inc: The Business of Democracy and Rights', in G. Anderson (ed.), *Rights and Democracy: Essays in UK–Canadian Constitutionalism*, London: Blackstone, pp.29–45.
Jacoby, R. (1999), *The End of Utopia: Politics and Culture in an Age of Apathy*, New York: Basic Books.
James, O. (1997), *Britain on the Couch: Treating a Low Serotonin Society*, London: Century.
Jay, E. (1979), *The Religion of the Heart*, Oxford: Oxford University Press.
Johnston, K. (1998), *The Hidden Wordsworth: Poet, Lover, Rebel, Spy*, New York: Norton.
Jolley, N. (1975), 'Leibniz on Hobbes, Locke's *Two Treatises* and Sherlock's *Case of Allegiance*', *Historical Journal*, 18, 21–35.
Kafka, F. (1953), *The Trial*, Harmondsworth: Penguin.
Kaldor, M. (2000), 'Civilising Globalisation?: The Implications of the Battle of Seattle', *Millennium*, 20, 105–14.
Kant, I. (1956), *The Critique of Practical Reason*, New York: Bobbs-Merrill.
Kant, I (1964), *Groundwork to the Metaphysics of Morals*, London: Routledge.
Kant, I. (1988), *The Critique of Pure Reason*, London: Dent.
Kant, I. (1991a), *The Metaphysics of Morals*, Cambridge: Cambridge University Press.
Kant, I. (1991b), *The Critique of Judgement*, Oxford: Oxford University Press.
Kant, I. (1991c), *Political Writings*, ed. H. Reiss, Cambridge: Cambridge University Press.
Kaplan, R. (1996), *The Ends of the Earth*, London: Vintage.
Klare, K. (1981), 'Labor Law as Ideology: Toward a New Historiography of Collective Bargaining Law', *Industrial Relations Law Journal*, 4, 450–82.
Klug, F. (2000), *Values for a Godless Age: The Story of the United Kingdom's New Bill of Rights*, Harmondsworth: Penguin.
Koh, H. (1997), 'Why Do Nations Obey International Law?', *Yale Law Journal*, 106, 2599–2659.
Koskenniemi, M. (1990), 'The Politics of International Law', *European Journal of International Law*, 1, 4–32.

Koskenniemi, M. (1995), 'The Police in the Temple. Order, Justice and the UN: A Dialectical View', *European Journal of International Law*, 6, 325–48.

Koskenniemi, M. (1996), 'The Place of Law in Collective Security', *Michigan Journal of International Law*, 17, 455–88.

Kott, J. (1967), *Shakespeare: Our Contemporary*, London: Routledge.

Kramnick, I. (1972), 'On Anarchism and the Real World: William Godwin and Radical England', *American Political Science Review*, 66, 114–28.

Krog, A. (1999), *Country of My Skull*, London: Vintage.

Laffan, B. (1998), 'The European Union: A Distinctive Model of Internationalization', *Journal of European Public Policy*, 5, 235–53.

Laws, J. (1995), 'Law and Democracy', *Public Law*, 72–93.

Leask, N. (1998), *The Politics of the Imagination: Coleridge's Critical Thought*, London: Macmillan.

Legrand, P. (1996), 'European Legal Systems are Not Converging', *International and Comparative Law Quarterly*, 45, 52–81.

Leibniz, G. (1973), *Philosophical Writings*, ed. G. Parkinson, London: Dent.

Leibniz, G. (1988), *Political Writings*, ed. P. Riley, Cambridge: Cambridge University Press.

Lindgren Alves, J. (1998), 'The United Nations, Postmodernity and Human Rights', *University of San Francisco Law Review*, 32, 479–532.

Lindgren Alves, J. (2000), 'The Declaration of Human Rights in Postmodernity', *Human Rights Quarterly*, 22, 478–500.

Lipschutz, R. (1992), 'Reconstructing World Politics: The Emergence of Global Civil Society', *Millennium*, 21, 389–420.

Locke, D. (1980), *A Fantasy of Reason: The Life and Thought of William Godwin*, London: Routledge and Kegan Paul.

Lyotard, J. (1988), *The Differend: Phrases in Dispute*, Manchester: Manchester University Press.

Lyotard, J. (1990), *Heidegger and the 'jews'*, Minneapolis: University of Minnesota Press.

Lyotard, J. (1993), 'The Other's Rights', in S. Shute and S. Hurley (eds), *On Human Rights: The Oxford Amnesty Lectures 1993*, New York: Basic Books, pp.135–47.

MacCormick, N. (1999), *Questioning Sovereignty: Law, State and Nation in the European Commonwealth*, Oxford: Oxford University Press.

MacIntyre, A. (1985), *After Virtue: A Study in Moral Virtue*, London: Duckworth.

MacIntyre, A. (1988), *Whose Justice? Which Rationality?*, London: Duckworth.

MacKinnon, C. (1994a), 'Turning Rape into Pornography: Postmodern Genocide', in A. Stiglmayer (ed.), *Mass Rape: The War Against Women in Bosnia–Herzegovina*, Lincoln: Nebraska University Press, pp.73–81.

MacKinnon, C. (1994b), 'Rape, Genocide, and Women's Human Rights', in A. Stiglmayer (ed.), *Mass Rape: The War Against Women in Bosnia–Herzegovina*, Lincoln: Nebraska University Press, pp.193–229.

Madison, J., A. Hamilton and J. Jay (1978), *The Federalist Papers*, ed. I. Kramnick, Harmondsworth: Penguin.

Mancini, F. (1991), 'The Making of a Constitution for Europe', in R. Keohane and S. Hoffmann (eds), *The New European Community: Decisionmaking and Institutional Change*, Boulder: Westview.

Marcuse, H. (1966), *Eros and Civilization*, London: Beacon Press.

Marcuse, H. (1991), *One-Dimensional Man*, London: Routledge.

Marks, S. (1997), 'The End of History?: Reflections on Some International Legal Theses', *European Journal of International Law*, 3, 449–77.

Marks, S. (2000), *The Riddle of All Constitutions: International Law, Democracy and the Critique of Ideology*, Oxford: Oxford University Press.

Marr, A. (1995), *Ruling Britannia: The Failure and Future of British Democracy*, London: Michael Joseph.

Marshall, D. (1984), 'Adam Smith and the Theatricality of Moral Sentiments', *Critical Inquiry*, 10, 592–613.

McCracken, D. (1969), 'Godwin's *Caleb Williams*: A Fictional Rebuttal of Burke', *Studies in Burke and his Time*, 11, 142–52.

McGlynn, C. (2000), 'Ideologies of Motherhood in European Community Sex Equality Law', *European Law Journal*, 6, 29–44.

Mertus, J. (2000), 'Considering Nonstate Actors in the New Millennium: Toward Expanded Participation in Norm Generation and Norm Application', *New York Journal of Law and Politics*, 32, 537–66.

Mill, J. (1989), *Autobiography*, Harmondsworth: Penguin.

Mill, J. (1994), *The Principles of Political Economy*, Oxford: Oxford University Press.

Mill, J. and J. Bentham (1987), *Utilitarianism and Other Essays*, Harmondsworth: Penguin.

Minnow, M. (2000), 'The Hope for Healing: What Can Truth Commissions Do?', in R. Rotberg and D. Thompson (eds), *Truth vs Justice: The Morality of Truth Commissions*, Princeton: Princeton University Press, pp.235–60.

Monnet, J. (1978), *Memoirs*, London: Doubleday.

Montaigne, M. de. (1993), *Essays*, Harmondsworth: Penguin.

Moosa, E. (2000), 'Truth and reconciliation as performance: spectres of Eucharistic redemption', in C. Villa-Vicencio and W. Verwoerd (eds), *Looking Back, Reaching Forward: Reflections on the Truth and Recon-*

ciliation Commission of South Africa, Cape Town: University of Cape Town Press, pp.113–22.

Moravscik, A. (1997), 'Taking Preferences Seriously: A Liberal Theory of International Politics', *International Organization*, 51, 513–53.

Morrow, J. (1991), 'Republicanism and Public Virtue: William Godwin's *History of the Commonwealth of England*', *Historical Journal*, 34, 645–64.

Niarchos, C. (1995), 'Women, War, and Rape: Challenges Facing the International Tribunal for the Former Yugoslavia', *Human Rights Quarterly*, 17, 649–90.

Nichols, A. (1998), *The Revolutionary 'I': Wordsworth and the Politics of Self-Presentation*, London: Macmillan.

Nietzsche, F. (1969), *Thus Spoke Zarathustra*, Harmondsworth: Penguin.

Nietzsche, F. (1979), *Ecce Homo*, Harmondsworth: Penguin.

Nietzsche, F. (1993), *The Birth of Tragedy*, Harmondsworth: Penguin.

Nussbaum, M. (1990), *Love's Knowledge: Essays on Philosophy and Literature*, Oxford: Oxford University Press.

Nussbaum, M. (1995), *Poetic Justice: The Literary Imagination and Public Life*, New York: Beacon Press.

Nussbaum, M. (1997), *Cultivating Humanity: A Classical Defense of Reform in Liberal Education*, Cambridge: Harvard University Press.

Ohmae, K. (1996), *The End of the Nation State and the Rise of Global Economics*, London: HarperCollins.

Onuf, N. (1994), 'The Constitution of International Society', *European Journal of International Law*, 5, 1–19.

Otto, D. (1997), 'Rethinking Universals: Opening Transformative Possibilities in International Human Rights Law', *Australian Yearbook of International Law*, 18, 1–36.

Paine, T. (1985), *The Rights of Man*, Harmondsworth: Penguin.

Paine, T (1987), *The Thomas Paine Reader*, eds M. Foot and I. Kramnick, Harmondsworth: Penguin.

Paxman, J. (1998), *The English: A Portrait of a People*, London: Michael Joseph.

Petersmann, E. (1999), 'Constitutionalism and International Adjudication: How to Constitutionalize the UN Dispute Resolution System?', *New York Journal of International Law*, 31, 754–70.

Phelan, D. (1992), 'Right to Life of the Unborn v Promotion of Trade in Services: The European Court of Justice and the Normative Shaping of the European Union', *Modern Law Review*, 55, 670–89.

Pope, A. (1978), *Complete Poetical Works*, Oxford: Oxford University Press.

Prodi, R. (2000), 'Shaping the New Europe', 15/2/2000 (*www.europa.eu.int/*).

Prodi, R. (2001), 'Poland and Europe: Building on the Past, Shaping the Future', 10/3/2001 (*www.europa.eu.int/*).
Pyle, F. (1995), *The Ideology of the Imagination: Subject and Society in the Discourse of Romanticism*, Stanford: Stanford University Press.
Ratner, S. (1998), 'International Law: The Trials of Global Norms', *Foreign Affairs*, 65–80.
Rawls, J. (1971), *A Theory of Justice*, Oxford: Oxford University Press.
Rawls, J. (1980), 'Kantian Constructivism in Moral Theory', *Journal of Philosophy*, 77, 515–72.
Rawls, J. (1993), 'The Law of Peoples', in S. Shute and S. Hurley (eds), *On Human Rights: The Oxford Amnesty Lectures 1993*, New York: Basic Books, pp.41–82.
Rawnsley, A. (2000), *Servants of the People: The Inside Story of New Labour*, London: Hamish Hamilton.
Read, H. (1974), *Anarchy and Order: Essays in Politics*, London: Souvenir Press.
Riley, P. (1976), 'Three 17th Century Theorists of Federalism: Althusius, Hugo and Leibniz', *Publius*, 6, 7–41.
Riley, P. (1996), *Leibniz' Universal Jurisprudence: Justice as the Charity of the Wise*, Cambridge: Harvard University Press.
Romano, C. (1999), 'The Proliferation of International Judicial Bodies: The Pieces of a Puzzle', *New York Journal of International Law*, 31, 709–51.
Rorty, R. (1989), *Contingency, Irony, and Solidarity*, Cambridge: Cambridge University Press.
Rorty, R. (1991), *Objectivism, Relativism and Truth*, Cambridge: Cambridge University Press.
Rorty, R. (1993), 'Human Rights, Rationality, and Sentimentality', in S. Shute and S. Hurley (eds), *On Human Rights: The Oxford Amnesty Lectures 1993*, New York: Basic Books, pp.175–202.
Rorty, R. (1998), *Achieving Our Country: Leftist Thought in Twentieth-Century America*, Cambridge: Harvard University Press.
Rorty, R. (1999), *Philosophy and Social Hope*, Harmondsworth: Penguin.
Rosenau, J. (1992), *Governance without Government*, Cambridge: Cambridge University Press.
Rosow, S. (2000), 'Globalisation as Democratic Theory', *Millennium*, 29, 27–45.
Ross, I. (1995), *The Life of Adam Smith*, Oxford: Oxford University Press.
Rotberg, R. (2000), 'Truth Commissions and the Provision of Truth, Justice and Reconciliation', in R. Rotberg and D. Thompson (eds), *Truth vs Justice: The Morality of Truth Commissions*, Princeton: Princeton University Press, pp.3–21.
Rousseau, J. (1953), *The Confessions*, Harmondsworth: Penguin.

Rousseau, J. (1968), *The Social Contract*, Harmondsworth: Pengiun.
Rousseau, J. (1984), *A Discourse Concerning Inequality*, Harmondsworth: Penguin.
Rousseau, J. (1991), *Emile*, Harmondsworth: Penguin.
Ruggie, J. (1998), *Constructing the World Polity: Essays on International Institutionalization*, London: Routledge.
Salzman, T. (1998), 'Rape Camps as a Means of Ethnic Cleansing: Religious, Cultural, and Ethical Responses to Rape Victims in the Former Yugoslavia', *Human Rights Quarterly*, 20, 348–78.
Sandel, M. (1996), *Democracy's Discontent: America in Search of a Public Philosophy*, Cambridge: Harvard University Press.
Santos, B. (1995), *Towards a New Common Sense: Law, Science and Politics in Paradigmatic Transition*, London: Routledge.
Sarkin, J. (1998), 'The Development of a Human Rights Culture in South Africa', *Human Rights Quarterly*, 20, 628–65.
Schachter, O. (1997), 'The Decline of the Nation-State and its Implications for International Law', *Columbia Journal of Transnational Law*, 36, 7–23.
Schama, S. (1989), *Citizens: A Chronicle of the French Revolution*, Harmondsworth: Penguin.
Scheiwe, K. (1994), 'EC Law's Unequal Treatment of the Family: The Case Law of the European Court of Justice on Rules Prohibiting Discrimination on Grounds of Sex and Nationality', *Social and Legal Studies*, 3, 243–65.
Schlesinger, A. (1997), 'Has Democracy a Future?', *Foreign Affairs*, 76, 2–12.
Schmitt, C. (1988), *The Crisis of Parliamentary Democracy*, Cambridge: MIT Press.
Scott, J. (1995), *Development Dilemmas in the European Community: Rethinking Regional Development Policy*, Milton Keynes: Open University Press.
Sedley, S. (1995), 'Human Rights: a Twenty-First Century Agenda', *Public Law*, 386–400.
Senarclens, R. de (1998), 'Governance and the Crisis in the International Mechanisms of Regulation', *International Social Science Journal*, 155, 91–104.
Sennett, R. (1998), *The Corrosion of Character: The Personal Consequences of Work in the New Capitalism*, New York: Norton.
Shakespeare, W. (1964a), *The Merchant of Venice*, London: Routledge.
Shakespeare, W. (1964b), *The Tempest*, London: Routledge.
Shakespeare, W. (1969), *Henry VI part 2*, London: Routledge.
Shakespeare, W. (1994), *Hamlet*, London: Routledge.

Shapiro, M. (1993), 'The Globalization of Law', *Indiana Journal of Global Legal Studies*, 1, 37–64.
Shaw, J. (1998), 'The Treaty of Amsterdam: Challenges of Flexibility and Legitimacy', *European Law Journal*, 4, 63–86.
Shaw, J. (2000), 'Process and Constitutional Discourse in the European Union', *Journal of Law and Society*, 27, 4–37.
Shaw, T. and C. Abide (1995), 'Africa and Global Developments in the Twenty-First Century', *International Journal*, 11, 1–26.
Shelley, P. (1971), *Complete Poetical Works*, Oxford: Oxford University Press.
Siedentop, L. (2000), *Democracy in Europe*, London: Penguin.
Singer, J. (1984), 'The Player and the Cards: Nihilism and Legal Theory', *Yale Law Journal*, 94, 1–70.
Sjolander, C. (1996), 'The Rhetoric of Globalization: What's in a Wor(l)d?', *International Journal*, 51, 603–16.
Slaughter, A. (1995), 'International Law in a World of Liberal States', *European Journal of International Law*, 6, 503–38.
Slaughter, A. (1997), 'The Real New World Order', *Foreign Affairs*, 76, 183–97.
Smith, A. (1976), *The Theory of Moral Sentiments*, Oxford: Oxford University Press.
Smith, A. (1978), *Lectures on Jurisprudence*, Oxford: Oxford University Press.
Smouts, M. (1998), 'The Proper Use of Governance in International Relations', *International Social Science Journal*, 155, 81–9.
Sofaer, A. (2000), 'International Law and Kosovo', *Stanford Journal of International Law*, 36, 1–21.
Sophocles. (1974), *The Theban Plays*, Harmondsworth: Penguin.
Soros, G. (2000), 'The New Global Financial Adventure', in A. Giddens and W. Hutton (eds), *On the Edge: Living with Global Capitalism*, London: Jonathan Cape, pp.86–92.
Spicker, P. (2000), 'A Third Way?', *The European Legacy*, 5, 229–39.
Spiro, P. (2000), 'Globalization, International Law and the Academy', *New York Journal of International Law and Politics*, 32, 567–76.
Steiner, G. (1971), *In Bluebeard's Castle: or Some Notes Towards a Redefinition of Culture*, London: Faber and Faber.
Stern, B. (1999), in M. Byers (ed.), *The Role of Law in International Politics: Essays in International Relations and International Law*, Oxford: Oxford University Press, pp.247–68.
Stiglmayer, A. (1994a), 'The War in the Former Yugoslavia', in A. Stiglmayer (ed.), *Mass Rape: The War Against Women in Bosnia–Herzegovina*, Lincoln: Nebraska University Press, pp.1–34.

Stiglmayer, A. (1994b), 'The Rape in Bosnia–Herzegovina', in A. Stiglmayer (ed.), *Mass Rape: The War Against Women in Bosnia–Herzegovina*, Lincoln: Nebraska University Press, pp.82–169.

Still, J. (1993), *Justice and Difference in the Works of Rousseau*, Cambridge: Cambridge University Press.

Strong, T. (1994), *Jean-Jacques Rousseau: The Politics of the Ordinary*, London: Sage.

Sullivan, R. (1989), *Immanuel Kant's Moral Theory*, Cambridge: Cambridge University Press.

Swift, J. (1985), *Gulliver's Travels*, Harmondsworth: Penguin.

Tariq Ali (2000), 'After the War', in Tariq Ali (ed.), *Masters of the Universe?: NATO's Balkan Crusade*, London: Verso, pp. ix–xviii.

Taylor, C. (1989), *Sources of the Self: The Making of Modern Identity*, Cambridge: Cambridge University Press.

Teson, F. (1998), *A Philosophy of International Law*, London: Westview.

Thompson, J. (1992), *Justice and World Order: A Philosophical Inquiry*, London: Routledge.

Thoreau, H. (1986), *Walden and Civil Disobedience*, Harmondsworth: Penguin.

Tocqueville, A. de (1994), *Democracy in America*, London: Fontana.

Toope, S. (1997), 'Cultural Diversity and Human Rights', *McGill Law Journal*, 42, 169–85.

Tushnet, M. (1984), *Texas Law Review*, 62, 1363–1403.

Tutu, D. (1999), *No Future Without Forgiveness*, London: Ebury Press.

Twining, W. (2000), *Globalization and Legal Theory*, London: Butterworths.

Verhoeven, A. (1998a), 'How Democratic Need European Union Members Be?: Some Thoughts After Amsterdam', *European Law Review*, 23, 217–34.

Verhoeven, A. (1998b), 'Europe Beyond Westphalia: Can Postnational Thinking Cure Europe's Democracy Deficit?, *Maastricht Journal of European and Comparative Law*, 5, 369–83.

Villa-Vicencio, C. (2000), 'Restorative Justice: dealing with the past differently', in C. Villa-Vicencio and W. Verwoerd (eds), *Looking Back, Reaching Forward: Reflections on the Truth and Reconciliation Commission of South Africa*, Cape Town: University of Cape Town Press, pp.68–76.

Voltaire (1994), *Political Writings*, ed. D. Williams, Cambridge: Cambridge University Press.

Waltz, K. (1959), *Man, the State and War*, New York: Columbia University Press.

Waltz, K. (1979), *Theory of International Politics*, London: Addison-Wesley.

Ward, I. (1996), *A Critical Introduction to European Law*, London: Butterworths.

Ward, I. (1997), *Kantianism, Postmodernism and Critical Legal Thought*, Dordrecht: Kluwer.

Ward, I. (1999), *Shakespeare and the Legal Imagination*, London: Butterworths.

Ward, I. (2000), *A State of Mind?: The English Constitution and the Popular Imagination*, Stroud: Sutton.

Ward, I. (2001), 'Tempted by Rights: The European Union and its New Charter of Fundamental Rights', *Constitutional Forum*, 11, 74–84.

Weiler, J. (1998), 'Bread and Circus: The State of European Union', *Columbia Journal of European Law*, 4, 223–48.

Weiler, J. (1999), *The Constitution of Europe*, Cambridge: Cambridge University Press.

Wellman, C. (2000), 'Solidarity, the Individual and Human Rights', *Human Rights Quarterly*, 22, 639–57.

Wendt, A. (1999), *Social Theory of International Relations*, Cambridge: Cambridge University Press.

Werhane, P. (1991), *Adam Smith and His Legacy for Modern Capitalism*, Oxford: Oxford University Press.

Whitman, W. (1996), *The Complete Poems*, Harmondsworth: Penguin.

Wilets, J. (1999), 'The Demise of the Nation-State: Toward a New Theory of the State Under International Law', *Berkeley Journal of International Law*, 17, 193–229.

Wingrove, E. (2000), *Rousseau's Republican Romance*, Princeton: Princeton University Press.

Woodring, C. (1970), *Politics in English Romantic Poetry*, Cambridge: Harvard University Press.

Woodward, S. (2000), 'War: Building States from Nations', in Tariq Ali (ed.), *Masters of the Universe?: NATO's Balkan Crusade*, London: Verso, pp.203–70.

Wordsworth, W. (1936), *Complete Poetical Works*, Oxford: Oxford University Press.

Yee, S. (1996), 'The New Constitution of Bosnia and Hercegovina', *European Journal of International Law*, 7, 176–92.

Zuern, M. (2000), 'Democratic Governance Beyond the Nation-State: The EU and other International Institutions', *European Journal of International Relations*, 6, 183–221.

Index